# The Developing Father

# The Developing Father

## EMERGING ROLES IN CONTEMPORARY SOCIETY

BRYAN E. ROBINSON, PH.D.
ROBERT L. BARRET, PH.D.
University of North Carolina at Charlotte

The Guilford Press
New York     London

© 1986 The Guilford Press
A Division of Guilford Publications, Inc.
200 Park Avenue South, New York, N.Y. 10003

Printed in the United States of America

**Library of Congress Cataloging in Publication Data**

Robinson, Bryan E.
  The developing father.

  Includes bibliographies and index.
  1. Fathers—United States.   2. Father and child.
3. Fathers—United States—Psychology.   I. Barret,
Robert L.   II. Title.   [DNLM: 1. Father–Child
Relations   2. Fathers—psychology.   WS  105.5.F2 R658d]
HQ756.R63   1986        306.8'742        86-4637
ISBN 0-89862-662-5
ISBN 0-89862-905-5 (pbk.)

*To Shirley Thompson Robinson and the memory of William Bryan Robinson—B. E. R.*

*To my daughters, Mary Ashley Barret, Amanda Byars Barret, and Laura Watkins Barret—R. L. B.*

# ACKNOWLEDGMENTS

The cooperation and help of many colleagues, friends, and family members have made this book possible.

We appreciate the steadfast personal and administrative support of Dr. Mary Thomas Burke, Chairperson of the Department of Human Services, and Dr. Harold W. Heller, Dean of the College of Education and Allied Professions at the University of North Carolina at Charlotte.

A special thanks to all the fathers and mothers who provided case material for our use: Jim and Lorne Boatright, Arnie Cann, Bill Dudley, Michael Finch, Ron Hall, Rod Houston, Dale Wachowiak, and our anonymous fathers. In addition, this book is enriched by the contributions of Mary Jane Brotherson, Ann Turnbull, Jean Ann Summers, and Rutherford Turnbull, who wrote the chapter on "Fathers of Disabled Children," and by Douglas Powers who wrote the poem "On Cold Feet." We wish to give special thanks to Dr. Robert Lewis for writing the foreword to this book.

We also benefited from the technical assistance of Joy Stewart, Libby Wilson, and Lorraine Penninger and the manuscript preparation skills of Betty Cauble.

We want to thank the staff and editors at The Guilford Press and particularly Seymour Weingarten, whose enthusiasm for and belief in this project helped make this book a reality.

B. E. R.
R. L. B.

# PREFACE

There has been a growing interest in the topic of fathering, an area largely ignored in the study of children and families until the past decade. Before this interest emerged, researchers focused all their attention on mothers. Studies, in fact, equated "mothering" with "parenting" and viewed fathers as unimportant in the process of child development. When sex roles were reevaluated during the '70s, men's issues in general and fatherhood in particular became a significant area of interest and research. The "age of paternal rediscovery," as one writer called it, led to a flood of fathering research during the late '70s and early '80s.

Nationwide support groups emerged for fathers in various situations, and professional journals began to devote special issues to the topic of fatherhood. In June 1982 top leaders in the field of men's studies and fatherhood met at Grove's Conference in Ocean City, Maryland, to share their research around the theme of "Men's Changing Roles and Relationships." About the same time, the Fatherhood Project was launched at Bank Street College of Education in New York City. The project is a national and international effort to determine how men can become more active in child rearing. Out of these studies a new profile of fathers has emerged. Fathers are no longer seen as distant, uninvolved family providers. Instead, men, as well as women, are beginning to recognize their innate nurturing instincts and to participate more in the processes of childbirth and child rearing.

This book presents the latest research findings about fatherhood in a novel way that uses case studies from the authors' interviews with a wide range of fathers and nonfathers to integrate the content and to add a human dimension otherwise obscured in studies of large groups. Special sections in each chapter on "suggestions to professionals" and "professional resources for working with fathers" make this book practical and useful for those employed in or preparing to enter a wide range of helping professions.

Section I examines four major topics: theories about fatherhood, choosing and preparing for fatherhood, traditional and newly emerging models of the father role, and fathering across the life span. Section II presents the findings about different kinds of fathers that have become a prevalent form of American family life: never-married single and adoptive fathers, fathers of broken homes (divorced and widowed) or blended families, gay fathers, teenage fathers, and fathers of disabled children (those with physical, emotional, and intellectual handicaps).

This book is intended as a resource for social workers, counselors, teachers, and other practitioners in the human services field. In addition, it is written for use as a supplemental text at the undergraduate and graduate levels for courses in social work, family life, parenting, child development, education, women's and men's studies, nursing, human services, and counseling psychology.

Bryan E. Robinson
Robert L. Barret

# FOREWORD

Back in 1975 my brother, Richard, and I began to envision a book addressed to and developed from interviews with househusbands. At the time he knew many engineers who were unemployed husbands and single fathers who stayed home to care for children and house. But try as we might, we were not successful in interviewing any of these "househusbands." Some men said that they were too busy to talk about their experiences as full-time fathers; others denied that they were unique in any way and therefore had nothing of value to contribute to others. Behind many of the excuses, however, my brother and I began to believe that these men were simply ashamed that they were not working full-time outside of the home—and were unable to believe that providing child-care and homemaking services were as important as being gainfully employed.

Times have changed since 1975. Family roles are constantly changing. But, of all family role changes, perhaps the most significant changes are occurring in fathers' roles. For example, many full-time fathers are no longer reluctant to admit that their most important and fulfilling roles relate to their being fathers. This new book by Robinson and Barret gives credence to these and many other changes which "developing fathers" are now experiencing.

To my way of thinking, the most exciting aspects of this book involve the great varieties of expressions that fatherhood experiences take. The authors describe a full spectrum of fathering styles from androgynous to traditional, and such special fathering roles as those of teenage fathers, recycled fathers, grandfathers, single fathers, and stepfathers, to name a few.

Not only do the authors make each of these fathering lifestyles real and fresh with quotations from fathers who have experienced them, but the authors also provide solid information on each fatherhood style from some of the best and most recent research. This volume will do much to counteract the trends that lead to popularized misconceptions of fatherhood—those distortions of data by media hype that document apparent "new trends" in fatherhood. For example, the findings of a study by Rebelsky and Hanks in 1971 reporting that a nonrepresentative sample of 19 fathers spoke an average of 37.7 seconds a day to their 0- to 3-month-old infants, has been popularized to the point where its interpretations overshadow new and more adequate data on fathers' involvement with their children. Consequently, this trivia has gravely distorted Americans' perceptions of how much time most fathers actually spend with their children. In contrast, actual data suggest that many fathers spend significant amounts of time with their children. As Robinson and Barret recognize, however, good data from controlled studies are providing reliable indications of new trends in fathering, information which they present for thoughtful examination.

Finally, one of the most valuable contributions of this book resides at the end of each chapter in the suggestion sections addressed to professionals. These sections and the following lists of resources will prove invaluable for all kinds of professional people who may work with "developing" fathers.

Robert A. Lewis

# CONTENTS

Section II. Types of Fathering Experiences

# I

# *Overview of Fatherhood*

# CHAPTER ONE

# *Theoretical Perspectives*

## THE CASE OF A FULL-TIME FATHER

Becoming a father has made a major impact on my life. Once our only child was born, I sold the modest house-painting business that I had run for 5 years, and I became the primary caregiver to our son. I did this without any regrets and looked forward to the unique opportunity of becoming a "househusband." Because I had worked my own hours as a house painter and my wife had a restricted schedule as a medical student, most of the household tasks were carried out either alone or by our combined efforts. We had planned our baby's birth to come at the start of a 5-month vacation period between the 3rd and 4th years of medical school so we would be able to begin our parenting adventure together. After that period I was home with the baby as primary caregiver for the next 5 years.

Those 5 years marked a period of intense emotional growth for me. I developed a deep understanding of the stresses involved in the role, and the intense pleasure of the deepest love I've ever known. Because I was experiencing many of the same successes and failures as my female neighbors who stayed at home with their children, I came to understand more fully the role of women in our society. I also learned how difficult it is for any parent to raise a child when his or her spouse is away for large blocks of time during the day.

My experience as a full-time father helped put me more in touch with many feelings. I am more free to express deep feelings to other full-time parents on the block. It is easier to ask for help, but sometimes it is more satisfying and surprising to find the strength within myself to deal with the often overwhelming feelings of anger that accompany the bond between parent and child. I also enjoy more fully physical contact with other people—children and adults. There is something profound in the love between a father and son. There is a tremendous freedom in feeling free to love, hold, and kiss your own child. It seems to awaken a more caring feeling to all children and their parents.

On another level, I have a keen awareness of what our children have lost, now that, first, Dad and, then, Mom have gone off to work. I believe that it is vital for a child to have that one-on-one, day-in–day-out involvement with both parents to develop a clear concept of personal identity. It has been especially moving for my son and me to spend so much time together. There is something in the strong feelings we share that I know will strengthen both of us for the rest of our lives.

*Bill Dudley*
*Charlotte, N.C.*

Until the 1970s fathers and the experience of fatherhood were largely taken for granted both in the popular culture and in the psychological literature. Fathers were accepted as necessary ingredients in family life, but few people really expected them to be deeply involved in day-to-day parenting activities. Margaret Mead's comment that "fathers are a biological necessity but a social accident" accurately described the limited role expected of men in families. Today, however, social scientists recognize that for biological and social reasons, "most children have two parents—one of either sex" (Lamb, 1979, p. 938). Although Bill Dudley is definitely an unusual example of a man committed to being a father, his experience indicates the deep attachment men can have toward their children.

The growing awareness of fathers' significant participation in their children's development has led researchers to devote more attention to this overlooked parent. Most studies contrast newly evident and more active fathering with the "traditional father," a term that is widely used but seldom defined. The traditional father is difficult to define partly because research reports on fathering have tended to reinforce a stereotypical role casting fathers in the amiable likeness of Dagwood Bumstead or the stridently authoritarian posture of Archie Bunker. The stereotypical father is involved with his family but obviously out of step with the family activities surrounding him. Other studies report parenting behavior but, in fact, only involve mothers as subjects. These researchers equate parenting with mothering (for example, Goode, 1965; Miller & Swanson, 1958; Sears, 1957).

The paucity of research on fathers is almost alarming. LeMasters and Defrain (1983) note that out of 1140 pages in the otherwise comprehensive *Handbook of Socialization Theory and Research* (Goslin, 1969), a major review of research, there are only five specific references to fathers. In a major work about child rearing, Sears (1957) interviewed 379 mothers and no fathers. Miller and Swanson (1958) based their findings in *The Changing American Parent* on interviews with 582 mothers; not a single father was included in this study. Goode (1965), in studying divorce and its effects on children and parents, interviewed 425 mothers and no fathers. A comprehensive anthology of research and commentary about infancy devotes 81 sections to maternal variables and the mother–child relationship but only two to fathers (Stone, Smith, & Murphy, 1973).

Many family experts criticize as a major deficit the slighting of fathers in research. Safilios-Rothschild (1969) used the term "wives sociology" to characterize most family studies. Josselyn (1956) stated:

> As long as men are seen as animated toys, mothers' little helpers, as powerful ogres who alone mete out rewards and punishment, the role of men in the family structure will be boring and/or depreciating. Being frustrated in their attempt to find qualification of their fatherliness, and dissatisfied with the watered down expression of themselves in the home, they will continue to seek release by diverting their available free energy into channels in which they feel more adequate, with a resultant overinvestment in the qualification they attain from activities away from the home. (p. 270)

The idea that such narrow participation in child rearing is dehumanizing was rare in the literature before the 1970s. The prevailing assumption was that women have an instinctive nurturing ability and men do not. During the 1970s the father was rediscovered (Lamb, 1979). Evidence has accumulated from men like Bill Dudley that men can function quite well as the primary care giver.

## PSYCHOLOGICAL AND SOCIOLOGICAL ROOTS OF CONTEMPORARY FATHERHOOD

Freud (1953) stressed that the father was the source of much of the content of the child's superego (i.e., the part of the personality that corresponds to conscience and includes moral and ethical restrictions). In Freud's view, the ideal father was a somewhat threatening authoritarian. Such masculine and emotional distance was seen as absolutely appropriate (Bronfenbrenner, 1960) to the son's working through of anxiety experienced in the oedipal stage (where boys compete with their fathers for their mother's attention and favor). Others in the psychoanalytic tradition underscored these views, stressing the positive role of the father in breaking up the infantile and potentially crippling mother–child relationship; too much nurturing, it was feared, caused the child to become overly dependent on the mother (Meerloo, 1956, 1968). Freud suggested that boys identify with their fathers out of fear and self-protection because the father appears so powerful (Freud, 1937). Several fathers we talked with believe that this is their major role. One said, "Yes, I love my son. But I never tell him that. I want him to grow up to be strong. And the best way to encourage strength is for me to be strong."

Freud's theories provided a rationale for traditional fatherhood and led researchers to study the mother as primary in the child's development. The major sociological studies of the mid-1950s depicted this traditional father role. English (1954) reflected the dominant sociological view:

> Traditionally, father has been looked on as the breadwinner. In times past so much of his time and energy was used in this role that at home he was thought of as taciturn and stern, albeit kind. He was respected but feared by his children who never learned to know him very well. He accepted the fact that he earned the money and mother cared for the home and raised the children. (p. 323)

Few questioned the appropriateness of such a division of labors.

Parsons (1954) furthered this view, labeling the mother's role as *expressive* and the father's as *instrumental* (Parsons & Bales, 1955): The mother nurtures her children with statements of empathy, offers the emotional security necessary for them to create healthy relationships with others, and teaches them about their emotions; the father, on the other hand, leaves the family to venture into an exciting and often dangerous world. In his instrumental role the father provides linkage between the emotional security provided by the mother and anticipated challenges in the outside world that require skill and intellect; he enables his children to gradually move from dependence on the mother toward the autonomy necessary to survive as an adult. In the words of one father: "I get lots of satisfaction from knowing I am the sole source of money in my family. And I like teaching the kids what the work world is like." Interpretations such as Parsons's effectively endorsed the status quo and justified the omission of fathers from research studies on parenting.

About 1960 a new focus became apparent—a more "modern" perspective of traditional fathering (Fein, 1978). Social learning theorists devoted attention to the importance of the father as a model of masculine behaviors for his children (Mowrer, 1950; Mussen, 1967). Essentially, these theorists translated Freud into behavioral language and encouraged fathers to display typical masculine behaviors so both boys and girls learn what men are like (Sears, 1957). Boys have been shown to model themselves after strong, domineering fathers (Hetherington & Frankie, 1967) and to consider dominance a major goal (Altucher, 1956, cited in Moulton, Burnstein, Liberty, & Altucher, 1966; Biller, 1969; Hetherington, 1965). Boys with dominant fathers tend to be more masculine, while those with dominant mothers tend to be more feminine. One father we interviewed commented, "I think one of the main things I do as a parent is teach my sons how to be men, and teach my daughter how to act with boys." This utilitarian view of the father's role was not widely challenged in the research literature of the 1960s. Another father we talked with reflected a frustration with this traditional perspective: "I've usually been an independent thinker. When I was in Air Force basic training, I remember being jolted when we were learning about wearing our uniforms. One of the rules that was stressed was that while in uniform we were *not* to carry a baby or push a baby stroller. When I pressed for a reason for such a strange rule I was told that if I had a baby in my arms I would be unable to salute a superior officer. Apparently such etiquette was more important than the love I could express to my child!"

## ANDROGYNY THEORY AND FATHERHOOD

Until the early 1970s, the prevailing view was that mothers and fathers modeled female and male behaviors in the home, providing the first and most powerful influence on gender roles. Masculinity and femininity were believed to be opposite, mutually exclusive traits. Cross-sex behavior was to be avoided, and a psychologically healthy individual was seen, in part, as a person who displayed stereotypical sex-role behavior. In the 1970s, however, a number of researchers began to suggest that masculine and feminine behaviors could not be as distinctly categorical as was once believed. They conceptualized role behaviors as a continuum, with femininity and masculinity at opposite extremes, along which an individual's degree of sex-typedness could be identified. This model accounted for the androgynous individual (from the Greek—andro, male, and gyne, female), one who combines characteristics of both sexes. The androgynous person can be assertive, competitive, and independent (usually viewed as male traits) as well as sensitive, gentle, and warm (usually viewed as female traits). According to Sandra Bem (1974, 1975; Bem & Lenney, 1976; Bem, Martyna, & Watson, 1976), who conducted most of the important research on androgyny, the androgynous person has the psychological freedom to engage in whatever behavior seems effective at the moment, regardless of roles typically assigned to the situation. Thus, androgyny expands the range of behavior and makes an individual more adaptable.

Bem's (1974) first group of subjects was given a choice between two stereotyped activities. They could prepare a baby bottle for two pennies or oil a squeaky hinge for double that amount. Highly feminine women more often took a loss of two cents and chose the "baby bottle" activity. Highly masculine men more often chose to oil the squeaky hinge. These subjects were willing to lose money to avoid behaving in ways that are characteristic of the opposite sex. When the men were forced to prepare the baby bottle and the women were only given the choice of oiling the squeaky hinge, masculine men and feminine women experienced discomfort and felt "nervous" or "peculiar." Androgynous men and women, in contrast, reported feeling more comfortable regardless of the role they performed. In another study Bem and her associates exposed a group of subjects to an infant. Each subject was left alone with the baby for 10 minutes. Masculine men played less with the baby; feminine women reacted very warmly. Both androgynous men and women responded warmly to the infant.

Although Bem's theory neatly resolves some of the limitations of the earlier sex-role theory, major questions, some fundamental to all personality research, remain unanswered: Doesn't Bem's dependence on traditional concepts of masculinity and femininity for her definition of androgyny inherently bias androgyny theory and make it just as limiting as other theories? Does the way androgyny is defined affect the research results? Couldn't the instruments used to measure androgyny actually be flawed and really measure some other subtle trait? As Bem struggled with some of these issues, she modified her theory and now speaks more in terms of "gender schema," a more cognitive (as opposed to personality) orientation: (Bem, 1981). Having an innate orientation toward masculinity and femininity, many people in particular instances may adopt behaviors generally associated with the opposite sex.

Lately, researchers in this field have offered another theory, "sex-role transcendence" (Robinson & Green, 1981). Based on a developmental model, individuals are seen moving from stage to stage toward the ultimate position where a new personality structure emerges. In this dynamic and flexible orientation, gender is irrelevant and behaviors are freely chosen from the total range of possible alternatives on the basis of what is useful and are chosen without consideration of masculinity–femininity issues.

A father we talked with reflected his development from a traditional father role toward a more androgynous position when he said:

> I don't have any regular child-care jobs. I like to be with my daughters at times. I like to be with them at home—at dinner or watching TV. I also like to touch them and tell them I love them. More than Nancy [his wife], I enjoy teasing them and joking around. Sometimes I help with their homework—especially math and science. Sometimes I put them to bed, and sometimes (usually on Saturdays) I like getting them up in the morning. I love sports and usually play tennis and basketball for recreation. That's not something I share with the girls that I probably would have shared with a son.

This father reflects a more traditional attitude toward his role in that he has no "regular child-care jobs." It is obvious, however, that he is deeply involved with his children. Being tender with them and nurturing them is more reflective of his androgynous nature.

## ADULT MALE DEVELOPMENT

Men's behavior as fathers is affected by their personal dynamics as they structure their adult lives. It is now recognized that personality continues to unfold throughout the life course. Internal issues sometimes influence a man's ability to father.

Daniel Levinson (1978) and his colleagues at Yale University published the results of their study of 40 men, *The Seasons of Man's Life*, a major contribution to the literature in adult male development. According to Levinson adult life is composed of three major periods, punctuated by transitions:

Age 17–22, early adult transition
Age 22–40, early adulthood
Age 40–45, midlife transition
Age 45–60, middle adulthood
Age 60–65, late adult transition
Age 65–80, late adulthood

Each period and each transition has associated tasks, which, if successfully mastered, contribute to a productive lifestyle. Two themes are constant throughout the life course: the life structure and the dream. From the life structure composed of work, home, friends, family, hobbies, and the like, one draws a sense of personal identity, and through it goals are formulated and achieved. The dream is the individual's idea of the life he or she wants. Formed during childhood and adolescence, the dream is first tested in early adulthood as the realities of adult living are encountered. One major element in adult life is reshaping the dream so that it conforms to the limits imposed by the life structure. The dream, like the life structure, is dynamic and is at the base of adult life.

In early adulthood both the life structure and the dream begin to emerge. As the 25-year-old moves into a career, establishes a home for himself away from his parents, builds a social network, and develops a primary relationship with a woman, he is fulfilling the tasks of this period in his life. Then, between the ages of 28–33, he takes stock of the extent to which his life structure is leading to his dream. There may have to be modifications in both; or a man may change his life structure so that his dream seems more attainable. For some men only minor changes or no changes at all usher them into the last half of young adulthood—settling down.

In this phase there are two major tasks: (1) establishing a stable and predictable life structure so that (2) "becoming one's own man," can be achieved. Thus, by age 40, the man has achieved certain goals so that his opinion is valued and his expertise is acknowledged.

The midlife transition is typically a time of unexpected and confusing upheaval (Brim, 1976). Men begin to become aware of fading youth and are forced by the passing of peers and parents to acknowledge the inevitability of their own deaths. They also must face the reality that some elements of their dreams will never be realized. Typically, men at this point begin to turn more inward, abandoning their previously held notion that the most fulfilling rewards are offered in the work world. Family assumes a new and important role at the same time that their children are beginning to move away, and their wives, experiencing a new freedom, likewise may have begun to explore the world outside the home (Farrell & Rosenberg, 1981; Jaques, 1965; Miller, 1971). Many men make major life changes in midlife in an attempt to revitalize their life structures or to have "one last shot" to attain their dreams. Others may adjust to the changes in their marriages entailed by the "empty nest" and find satisfaction in using their new freedom to explore new interests.

Levinson (1978) does not provide as detailed a map for middle adulthood, because most of the men in his sample were in the early stages of that period. The task of middle adulthood seems to be to integrate the new or modified midlife structure into a secure lifestyle:

Both father and offspring must give meaning to the fact that they are approaching early adulthood while he is leaving it behind. No longer a youthful father raising small children, he is a father entering middle age and seeking new ways of relating to his adolescent and young adult offspring. As their generational status changes, he faces new responsibilities and new opportunities. At best they can form mutually satisfactory relationships that include some degree of loving, teaching, learning, supporting, working, and playing together. But this is not easy, and it is more the exception than the rule. (Levinson, 1978, p. 254)

A man's success or failure in fulfilling his own dream has implications for his fatherly response to supporting his children's dreams. If he feels lost or betrayed, he may resent their optimisms and successes. However,

. . . as midlife issues are resolved, a father can respond with more care and wisdom to the needs of his offspring. He can value their youthful hopes, accept their youthful awkwardness, and offer his gifts with respect for their individuality. (Levinson, 1978, p. 256)

Knowledge about adult development provides a framework through which to view fathers interacting with their children. There is danger in isolating the father role and drawing conclusions without seeing fathers as men who are deeply involved in a larger maturing process that influences everything they do.

## FAMILY SYSTEMS THEORY AND FATHERHOOD

In the mental health professions there is a current emphasis on treating the entire family, which is seen as more effective than simply treating the individual who has been identified as "having problems." This family treatment emphasis grew out of the experience of several practitioners in the 1950s and 1960s with patients in mental institutions. It was noticed that in some cases a highly disturbed individual would respond to treatment, return home, and then in a short period of time, would be brought back to the hospital as dysfunctional as before treatment (Bronfenbrenner, 1979; Carter & McGoldrick, 1980; Jackson, 1965a, 1965b; Nichols, 1984).

Curious about the patient's rapid regression, therapists began to invite the families in for consultation before release to try to smooth the transition home. Once a family was together, it was observed that the pattern of communication and family structure required that at least one family member (usually the patient) behave in a dysfunctional manner. The patient's "sickness" served a purpose in the family context. In some cases if the patient could find appropriate resources to regain mental health, another family member would become distressed and require hospitalization.

In searching for a theoretical explanation for this situation, researchers turned to the work of Bertalanffy (1968), who suggested that systems are characterized as sets of elements interacting in such a way that there is a hierarchical order among them that maintains a balance, or *homeostasis*, so that unity is maintained. The system functions in such a way that it has a wholeness which transcends the qualities of its parts and is more than the simple sum of them. When a couple joins together a system is created that is made up of dynamics contributed by both; as children are born, the system changes, readjusting itself and its dynamics to maintain homeostasis. These family systems have a past and a future that affect whatever is seen at any given moment. In order for the systems to function well, there must be equilibrium, which is achieved through family rules, roles, and characteristic patterns of reaction to stress. Some families demand high levels of stress and turmoil; others collapse if too much pressure is applied.

The implications of family systems theory for the purposes of this discussion are that in order to understand the behavior of a father, information about the family as a whole often must be obtained. Some of the men we talked with wanted more involvement with their children, but were rebuffed by wives who saw parenting as their domain and kept their husbands out in order to maintain complete control. A case example is the "Helms" family (a pseudonym): The parents brought their 15-year-old son for counseling because he was failing in school. Although the son was not rebellious and was a valued worker at his job, courteous and easygoing at home, and active in sports and church, he did not study or complete school assignments. In one session his parents continued to express their anger at and frustration with him until he suddenly blurted out, "You know, the only time you two talk to each other is when you are worrying about my grades!" A long silence followed before his parents acknowledged the truth of his statement. Subsequently, he was dismissed from counseling, and we began to work with the parents on their relationship. As they found new ways of relating to each other, the son's problems disappeared. He had been acting out the tension in his parents' relationship by not doing his schoolwork. This behavior was not consciously chosen, but had developed over the years as he tried to get his parents to interact with each other. On superficial observation one might have concluded that the father was involved and caring toward an unresponsive son. In fact, the father did care a lot about his son, yet unconsciously even subtly encouraged his son's school failure because he knew no other way to relate to his wife.

Another aspect of family systems theory is Bowen's suggestion (1966) that families can be either too closely *fused* together or so highly *differentiated* that little relating occurs (Okun & Rappaport, 1980). It is healthy for individuals to function within the family and yet, at the same time, be aware of personal strengths and attitudes that define their differentness from the family. One of the tasks of parenting is to allow children to develop their differentness so that they are able to separate from the family and move into the adult world without abandoning the family entirely.

The kind of fathering evident in any particular family reflects the unique qualities of that family system. This understanding will be especially crucial in the discussion of stepfathering (Chapter 6), a situation in which a man enters a functioning system, necessarily forcing changes that may be resisted by members of the old system.

## CONCLUSION

Most men are encouraged to perform as highly traditional fathers, and much of the psychological and sociological literature prior to the 1970s has generally validated such a restricted role. Many men feel they must restrict or sacrifice their father role in order to be successful breadwinners (Moreland & Schwebel, 1981). However, as androgyny theory suggests (Bem, 1975), some men are uncomfortable with restricting their parenting activities to providing income for the family. It may be that more fathers will try to create a balance between their breadwinner role and their own need to be involved with their children. One father told us:

> I came from a family of an older sister, younger brother, and my mother. My Dad died when I was 6. As a family we got along OK. But we were never really close. When Nancy and I married, she had already worked for several years, so we knew she could support herself. We just sort of evolved a pattern of parenting over the years. Nancy was happy to be at home, and I was working hard in my career. Now that the kids are older, she has gone to work and back to school. We are both traditional people, but I would say that right now we are in transition. The kids will be gone in a few years, and I understand why she wants a career to be involved with outside our home.

A particular father's level of involvement in parenting must be examined in terms of its social benefits and pressures, the family system, and internal developmental issues. Some men do ignore the father role because the rewards of activities outside the home are so strong. Other men may be closed out by their family system or traditions, or they may be struggling with internal issues that consume all their energy. More information needs to be available to men, so that they can make better decisions about the kind of involvement they want to have with their children.

## PROFESSIONAL RESOURCES FOR THEORETICAL PERSPECTIVES ON FATHERHOOD

Anderson, C. P. *Father: The figure and the force.* New York: Warner, 1983.

Benson, A. *Fatherhood: A sociological perspective.* New York: Random House, 1968.

Butler, H., & Meredith, D. *Father power.* New York: McKay, 1974.

Cath, S. H., Gurwitt, A. R., & Ross, J. M. *Father and child: Developmental and clinical perspectives.* Boston: Little, Brown, 1982.

Greene, M. *Fathering.* New York: McGraw-Hill, 1976.

Kaplan, A. G., & Sedney, M. A. *Psychology and sex roles: An androgynous perspective.* Boston: Little, Brown, 1980.

Kastenbaum, R. (Ed.). *Men in their forties.* New York: Springer, 1982.

Kemper, S., Rappaport, D., & Spirn, M. *A man can be. . . .* New York: Human Sciences Press, 1981.

Lamb, M. *The role of the father in child development* (2nd ed.). New York: Wiley, 1980.

Lamb, M. E., & Sagi, A. (Eds.). *Fatherhood and family policy.* Hillsdale, N.J.: Erlbaum, 1983.

Lenny, E. (Guest Ed.). Special issue on androgyny theory. *Sex Roles: A Journal of Research, 5,* 1979.

Lynn, D. B. *The father: His role in child development.* Monterey, Calif.: Brooks/Cole, 1974.

Mead, M. *Male and female: A study of the sexes in a changing world.* New York: Morrow, 1952.

Mead, M. Fatherhood. In S. A. Richardson & A. F. Guttmacher (Eds.), *Childbearing—Its social and psychological aspects.* Baltimore: Williams & Wilkins, 1967.

Parke, R. *Fathering.* Cambridge, Mass.: Harvard University Press, 1981.

Singer, J. *Androgyny: Toward a new theory of sexuality.* Garden City, N.J.: Anchor, 1976.

# REFERENCES

Bem, S. L. Gender schema theory: A cognitive account of sex typing. *Psychological Bulletin*, 1981, *88*, 354–364.

Bem, S. The measurement of psychological androgyny. *Journal of Consulting and Clinical Psychology*, 1974, *42*, 155–162.

Bem, S. Androgyny vs. the tight little lives of fluffy women and chesty men. *Psychology Today*, 1975, *9*, 58–62.

Bem, S., & Lenney, E. Sex typing and the avoidance of cross sex behavior. *Journal of Personality and Social Psychology*, 1976, *33*, 48–54.

Bem, S., Martyna, W., & Watson, C. Sex typing and androgyny: Further explorations of the expressive domain. *Journal of Personality and Social Psychology*, 1976, *34*, 1016–1023.

Bertalanffy, L. von. *General systems theory: Foundation, development, applications.* New York: Brazillier, 1968.

Biller, H. Father dominance and sex role development in kindergarten boys. *Developmental Psychology*, 1969, *1*, 87–94.

Bowen, M. The use of family therapy in clinical practice. *Comprehensive Psychology*, 1966, *7*, 345–374.

Brim, O. Theories of the male mid life crisis. *The Counseling Psychologist*, 1976, *6*, 1–9.

Bronfenbrenner, H. Freudian theories of identification and their derivatives. *Child Development*, 1960, *31*, 51–40.

Bronfenbrenner, U. *The ecology of human development.* Cambridge, Mass.: Harvard University Press, 1979.

Carter, E., & McGoldrick, M. The family life cycle and family therapy: An overview. In E. Carter & M. McGoldrick (Eds.), *The family life cycle: A framework for family therapy.* New York: Gardner Press, 1980.

English, O. The psychological role of the father in the family. *Social Casework*, 1954, 323–329.

Farrell, M., & Rosenberg, S. *Men at midlife.* Boston: Auburn House, 1981.

Fein, R. A. Research of fathering: Social policy and an emergent perspective. *Journal of Social Issues*, 1978, *34*, 12–135.

Freud, A. *The ego and the mechanisms of defense.* London: Hogarth, 1937.

Freud, S. The taboo of virginity (Contributions to the psychology of love. III). In J. Strachey (Ed. and Trans.), *The standard edition of the complete psychological works of Sigmund Freud* ( Vol. XI, pp. 191–208). London: Hogarth Press, 1953. (Original work published 1918).

Goode, W. *After divorce.* New York: The Free Press, 1965.

Goslin, D. A. ( Ed.). *Handbook of Socialization Theory and research.* Chicago: Rand McNally & Co., 1969.

Hetherington, E. A developmental study of the effects of the dominant parent on sex-role preference, identification, and imitation in children. *Journal of Personality and Social Psychology*, 1965, *2*, 188–194.

Hetherington, E., & Frankie, G. Effects of parental dominance, warmth, and conflict on imitation in children. *Journal of Personality and Social Psychology*, 1967, *6*, 119–125.

Jackson, D. Family rules: Marital quid pro quo. *Archives of General Psychiatry*, 1965, *12*, 589–594. (a)

Jackson, D. The study of the family. *Family Process*, 1965, *4*, 1–20. (b)

Jaques, E. Death and the midlife crisis. *International Journal of Psychoanalysis*, 1965, *46*, 203–514.

Josselyn, I. Cultural forces, motherliness and fatherliness. *American Journal of Orthopsychiatry*, 1956, *26*, 264–271.

Lamb, M. Paternal influences and the father's role: A personal perspective. *The American Psychologist*, 1979, *34*, 938–943.

LeMasters, E., & DeFrain, J. *Parents in contemporary America: A sympathetic view*. Homewood, Ill.: The Dorsey Press, 1983.

Levinson, D. J. *The seasons of a man's life*. New York: Ballantine, 1978.

Meerloo, J. The father cuts the cord. *American Journal of Orthopsychiatry*, 1956, *10*, 471–480.

Meerloo, J. The psychological role of the father: The father cuts the cord. *Child and Family*, 1968, 102–114.

Miller, D., & Swanson, G. *The changing American parent*. New York: Wiley, 1958.

Miller, S. The making of a confused middle aged husband. *Social Policy*, 1971, *2*, 2.

Moreland, J., & Schwebel, A. A gender role transcendent perspective on fathering. *The Counseling Psychologist*, 1981, *9*, 45–54.

Moulton, R. W., Burnstein, E., Liberty, P. G., & Altucher, N. Patterning of parental affection and disciplining dominance as a determinant of guilt and sex typing. *Journal of Personality and Social Psychology*, 1966, *4*(4), 356–363.

Mowrer, O. *On learning theory and personality dynamics*. New York: Ronald, 1950.

Mussen, P. Early socialization: Learning and identification. In T. M. Newcomb (Ed.), *New directions in psychology* (Vol. 3). New York: Holt, Rinehart, & Winston, 1967.

Nichols, M. *Family therapy: Concepts and methods*. New York: Gardner Press, 1984.

Okun, B., & Rappaport, L. *Working with families: An introduction to family therapy*. North Scituate, Mass.: Duxbury Press, 1980.

Parsons, T. The father symbol. An appraisal in the light of psychoanalytic and sociological theory. In L. Bryson, L. Kinkelstein, R. MacIver, & R. McKeon (Eds.), *Symbols and values*. New York: Harper & Row, 1954.

Parsons, T., & Bales, R. *Family socialization, and interaction process*. Glencoe, Ill.: Free Press, 1955.

Robinson, B. E., & Green, M. G. Beyond androgyny: The emergence of sex role transcendence as a theoretical construct. *Developmental Review,* 1981, *1*, 247–265.

Safilios-Rothschild, C. Family sociology or wives' family sociology? A cross-cultural examination on decision-making. *Journal of Marriage and the Family,* 1969, *31*, 290–301.

Sears, R. Identification as a form of behavior development. In P. B. Harris (Ed.), *The concept of development.* Minneapolis: University of Minnesota Press, 1957.

Stone, L., Smith, H., & Murphy, L. (Eds.), *The competent infant: Research and commentary.* New York: Basic Books, 1973.

# CHAPTER TWO

# Preparing for Fatherhood

## THE CASE OF A CHILDLESS MAN

I'm not really sure when we made the decision to be childless. The finalizing of the decision was marked by my vasectomy, but I believe the choice had already been made long before then. I don't remember talking about raising a family during the early years of our marriage. It wasn't a case of deciding *not* to have children, rather it was a case of *not deciding* to have children. I was scheduled to enter graduate school a few weeks after we were married, and Helene was going to be the primary income producer until I had my degree. The circumstances made having children an impossibility, at least in our view. A second factor was that Helene still hadn't decided on a career. She had always expected to be a professional, the only question was, what type of professional? As the years passed, I finished my degree and took a job and Helene returned to school, still searching for an appealing career. Our lifestyle developed around our careers and became quite comfortable with just the two of us. As Helene approached an age when childbearing became more of a risk and where continuing to use birth control pills became more dangerous, we decided we had to act. Our decision was not easy and was not made with complete confidence. But it was clearly our best at the time, and delaying seemed unacceptable.

Sometimes I feel like I am cheating my parents out of an experience they would greatly value. It's funny, but if they have questions about our having children they are more likely to ask Helene instead of me. Most of our friends had had children by now, so we were aware that we were different. Friends seem to take one of three approaches once they accept that we probably will remain childless. Some guard us from their children assuming, I guess, that childless couples dislike children, an invalid assumption in our case. Others encourage our interactions with their children, seemingly in the hope that this will show us the error of our decision. The third group of friends pay us no special attention, treating us as if we were a normal couple, except for our childless state.

In looking back over the years, I think the decision has been more difficult for Helene than for me. In social situations, men are less likely to discuss their children. But for women that often becomes the main topic of conversation. This either leaves Helene out or creates an awkwardness as the others realize she doesn't have children. In general, we have become closer as a couple because there are no children to take up our time. We are good friends and seem to share more activities than most of our friends who have children. We are still pretty young, and we may some day grow to regret our decision, but our lives, so far, have been happy and full. There are days when we think it would be fun to have children, to share some event that they would most probably enjoy. But there are also days when we are quite thankful that we decided to remain childless.

**Arnie Cann**
*Charlotte, N.C.*

Increasing numbers of men are opting for childless marriages to enable their wives to pursue an uninterrupted career, a decision facilitated by the availability of effective birth control. The current estimate of couples deciding not to become parents is between 15% and 20% (Veevers, 1982), a percentage that is estimated to triple in the next generation. According to a 1982 Census Bureau report, young men and women today are marrying later and having fewer children; if they decide to have children they are having them later in their adult years. This same trend is evident in the Netherlands and other countries (Den Brandt, 1980).

## ATTITUDES TOWARD CHILDLESS MEN

Men who decide they do not want the experience of fatherhood are often viewed with suspicion. Disappointed parents and concerned friends subject them to subtle or sometimes painfully blunt pressures with questions like "Isn't it time you thought about starting a family?" or "When do you think your wife will quit that ridiculous job and settle down to raise children?" Society rarely confronts fathers with the demand that they justify their decisions to have children, but non-fathers are treated as a threat and often called to account for this decision. Childless men have been described as selfish, immature, disturbed, sexually inadequate, and incomplete (Greenbaum, 1973; Pohlman, 1970). A 1979 Gallup Poll revealed that in spite of the increasing number of childless couples there was virtual unanimity that "childlessness is a disadvantage for men" (Blake, 1979). This same attitude is reflected in the policy statement on vasectomies adopted in 1969 by the Margaret Sanger Research Bureau, the first medical clinic to offer the procedure on an outpatient basis.

> The candidate must be at least twenty-five years old, married or in a stable relationship, he must have at least three children if less than forty years old, two children if he is between the ages of forty and forty-five, and one child if between forty-five and fifty years old, and if over fifty, he is eligible without any children. (Lieberman *et al.*, 1979, p. 181)

Today most agencies have adopted policies more accepting of child-lessness. The perspective of the general public has changed little, however.

Childless marriages are viewed as incomplete and the lifestyles of childless couples as self-centered. Children are popularly considered a social investment against loneliness in old age, and are held to add meaning to life, cement marriages, and guarantee fulfillment in life to women (Blake, 1979). Similar attitudes exist even among young adults, who perceive fathers as less disturbed than nonfathers (Calhoun & Selby, 1980).

Given society's generally negative views toward childlessness, it is surprising that men choose to forego parenthood. The negative aspects of child rearing deter a large proportion of childless men. For some, the major factor is financial: Children are seen as too expensive. Not only would the child consume a major portion of the couple's resources, but a baby would mean a loss of income during the time the mother is away from her career. Others fear that children will somehow weaken a strong and rewarding relationship or that because of the child's demands, tension between the spouses will increase. Other reasons include uncertainty about the marital relationship itself and a fear that children would only complicate both spouses' lives should divorce occur. Many men are simply afraid of the responsibility of raising a child, and for some this fear is intense enough that they avoid marriage altogether (Leader & Mumford, 1975). Positive reasons are also given for not becoming a parent. Some men feel that they are not emotionally equipped to deal with the "hassles" of children and do not want to take on a responsibility they cannot fulfill. For others, there is an awareness that they and their spouses will be happier without children (Pupo, 1980). Veevers (1980) suggests that childless men fall into two categories: "Rejectors," or those who chose childlessness as a reaction against the burdens of having children, and "aficionados," or those who made their decisions on the basis of perceived benefits from remaining childless.

Whether the decision to remain childless is made before, early, or late in the marriage, most men are unable to put the issue aside permanently. There are periods of intense ambivalence, possibly because of the relentless pressure to conform to society's expectations (Pohlman, 1970). Some men may give in and decide to become fathers in spite of an awareness that they would prefer to remain childless (Peterson, 1983). These attitudes can be seen in the comments of a childless man who is reconsidering his decision: "We decided not to have children 5 years ago, so I had a vasectomy. But somehow the idea of being a parent just wouldn't go away. My dad is getting older, and I know he would like to know the family name is being passed on. And I'm afraid I may be missing out on an important experience. I recently had surgery to try to undo the vasectomy. I'm still not sure I want to have children, but I want to keep the choice open for me." Many couples do stick to the decision to remain childless. Others delay making a final decision until it is too late for them to safely become parents; these couples have decided by not deciding. Overall, childless men report that they are satisfied with their decision, and even in old age they appear to be as well adjusted as fathers (Bachrach, 1980; Kivett & Learner, 1980; Smith & Williams, 1981).

## CHARACTERISTICS OF CHILDLESS MEN

Even though childless men may say that they are happy with their lives, the perception of the public is that there must be something wrong with these men or with their upbringing. Surely they must have had unhappy childhoods or parents who were not nurturing, or perhaps their marriages are not healthy. Actually, research studies (Feldman, 1981; Schapiro, 1980) reveal a positive personality profile that challenges this negative stereotype. Very few differences are found between the personality characteristics of fathers and nonfathers.

Childless men are more highly educated and are likely to be in higher-status professions (Schapiro, 1980). They like to experiment, show greater independence (a trait that serves them well, especially in old age), and are better able to defend themselves against social disapproval. Childless men feel more in control of their lives and do not suffer from severe mental health deficiencies in numbers greater than fathers do. Childless men generally are normal men who choose to remain childless because of personal, rather than antisocial, reasons. They grow up in families that are just as stable and equally balanced with positive parental interactions; their childhoods were just as happy as those of fathers (Feldman, 1981). When the marriages of childless men are compared with those of fathers, the differences are positive for the childless marriages. Not surprisingly, childless couples have less-traditional attitudes toward women; they also value assertiveness and create marital relationships that are characterized by frequent and more positive interactions (Feldman, 1981). Further, the marriages of nonfathers are no more prone to divorce than those of fathers (Leete, 1976). Other studies support this positive description of non-fathers (Magarick & Brown, 1981, Veevers, 1982). Compared with fathers, childless men are no different in their marital satisfaction, self-esteem, or level of psychological adjustment.

## UNINTENTIONALLY CHILDLESS MEN

One group of nonfathers has a more difficult experience than most other married men: men who want to become fathers but discover that they or their spouses are infertile. It is estimated that one out of six couples in the United States experience fertility problems (Menning, 1975). Childless couples struggling with infertility encounter all of the negative pressures directed toward intentionally childless couples as well as the additional burdens of feeling inadequate and experiencing greater stress in their marriages (Pohlman, 1970). Sexual intercourse may become a high pressured attempt to "make a baby" as opposed to a natural expression of intimacy. Efforts to overcome infertility may involve emotionally draining medical procedures or rearrangement of business travel plans in order to be available for intercourse during the most fertile period of their wives' menstrual cycle.

Although many of these couples eventually adjust to their infertility, others experience a lifetime characterized by self-blame and defensiveness. Having to respond to the question "How many children do you have?" can be extremely painful and awkward. One man who wants to become a father told us:

> This has been an awful time for me. I'd always expected children would naturally come at the right time. After 6 years of trying we knew something had to be wrong. We've been to lots of experts and for the past few months have been working with a doctor who is not real optimistic. Sex has become work for us, and every month when my wife has her period, we both feel let down. Just thinking about never having children is bad enough, but on top of that our relationship is suffering, and our families and friends continue to expect us to start our family! If they only knew half of what we are going through, they wouldn't say a word! We don't know what to tell them.

Men in the process of adopting a child also experience increased stress. Forced to endure a seemingly endless process of interviews and scrutiny by outsiders, they must maintain an appearance of wholesomeness and stability. They fear that their least fault may lead to disqualification by the adoption agency. This situation is further complicated for those fathers who are still involved in fertility counseling;

### THE CASE OF AN EXPECTANT FATHER

I can't say that I remember making a decision to become a father. As I write about it now 20 years later, it mostly seems like I just grew up knowing or, maybe even looked forward to, raising kids. My wife and I married when we were still in graduate school, having decided not to have children for a few years. But after we had been out of school for about 6 months, and both of us had jobs, I found myself thinking more and more about starting a family. We had accumulated enough money for the essentials and were having a great time with the 2-year-old who lived next door. I'm sure the availability of a baby kept the thought in front of my mind.

As I remember it, on Diane's birthday her mother called and said something like, "Well, you've been married over a year now. When am I going to be a grandmother?" That seemed like just the pressure we needed. In any event, a month later Diane was pregnant, and both of us were real excited about becoming parents.

Looking back, I can see that this pregnancy was important to me, but no less exciting than the two others that followed. I went through times when I felt very left out because family and friends favored my wife so much. It was almost like my job was over now that she was pregnant, and even worse, that whatever feelings I was having were of no importance. At times I was depressed and not sure I would like being a father. I know many agencies will not approve an adoption if there is any chance the couple may become pregnant. For men in this predicament, clandestine visits to physicians who assist them with their fertility without notifying adoption agencies offer a means to keep their options open.

Unintentionally childless men, whether struggling with infertility, adoption, or both, have marriage relationships that are more highly stressed than those of intentionally childless men and fathers. Fortunately for some of these unintentionally childless couples, being involved in either attempting to conceive or adopt forces them into greater intimacy as they work together.

## EXPECTANT FATHERS

Bob's feelings are typical of those men who are expecting babies: They have a deeply complex emotional and physical response to pregnancy that researchers (Barnhill, Rubenstein, & Rocklin, 1979; Greenburg & Morris, 1974) are just discovering (see "The Emotional Transition to

Diane didn't understand my reactions; after all, it was her body that was getting larger, and she had to put up with the usual aches and pains that caused her real discomfort. Lots of times I felt very distant from her and, maybe, a little bit jealous about all the attention she was getting.

When our daughter was born I felt so proud! Those days in the hospital seemed to last forever; I was anxious to get the three of us home so I could learn about being a father and so Diane could begin to give me a little more attention. One of the hardest things was that in our excitement and anticipation over having a baby, neither of us ever gave much thought to how to take care of our newborn. I remember arriving at our apartment after a 50-mile ride from the hospital, Diane collapsing into the bed, and being left with a helpless baby who went through three diapers in a 3-minute period! I learned how to tend to those kinds of needs real fast!

The next few weeks were maybe the best and worst in my life. I loved to come home, feed, and just hold my daughter. But often I was depressed. We were so tied down and were losing lots of sleep. My wife had her lows and needed me to boost her up. Before the baby if we were low we would go to a movie or out with friends, but a baby made that more complicated. I suppose we were really overwhelmed at first. Of course, it eventually got much easier. After a few months all of us were getting along well.

**Bob Barret**
*Charlotte, N.C.*

Fatherhood" below). One reason this response has been unacknowl-
edged is that the new father's responses occur at a time when the
mother receives most of the attention and concern. Awareness of
fathers' emotional reactions to pending parenthood has increased as
prepared childbirth classes have structured a role for fathers in the
birth process.

## Emotional Reactions During Pregnancy

Expectant fathers have emotional experiences with extreme highs and
lows (see "The Emotional Transition to Fatherhood" below). The initial

---

### THE EMOTIONAL TRANSITION TO FATHERHOOD

Research has revealed that expectant fathers have a wide range of emotions before, during, and after childbirth that were once believed to be
exclusively maternal reactions. These emotions range from empathy and
elation to depression.

**Before Childbirth**
Perhaps the most common initial emotions fathers have are excitement
about and anticipation for the upcoming birth. But after approximately
1 month, the "high" begins to decline, and the expectant father shifts his
attention toward his wife and her well-being. The father's concern takes
the form of empathy for the expectant mother. Episodes of morning
sickness or other physical and psychological complaints can occur among
men during their wife's pregnancy. Empathy sometimes appears because
the father feels cut-off from the physical sensations of the baby's growth
as well as from his wife's attention surrounding her pregnancy and the
upcoming childbirth. As childbirth draws nearer, feelings of helplessness
and isolation emerge as many fathers become "the peripheral person" in
the family (Barnhill, Rubenstein, & Rocklin, 1979).

**During Childbirth**
The childbirth experience is usually an "up" time for new fathers, although characterized by anxiety as well as elation. Anxiety stems from the
wish to perform well during labor and delivery, concern about possible
danger to wife or baby, or fears of deformities or miscarriages. Nevertheless, childbirth is also a time of elation for many expectant fathers, who
experience increased self-esteem and closer ties to their newborns after
childbirth participation (Greenberg & Morris, 1974).

excitement and feelings of anticipation quickly give way to deeper and more stressful concerns that are fairly constant throughout the pregnancy and early weeks of parenthood. Liebenberg (1969) was among the first to publicize the reactions of men during pregnancy. In her study of "pregnant" men, symptoms were reported that are very similar to many of the complaints of women during pregnancy, for example, "Edith didn't have morning sickness. I did. For months. I didn't throw up, I just didn't feel like eating breakfast" (Daniels & Weingarten, 1982, p. 147).

In other cultures men also experience symptoms similar to their pregnant wives. In a study of the Black Carib indians of Honduras, almost every man interviewed reported experiencing symptoms dur-

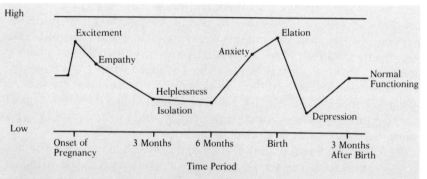

**Figure 1.** The emotional reactions of the father during pregnancy.

### After Childbirth

Not only do fathers share the highs, they also share the lows. A recent study of new fathers indicated that 62% experienced postbirth blues or depression similar to the emotional letdown reported by 89% of new mothers (Zaslow & Kramer, 1981). These fathers felt frustrated in their inability to help their wives cope with the baby or felt helpless in caring for the baby themselves. Some men who experienced more prolonged depression described themselves as "overwhelmed" by their wives' problem of caring for the infant. After childbirth the most important tasks facing the new father are adjustment to the new baby and integration of fathering and husbanding responsibilities (Barnhill et al., 1979). The expectant father usually resolves his task of emotional transition to parenthood within 6 weeks of birth, and the emotional extremes usually level off.

ing his wife's pregnancy, including food cravings, daytime sleepiness, fatigue, vomiting, headaches, fever, dizziness, and toothaches (Munroe, Munroe, & Whiting, 1973). Psychologists believe the *couvade* (the time when husbands show some of the symptoms of pregnancy) provides emotional compensation for being unable to bear children (Bettelheim, 1954). The *couvade* varies among cultures, but in primitive societies it may include taking to bed prior to the wife's childbirth or dressing in women's clothing, entering a darkened room, and simulating groans and other sounds of pain that often accompany birth. Today most of these practices have become ritualized and may no longer be actual expressions of internal emotional states. Their importance lies in the fact that they provide a way for men to be involved in the birth experience.

In Western society the range of changes men experience during pregnancy is equally broad. For some, pregnancy may only cause them to be more likely to grow a moustache or beard for the first time (Bittman & Zalk, 1978); for others the stress can be great enough to cause an emotional breakdown or psychotic episode (Fishbein, 1981). Expectant fathers in the military report physical ailments, but have also been observed to engage more frequently in reckless behavior involving physical daring. Some men withdraw from their wives by throwing themselves into their work with increased vigor; for others, weight changes occur (Curtis, 1955). Complaints like these are typical of expectant fathers early in the pregnancy, and along with aches and pains, they usually fade after childbirth (Gearing, 1978).

Research by Barnhill and his associates (1979) shows that the last half of the last trimester of the wife's pregnancy can be a highly stressful time for expectant fathers. Many expectant fathers experience a loss of personal freedom and the wife's time and attention. "From conception to delivery and through early infancy, fathers report feeling 'discounted,' a sense of being in the background, although these losses are often not noticed or mourned until much later after the highs of "birth" (Barnhill *et al.*, 1979, p. 232).

As men demand increased attention, they may also become more sensitive to and supportive of their wives. This may take the form of additional pampering, back rubs, and other efforts to lessen physical demands as the woman's body changes. Behaviors like these add a positive dimension to the marriage (Bittman & Zalk, 1978). Certainly the onset of pregnancy affects the couple's relationship in subtle ways. Sexual intercourse may become more frequent as an expression of renewed intimacy and closeness as the baby grows. For other couples, intercourse becomes less frequent, possibly as a reflection of a fear of hurting the baby or because men are subconsciously reminded of oedipal feelings toward their own mothers and feel that sexual intimacy would be a kind of incest (Liebenberg, 1969).

Other, more permanent changes in the couple's relationship are necessary. Grieving must occur as the freedoms of a childless and couple-centered lifestyle are given up. The couple must come together as they separate themselves more clearly from their own families. In order for this transition to be most meaningful, they integrate the new roles of mother and father into their relationship. This change requires the development of a sense of trust in the new baby, mother, and father.

## Men in Childbirth

Once the medical establishment acknowledged that men had a role in childbirth, expectant parents have been flooded with options for men to participate in childbirth. Not long ago most men anxiously awaited the birth of their children in dreary and often smoke-filled rooms; today they may be actively involved in coaching their wives through labor and delivery or even delivering their babies themselves at home. Barnhill and his associates (1979) says the father's most acute and overt anxiety now concerns his performance as a competent husband during labor and childbirth, "Though there is little for him to do, he has a high sense of risk and many questions about how to do things right" (p. 233). The fact that so many fathers are now present in the delivery room indicates an interest and an ability to nurture that has not been recognized before.

Prepared childbirth classes, such as the Lamaze technique, provide a new and exciting dimension for the advent of parenthood. Learning about the physiological aspects of labor and delivery and practicing birthing exercises allow mothers to deliver their babies with a minimum of pain and pain-inhibiting medication. The father is provided an opportunity to directly and more actively experience the birth of his child. He becomes both a coach and a source of emotional support throughout the labor. These mothers report less pain, receive less medication, and feel more positive about the birth experience than women whose husbands are not present (Henneborn & Cogan, 1975). Although there is no definite research evidence, it appears that fathers present at birth do develop a strong emotional commitment, bonding, with their babies.

Some professionals have recently encouraged men to deliver their babies under the guidance of obstetricians in their homes (Flake-Hobson, Robinson, & Skeen, 1983). Many hospitals have created birthing centers where babies are born in home-like settings where the father may participate in the birth. Being active in the birth process may influence men to spend more time in child-care activities once the mother and baby go home (Parke & Sawin, 1976). Some men even report wishing they could breast-feed their babies (Viesti, 1980).

Studies generally indicate that fathers, regardless of economic status or degree of active involvement in childbirth are just as emotionally involved with their babies as are the mothers (Greenberg & Morris, 1974; Knox, 1975; Parke & Sawin, 1976). Researchers have observed that newborns obviously exert a powerful influence on their fathers (Greenberg & Morris, 1974). The men in one study reported by Greenberg and Morris enjoyed gazing at their babies, perceiving them as attractive, pretty, or beautiful. They delighted in physical contact with their babies and in describing their physical features. These men were "engrossed" in their new babies and clearly perceived the children as the center of their attention. Many of these fathers found their reactions to be a meaningful surprise (Greenberg & Morris, 1974):

> Something changed in me the minute she was born. It was like that (*Snaps fingers*). I was stunned by my aesthetic reaction. I had gone by the nursery window before Rebecca was born, and I hadn't found newborns very attractive. I didn't have the urge to pick up my camera and photograph them. But I was with Dale during the delivery, and the minute Rebecca came out, I thought she was beautiful. I was amazed. I had not expected her to be so beautiful and substantial, and really very much like a person . . . it was unbelievable to me. My whole perspective changed. When I went past the nursery window afterward with all the babies, one or two days old, lined up behind the window in their little bins, I looked again. They were still all red and puckery, but appealing, too, and I said to myself, "that's really nice!" (Daniels & Weingarten, 1982, p. 182)

With increasing frequency professionals are suggesting that a paternal instinct is present at birth and is a natural (but long-suppressed) urge common to most men (Hale, 1979). The moment of creating a new family, which had once been an activity exclusively for women, is rapidly expanding into a mutual endeavor in which husbands and wives join together.

Professionals have previously described childbirth as a time of crisis (Dyer, 1963; LeMasters, 1957). Perhaps this sense of crisis merely reflects the increased demands on the mothers (Miller & Sollie, 1980). Some researchers found that fathers experience less stress than mothers in adjusting to parenthood (LaRossa & LaRossa, 1981). The research of Fein (1976) determined that marital stress remained at the same level for fathers 6 weeks and 8 months following the births of their children. The crisis for fathers, if there ever was one, seems to have dissipated by the time babies are 2 weeks old (Fein, 1976). The level of tension in fathers has been shown to be much less postbirth than prenatally (Bycott, 1981). Rather than crisis, this is a time of transition accompanied by varying levels of stress (Rossi, 1968). Much of the stress during the early weeks seems to be associated with the scarcity of free time and the struggle between the spouses for release from the "drudgery" of child care (LaRossa & LaRossa, 1981).

## CONCLUSION

We are learning that "daddies make good mommies, too" (Flake-Hobson, Robinson, & Skeen, 1983). Parenting can no longer be equated with mothering and labor and delivery are no longer the exclusive domain of women. Fathers are demonstrating that the experience of parenthood is dramatic and powerful for them. As social institutions like hospitals, day-care facilities, and schools begin to expect father participation in decisions regarding their children, there will likely be a corresponding increase in the participation of fathers who are eager to be involved.

No longer can it be said that the father's only role is to be the financial provider for his family. Today men have an opportunity to express their natural nurturing instinct more fully.

## SUGGESTIONS TO PROFESSIONALS

Professionals who interact with expectant fathers can have the greatest impact on helping them and society in general become more aware of the meaning of their fathering experiences.

*1.* Researchers and speakers frequently equate parenting with mothering and totally neglect the father's role. Professionals could help by including the father's role more fully and by using more precise language concerning the possible activities of fathering.

*2.* Because men who choose not to be fathers are often exposed to criticisms and pressures from their families and friends, special sensitivity is needed when talking with them about their lives. Deliberate efforts should be made to help them identify the strengths that being childless creates for them.

*3.* Some institutions have developed structured group experiences that provide opportunities for young people to grapple with the par-

enting issue (Kimball & McCabe, 1981). Parenting topics should also be
included in courses in family life education that could be offered in
high schools, churches, and on college campuses. It is important that
these groups provide opportunities for individuals to make informed
decisions about becoming parents.

4. Men involved in fertility counseling or the adoptive process may
have deep feelings of inadequacy and may simultaneously be under
extreme stress as they attempt to become fathers. Helping them express their feelings and communicating understanding about their
plight can likewise help them deal with their situations more effectively. Professionals also need to sensitize physicians and adoption
agency policy makers about the emotional needs of these men.

5. Men and women who interact with public and private agencies
for adoption and pregnancy counseling often encounter policies that
may be insensitive to their feelings or may ignore the male's role
completely. Policies should be carefully reviewed to ensure that the
rights of all parties are appropriately covered.

6. High schools, churches, and other institutions may begin to structure roles for men that allow them outlets for their nurturing instincts.
When schools expect fathers to be present at parent conferences and
invite fathers to come into the classroom to talk about parenting or
other experiences, they are suggesting that male involvement with
children is natural. Likewise, churches could routinely include fathers
at critical points in the development of religious education. The Bank
Street School in New York City recently offered opportunities for
junior high school boys to play with and care for babies. Opportunities
like these allow young boys to learn how to nurture children long
before they become parents.

7. Prechildbirth classes for expectant fathers can provide information that helps men know what to expect during pregnancy and the
early months of parenthood (Resnick, Resnick, Packer, & Wilson,
1978). Pregnant fathers and new fathers experience a unique form of
stress; discussing the sources of it with the couple during and after
childbirth might help them to feel more in control of their lives.
Professionals could play a major role as they help these couples learn
how to talk about their feelings and focus on the needs of both
spouses.

8. Postchildbirth classes are a unique and sensible extension of
prepared childbirth training. Mothers and fathers who participate
could learn about effective parenting practices while supporting each
other through the adjustment to parenthood. New fathers should be
encouraged to talk about the emotional aspects of fatherhood. Too
often men do not express feelings because they are not expected to

have any, and accordingly, learn to ignore them. The emotional power of fatherhood provides an opportunity for men to learn to express their feelings. Emotional expression could be facilitated by churches, hospitals, and other institutions involved in parent training that encourage new parents to gather in small groups to share their experiences.

*9.* Male professionals who have not been present at the birth of their children could observe classes in prepared childbirth and may even observe labor and delivery. Such direct experience would undoubtedly increase the professional's sensitivity to the emotional aspects of the birth experience. Familiarity with the many choices available to a couple anticipating childbirth is essential for those who routinely interact with men and women during pregnancy.

*10.* Services providing emotional support for infertile and adoptive couples need to be increased. Physicians, nurses, and other medical personnel can play a key role in bringing these people together. Churches and other social institutions could provide teachers and counselors to assist childless couples with information and emotional support.

*11.* Above all, it is essential that professionals not encourage one model for expectant fathers. Many men prefer to await parenthood in hospital waiting areas, yet may be just as involved with their children after birth as men who are present in the delivery room.

## PROFESSIONAL RESOURCES FOR WORKING WITH CHILDLESS MEN AND EXPECTANT FATHERS

### Books

Alliance for Perinatal Research and Services. *The father book: Pregnancy and beyond.* Washington, D.C.: Acropolis Books, 1981.

Biller, H., & Meredith, D. *Father power.* New York: David McKay, 1974.

Brazelton, T. B. *On becoming a family.* New York: Delacorte, 1981.

Borg, S., & Lasker, J. *When pregnancy fails: Families coping with miscarriage, stillbirth, and infant death.* Boston: Beacon, 1981.

Daniels, P., & Weingarten, K. *Sooner or later: The timing of parenthood in adult lives.* New York: Norton, 1982.

Gresh, S. *Becoming a father: A handbook for expectant fathers.* New York: Butterick, 1980.

Hale, N. C. *Birth of a family: The role of the father in childbirth.* New York: Anchor Broom, 1979.

Heinowitz, J. *Pregnant fathers: How fathers can enjoy and share the experiences of childbirth.* Englewood Cliffs, N.J.: Prentice-Hall, 1982.

Phillips, C. R., & Anzalone, J. T. *Fathering: Participation in labor and birth.* St. Louis: Mosby, 1978.

Redman, A. S. *Fatherhood: To be a father.* Satellite Beach, Fla.: Redmonth Associates, 1983.

Shield, R. R. *Making babies in the 80s.* Boston: The Harvard Common Press, 1984.

Trimmer, E. *Father-to-be: Questions and answers about pregnancy, birth and the new baby.* Tucson: HP Books, 1983.

Veevers, J. E. *Childless by choice.* Toronto: Butterworth, 1980.

## Audiovisuals

*Becoming.* A prepared conscious, cooperative labor and delivery are shown with emphasis on the support of the husband and reaction of the mother to labor and delivery. Joseph T. Anzalone Foundation, P.O. Box 5206, Santa Cruz, Calif. 95063. 16 mm, 27 minutes, color.

*Fathers.* Documentary on the lives and homes of contemporary American men who share their innermost feelings about childbirth and parenthood. American Society for Psychoprophylaxis in Obstetrics, 1411 K Street, N.W., Suite 200, Washington, D.C. 20005. 16 mm, 26 minutes, color.

*Pregnant fathers.* This film is a sensitive, beautifully filmed presentation of a prepared childbirth, concentrating on the father's role in pregnancy and birth. It reveals the changing role of men in today's society and encourages men to participate in physical, emotional, social, and cognitive preparation for birth and parenthood. Joseph T. Anzalone Foundation, P.O. Box 5206, Santa Cruz, Calif. 95063. 16 mm, 18 minutes, color.

*To be a man.* Perspective Films, 369 W. Eric Street, Chicago, Ill. 60614.

## Organizations

American Society for Psychoprophylaxis in Obstetrics, 36 West 96th Street, New York, N.Y. 10025.

Association for Voluntary Sterilization, 708 Third Avenue, New York, N.Y. 10019.

Center for Population Options (Teen Programs), 2031 Florida Avenue, N.W., Washington, D.C. 20009.

The *National Organization for Optional Parenthood* has recently closed its office because of lack of funding. This group sought to provide information so that nonparenthood could become an option. Their publications, *"Am I Parent Material?"* (1976), *The Parenthood Option: A Manual for Professionals Helping People Decide Whether to Have Children or Remain Childfree* (1968), *Exploring the Parenthood Choice: An Activities Guide for Education* (1981), are available from ETR Associates, 1700 Mission Street, Suite 203, Santa Cruz, Calif. 95060.

Parents as Partners, 1227 Fort Stockton Avenue, San Diego, Calif. 92103.

Zero Population Growth, 1346 Connecticut Avenue, N.W., Washington, D.C. 20036.

## Home Birth Agencies

American College of Obstetrics, 2821 Rose Street, Franklin Park, Ill. 60601.

Association of Childbirth at Home, 16705 Monte Christo, Cerriton, Calif. 90701.

Birth Day, Box 388, Cambridge, Mass. 02138.

Birthwork, 55 Loomis Street, Burlington, Vt. 05401.

National Association of Parents and Professionals for Safe Alternatives in Childbirth, P.O. Box 1307, Chapel Hill, N.C. 27514.

## REFERENCES

Bachrach, C. A. Childlessness and social isolation among the elderly. *Journal of Marriage and the Family*, 1980, *42*, 627–636.

Barnhill, L., Rubenstein, G., & Rocklin, N. From generation to generation: Fathers-to-be in transition. *The Family Coordinator*, 1979, *28*, 229–235.

Bettelheim, B. *Symbolic wounds*. New York: Free Press, 1954.

Bittman, S. J., & Zalk, S. R. *Expectant fathers*. New York: Hawthorne Books, 1978.

Blake, J. Is zero preferred? American attitudes towards childlessness in the 1970's. *Journal of Marriage and the Family*, 1979, *41*, 245–257.

Bycott, L. T. Transition to fatherhood: Birth order and related factors. Ann Arbor, Mich.: *Dissertation Abstracts International*, 1981, *41*, 4635B. (University Microfilms No. 8110148)

Calhoun, L. G., & Selby, J. W. Voluntary childlessness, involuntary childlessness, and having children: A study of social perceptions. *Family Relations*, 1980, *29*, 181–183.

Curtis, J. A psychiatric study of fifty-five expectant fathers. *U.S. Armed Forces Medical Journal*, 1955, *6*, 937–950.

Daniels, P., & Weingarten, K. *Sooner or later: The timing of parenthood in adult lives*. New York: Norton, 1982.

Den Brandt, M. Voluntary childlessness in the Netherlands. *Alternative Lifestyles*, 1980, *3*, 329–349.

Dyer, E. D. Parenthood as crisis: A restudy. *Marriage and Family Living*, 1963, *25*, 196–201.

Fein, R. A. Men's entrance to parenthood. *The Family Coordinator*, 1976, *25*(4), 341–350.

Feldman, H. A comparison of intentional parents and intentionally childless couples. *Journal of Marriage and the Family*, 1981, *43*, 593–600.

Fishbein, E. G. Fatherhood and disturbances of mental health: A review. *Journal of Psychiatric Nursing and Mental Health Services*, 1981, *19*, 24–27.

Flake-Hobson, C., Robinson, B. E., & Skeen, P. *Child development and relationships*. Reading, Mass.: Addison-Wesley, 1983.

Gearing, J. Facilitating the birth process and father–child bonding. *The Counseling Psychologist*, 1978, *7*, 53–56.

Greenbaum, H. Marriage, family, and parenthood. *American Journal of Psychiatry*, 1973, *130*, 1262–1265.

Greenberg, M., & Morris, N. Engrossment: The newborn's impact upon the father. *American Journal of Orthopsychiatry*, 1974, *44*, 520–531.

Hale, N. C. *Birth of a family: The new role of father in childbirth*. Garden City, N.Y.: Anchor, 1979.

Henneborn, W. J., & Cogan, R. The effect of husband participation on reported pain and probability of medication during labor and birth. *Journal of Psychosomatic Research*, 1975, *19*, 215–222.

Kimball, K. K., & McCabe, M. E. Should we have children? A decision-making group for couples. *Personnel and Guidance Journal*, 1981, *2*, 53–159.

Kivett, V. R., & Learner, R. M. Perspectives on childless rural elderly: A comparative analysis. *The Gerontologist*, 1980, *20*, 708–716.

Knox, D. Fatherhood—the first time—the first year. *American Baby*, 1975, *40*, 32–33.

LaRossa, R., & LaRossa, M. *Transition to parenthood*. Beverly Hills: Sage, 1981.

Leader, A. J., & Mumford, S. D. Vasectomy: Informed consent. *Texas Medicine*, 1975, *71*:B.

Leete, R. Marriage and divorce. *Population Trends*, 1976, *10*, 17.

LeMasters, E. E. Parenthood as crisis. *Marriage and Family Living*, 1957, *19*, 352–355.

Liebenberg, B. Expectant fathers. *Child and Family*, 1969, *8*, 265–277.

Lieberman, R., Kaufman, A., Heffron, W., DiVasto, P., Voorhees, J., Williams, K., & Weiss, L. Vasectomy for the single childless man. *The Journal of Family Practice*, 1979, *8*, 181–184.

Magarick, R. H., & Brown, R. A. Social and emotional aspects of voluntary childlessness in vasectomized men. *Journal of Biosocial Science*, 1981, *13*, 157–167.

Menning, B. The infertile couple: A plea for advocacy. *Child Welfare*, 1975, *54*, 454–460.

Miller, B. C., & Sollie, D. L. The transition to parenthood as a critical time for building family strengths. In Stinnett, N., Chisser, B., DeFrain, J., & Knaub, P. (Eds.), *Family strengths: Positive models for family life*. Lincoln, Neb.: University of Nebraska Press, 1980.

Munroe, R. L., Munroe, R. H., & Whiting, J. The couvade: A psychological analysis. *Ethos*, 1973, *1*, 30–74.

Parke, R. D., & Sawin, D. B. The fathers role in infancy: A re-evaluation. *The Family Coordinator*, 1976, *35*, 325–372.

Peterson, R. A. Attitudes towards the childless spouse. *Sex Roles: A Journal of Research*, 1983, *9*, 321–332.

Pohlman, E. Childlessness, intentional and unintentional. *Journal of Nervous and Mental Disease*. 1970, *151*, 2–12.

Pupo, A. M. A study of voluntary childless couples. Ann Arbor, Mich.: *Dissertation Abstracts International*, 1980, *41*, 1095-B, 99. (University Microfilms No. 8019782)

Resnick, J. L., Resnick, M. B., Packer, A. B., & Wilson, J. Fathering classes: A psychoeducational model. *The Counseling Psychologist*, 1978, *7*, 56–60.

Rossi, A. S. Transition to parenthood. *Journal of Marriage and the Family*, February, 1968, *30*, 26–39.

Schapiro, B. Predicting the course of voluntary childlessness in the 21st century. *Journal of Clinical Child Psychology*, 1980, *9*, 155–157.

Smith, B., & Williams, J. Childlessness and family satisfaction. *Research on Aging*, 1981, *3*, 218–227.

U.S. Bureau of the Census. *Current population reports*. Washington, D.C.: U.S. Government Printing Office, 1982.

Veevers, J. E. *Childless by choice*. Toronto: Butterworth, 1980.

Veevers, J. E. Researching voluntary childlessness: A critical assessment of current strategies and findings. In Macklin, E., & Rubin, R. (Eds.), *Contemporary families and alternative lifestyles*. Beverly Hills, Calif.: Sage, 1982.

Viesti, C. R. An exploration of the psychological experience of expectant fatherhood. *Dissertation Abstracts International*, 1980, *41*, 715B 315. (University Microfilms No. 8017900)

Zaslow, M., & Kramer, E. Postpartum depression in new fathers. Paper presented at the Society for Research in Child Development, Boston, Mass., April 1981.

# CHAPTER THREE

# Changing Roles of Fathers

## THE CASE OF A MODERN-DAY FATHER CAUGHT IN A TRADITIONAL WORLD

*"A father is a banker provided by nature."*
—old French proverb

When Jane and I married in 1961, I looked forward to having babies and being a father. We got pregnant a little over a year later; I know I was a terrible burden to Jane during that time. None of her friends had to put up with a husband who wanted to be involved in every aspect of those prenatal months.

I read all the books about childbirth and watched her slowly changing body with keen interest. When I began to talk about wanting to be present at the delivery, she and her physician let me know that I was way out of line. I suppose we had our babies 10 years too soon for, in the early 60s, in the South at least, no hospitals I knew of recognized the father as a major participant in childbirth, and most women were simply put to sleep to have their babies. I could never understand how a woman would allow her conscious presence at the birth of her child to be taken from her—unless the delivery was complicated by unusual factors.

And so Jane and I were not together in those exciting hours before our baby was born. I was told to wait in her room which, like most small rural hospitals, provided few distractions. Those hours were agony for me. I constantly pestered the nurses with questions, and I can remember standing by the doors leading to the labor and delivery rooms and thinking, "One of the most important events of my life is happening right now behind those doors. What am I doing out here alone?"

Later, sitting in the room, I heard the sound of a cart being rolled down the hall. Suddenly in came the doctor pushing an incubator which contained my daughter, already quietly sleeping. As I reached out to touch her, he said all I could do was look—not touch until we went home from the hospital! I was so frustrated for I wanted so much to pick her up and hold her close. After maybe a minute she was taken to the nursery where she was safely protected from me by a window and a stern nurse.

The next day I decided that somehow I was going to at least touch her hand. As I stood at the "viewing" window, I realized the door to the nursery was open and there were no nurses around. I crept into the room and was just about to touch her when the nurses descended on me, whisked me out the door, and told me that I would lose my viewing privileges if I refused to obey the rules.

We had a 50-mile ride home from the hospital, and, once we got home, Jane fell into the bed leaving me to face my first diaper change alone. I was prepared to be a father; I was not prepared to take care of a baby. After we got home, of course, I had more than enough time to hold Mary and to play with her; I learned how to feed and change her, and loved to simply cuddle and rock her for hours. I was different from most of the other fathers I knew. They seemed awkward and not at all willing to change a diaper or do other things with their babies. I suppose over the years everyone came to accept that I was different and demanded greater than usual involvement with my daughter. I don't think I was hovering and overly fastidious. I just wanted to have a part in raising her and wanted her to be sure of my love. Later, I helped her learn to walk and vividly remember her excitement as she finally "got it together" and rode away from me on her bicycle! And now that she is 20, I am proud of her for all of her successes; I love her for being the wonderful and interesting person she is, and I like her because she is fun!

And so she grew up. And our family also grew to include her two sisters, both providing me with similar birth experiences. I had come to accept the fact that my absence at their births was simply "the way things are," but I still was not happy about it. I believe all of us missed something very important by not being together to share that time.

As the years have passed and I have seen fathers become more and more involved in birthing, I have really been envious. Fortunately, I did not allow that original distance from Mary's birth to carry over into the close relationship we have shared over the years.

**Anonymous**
*Asheville, N.C.*

The father in the case study is an exceptional example of the more family-involved androgynous fathers seen today. We interviewed many fathers who are less involved with everyday care of children than their wives, yet who would be insulted by the suggestion that, therefore they love their children less than their wives do. These fathers believe their major parental task is to provide financial security and to exercise paternal authority, leaving most of the nurturing activities to their wives. They prefer the *breadwinner,* or instrumental, role (Parsons, 1954). We also interviewed many more highly involved fathers who struggle to keep the demands of their work from excessively dominating their family lives and must often overcome the attempts of their families and friends to push them into roles that they perceive as confining. With the increasing dissemination of research about fathers (Bozett & Hanson, 1985; Lamb, 1981; Lamb & Sagi, 1983; Parke, 1981), more men are speaking out about the rewards of fathering that blend both the breadwinner and nurturing roles. In this chapter we explore both these roles.

## TRADITIONAL FATHERS

Much of the research on traditional fathers has grown out of the long-standing belief that fathers have a limited role in the family (see Chapter 1), namely to provide a solid economic base and to assist their children, especially sons, in the acquisition of appropriate sex-typed behavior to perform as breadwinners and authority figures.

Only a handful of studies provide glimpses of traditional fathers, (Heath, 1978; Spence & Helmrick, 1978; Yankelovich, 1974). In a recent study (Heath, 1978) parenting was mentioned as an important life experience by only 30% of professional men in New England. Those who included the parent role on their list placed it third, choosing wife and occupation as more powerful (Heath, 1978). The primacy of career pursuits is underscored in a 1974 survey that showed that young adults value income more than any other family contribution from men (Yankelovich, 1974). When asked to equate a list of characteristics with the father role, another group of young adults chose the masculine traits of competitiveness and work (Spence & Helmrick, 1978). In general, breadwinner or traditional, fathers value assisting in their children's cognitive development and acquisition of social skills, and encouraging moral values and the demonstration of socially acceptable behavior (Gilbert, Hanson, & Davis, 1982).

A detailed investigation of family pressures during the months following the birth of a baby showed that most fathers "helped with" rather than shared child care, and they generally viewed caring for babies as women's work (LaRossa & LaRossa, 1981). Some of the mothers in this study were unwilling to force the issue of shared child care with their husbands because the "price would be too high." These traditional attitudes were firmly entrenched, even among couples who at first stated they had more egalitarian relationships. Household labor is divided on the basis of indoor (women) and outdoor (men) activities. Child rearing, especially during infancy, is more likely to be an indoor, and hence a woman's task (Tognoli, 1979). The notion of parenting, or actually giving up free time to take care of children, continues to be alien to most men (Feigen-Fasteau, 1974). Men may be willing to help their wives with parenting, but not equally (Liss-Levinson, 1981).

Other studies have examined the kinds of parenting activities fathers choose. Fathers are especially likely to play with their children (Parke, 1979). Appropriate father involvement with children is believed to occur spontaneously, such as when the time is available or when he puts children to bed on the weekend or holiday (Benson, 1968). Fathers may also be more involved when their wives need "down time" or are depressed about the confinements of motherhood (LaRossa & LaRossa, 1981).

Many men experience deep fulfillment in providing for their families (Maxwell, 1976). These fathers believe they make a better contribution (usually financially) to their children's lives by focusing on their careers. One father, a physician, told us:

> I'm so proud of Mark. He's been all I could ever hope for in a son, succeeding academically, athletically, and in leadership. Sometimes I'm amazed at how hard he works; maybe that comes from watching me. I'm not sure. . . . I missed many of his ball games and rarely saw him get awards. I wish I knew how to tell him how much I love and respect him. We do lots of things together when I have time, but I've never really talked with him. I think his mother got to know him better because she spent so much time with him while I was working. I want him to have every opportunity I can possibly provide.

However, some of these men resent that they are "shadowy figures" in the backgrounds of their children's lives (Elliot, 1978). Other men feel pressured by the attempts of others (wives, family members, etc.) to involve them more actively. Some are afraid of losing their masculinity if they enter the mother's world. Employers, realizing that their employees' families have the potential to take energy away from work, often give lip service to increased family involvement; however, workers usually know that a choice has to be made between family and career if a man desires promotion (Colman & Colman, 1981). As men advance in careers they experience even greater pressure to put work first (Bear, Berger, & Wright, 1979). Most traditional fathers would agree that increased family involvement could only come at the cost of career advancement and income.

There appears to be evidence that some traditional fathers want to be more involved with their children (Erikson, 1969; Ross, 1982). Perhaps as father roles are studied more completely, evidence will be found that indicates that the instrumental role has negative effects on the emotional lives of men and their children (Nash, 1965; Pleck, 1980). The evidence to date, however, does not support this conclusion, and many men who call themselves traditional fathers would perhaps argue that this role is fulfilling to them and offers their children the best kind of parenting. One father said, "I love my children and I enjoy being a father who can teach them how to succeed in the workplace. I've learned valuable lessons from my career and I want to share that with the kids."

## ANDROGYNOUS FATHERS

Androgynous fathers differ from traditional fathers in that they try to protect their children from the influence of sex-role stereotyping. They encourage their children to pursue their interests without regard to role appropriateness. Androgynous fathers are more nurturant, are more involved in everyday child-care activities, and interact more with their children than men who have only "masculine" traits (Cordell, Parke, & Sawin, 1980; DeFrain, 1979; Russell, 1978). Androgynous fathers generally prefer that their children grow up to be androgynous (Flake-Hobson, Robinson, & Skeen, 1981). In situations where fathers spend the same amount of time caring for their infants as mothers, fathers interact with their babies in similar fashion as their wives (Field, 1978).

Sometimes new fathers, because of their own upbringing, are unfamiliar and even uncomfortable with an androgynous role. To help fathers adapt to this role, one group of social scientists set up training sessions for new fathers (Parke, Hymel, Power, & Tinsley, 1979) that featured education about young infants and modeling of infant care and social interaction. The training facilitated new behavioral options for fathers: participating in infant care and being more understanding of the strains on mother and infant. Three months later, trained fathers were more involved in caring for their babies and helping with housework. In contrast, untrained fathers and their wives rarely saw themselves as having any choices other than the traditional roles of female care giver and male breadwinner.

In laboratory settings androgynous men touch their babies more, sit closer to them, smile more, and talk to them more than masculine men do (Bem, 1974, 1975; Bem & Lenney, 1976; Bem, Martyna, & Watson, 1976). Russell (1978), reporting on interviews with 43 Australian families, suggests that androgynous men are more involved in day-to-day activities and play with their children more than masculine men do. Russell cautions, however, that it is too early to know if these nurturant behaviors reflect an androgynous personality; it may be that the experience of nurturing children combines with a set of values to lead men to respond androgynously on psychological tests.

Androgynous parents are likely to share child-care and breadwinner roles equally. Bem *et al.* (1976) found that androgynous parents are more flexible, have higher self-esteem, and function more effectively at home and work than traditional couples do. These couples tend to succeed in both roles because early in their marriages they developed flexible and relaxed methods of assigning jobs (DeFrain, 1979; Russell, 1978). In one study androgynous men were found to be college-educated politically moderate professionals with flexible work schedules (DeFrain, 1979). The mothers in this study devoted 54% of their time to child care, while the fathers devoted 54% of their time to jobs, careers, and/or education. Some of the reasons parents gave for role sharing included positive modeling for children, demands of wife's career, father's perception of working mothers as more interesting persons, and father's desires to be more involved in child care as an expression of love. The parents of these couples were described as role models for increased sharing—but not always positive models. One father reported he had such a strong dislike for his own father's "chauvinistic antics" and refusal to help out that he decided to be different. On the whole these couples believe they are personally happier and that their marriages and family lives are happier than those of their own parents.

Other researchers have focused on the characteristics of children of androgynous couples. Baumrind (1982) studied both traditional and child-centered (androgynous) fathers to see the effects of fathering styles on children's achievement. Traditional fathers in this study were firm and demanding, authoritarian, and possessed the bulk of the power in their families. The children of these men, who were self-confident and comfortable in their paternal roles, fared better in the outside world, were more assertive, were better adjusted, and achieved at a higher level than children of androgynous parents. Contrary to expectations, children of androgynous parents were less competent than the children of sex-typed parents. This study indicates the need for a more thorough examination of instrumental fatherhood. In contrast, a child psychologist at Yale (Carro, 1983) found that infants with stay-at-home fathers could solve problems on the level of babies 6–12 months older and had social skills that were 2–10 months more advanced. These babies flourished "because, instead of having one-and-a-quarter or one-and-a-half parents, they have two real parents" (Carro, 1983, p. 71).

As men and women find new ways of parenting, stress may increase, especially for dual-career couples (Hopkins & White, 1978). DeFrain (1979, p. 242), in his study of androgynous fathers, identified the following needs expressed by a percentage of those fathers:

- More flexible work schedule, 64%
- Better-paying part-time jobs, 58%
- Better day care, 52%
- More part-time jobs, 36%
- Four-day work week, 64%
- More benefits for part-time workers, 42%
- Public school day care, 36%

Some institutions are trying to respond to these needs. "Flexi-time," when employees work varying hours, have longer blocks of leisure time, and have paternity leave for new fathers are less rare than previously. However, even in Sweden and other European countries that have attempted to increase their populations by government policies that reward childbirth, men are still reluctant to take full advantage of them (Lamb, 1982; Lamb & Levine, 1983). Swedish fathers can take up to 9 months off with partial pay, but most (95%) do not request leave, citing fear of employer retaliation. In a study of 52 middle-class Swedish couples, 26 men said they would take paternity leave, but only 17 actually did (Lamb, 1982). In the United States as late as 1981, only two organizations, the Ford Foundation and the Bank Street College of Education, offered paid paternity leave. Ten percent of corporations in the United States provide unpaid paternity leave, but here, as in Sweden, few men take advantage of it (Lamb, 1982).

The future of paternal roles is not clear, but there is good reason to reject the desirability of an era of "androgynous unisexuality." One author, Lamb (1979), suggests that role changes should occur within the context of secure gender identification:

Long established assumptions, values, and attitudes concerning children, their care, and their needs are changing. . . . increasing numbers of men appear eager to play an active and important role in child rearing.... (p. 928) ... given a secure gender identification, a wide range of gender roles can be assumed. ... the fathers of tomorrow will share in the joys and the sorrows of parenthood much more than they have in the past. In my view, this represents a wholly admirable evolution within our society and as the fathers' role changes, the formative significance of fathers in children's lives is likely to expand greatly. (p. 942)

Studies of young adults do support this view. In a comparison of 277 families with college-age males, sons valued the nurturing dimension of fatherhood more than their fathers. Both parents emphasized the breadwinner and societal model, while their sons valued the recreational role more (Eversoll, 1979). Macklin (1980) suggests these changes flow from both the men's and women's movement and the popularity in the 1970s of books such as *Open Marriage* (O'Neill & O'Neill, 1972), which encouraged more role flexibility, equal sharing of power, and mutual trust. Perhaps the most important contribution androgynous fathers make is that they provide a clear alternative to traditional fatherhood.

## TYPICAL FATHERS

Traditional and androgynous fathers represent the extremes of fatherhood. The "typical" father is less clearly defined by research studies. Researchers who have attempted to locate and write about them present an array of types (Abt, 1979; Pleck, 1979; Colman & Colman, 1981). With the diversity that one expects to find near the center of any group, it is unlikely that discrete types can ever be adequately described.

Most men develop father behavior that blends instrumental and expressive roles. The women's movement in the early 1970s changed men's roles as well as women's. Many fathers continue to give their role as breadwinner highest priority but also want to be involved with their children:

My job can easily gobble up many more hours than the standard work week.... When I can I try to juggle trips around big events in my children's life such as birthdays, little league championships, games, or water ballet shows. Last year I scheduled my visit to our European operations during the time in which my children were in summer camp.... Although time with my children is precious, I'm not willing to sacrifice my executive career in order to be home every night at 5:30. Aside from spending loads of time with my children, I also want to serve as a person they can emulate—a guy who's making it in the big, tough, outside world. (DuBrin, 1976, p. 78)

This father's views reflect the dynamics of many modern fathers.

In other cases, economic pressures have meshed with the women's movement, so that many women are no longer able, or willing, to spend the bulk of their energy on household and parenting activities. As men see the benefits of two paychecks, many are more willing to give up some of their freedom to "help out" at home.

Some men find themselves forced to assume larger roles because their wives are dissatisfied with motherhood or suffering from post-natal depression (Baruch & Barnett, 1981; Grossman, 1981). In a survey of 1500 families by the General Mills Corporation, 8 out of 10 men whose wives had jobs outside the home argued that both parents should share in child care (A new kind of life with father, 1981).

Although at first uncomfortable as nurturing fathers, many men soon find themselves looking forward to time with their children. The following father, a welder, illustrates this change:

Don't lay on me that "I see you help your wife with the children" bit on me. If anything Darlene helps me out. Working the second shift frees up loads of time that I can spend with my son or daughter. When one of the kids gets a fever, it could be me as well as my wife who puts the thermometer into his mouth. (DuBrin, 1976, p. 63)

Sometimes men report difficulty in talking about their parenting activities. Hood and Golden (1979) offer the comments of one man whose wife had gone to work to help supplement their income.

It was, kinda mixed emotions . . . kind of an economic deal . . . in our situation. I imagine, somebody with a doctor for a husband, it would be more or less something to do [for the wife to work] . . . It wasn't that much. You know, I helped out before. Just the first time I had them all to myself all day. It wasn't much of an adjustment. Diapers, I could never get used to that. (Hood & Golden, 1979, p. 579)

Five years later when Hood and Golden (1979) interviewed this father again, he had just returned from taking the children for a picnic lunch on his wife's lunch hour and was about to take his son to the doctor. Now he could talk about his experience more comfortably and clearly:

Yeah, I see situations like that, where the wife doesn't work. It seems the wife is "the parent." The father is always working. Whereas the situation we have . . . I never really thought . . . it might be just the way the situation was out of necessity . . . I was brought closer to my kids . . . some days you feel like knocking their heads together. I think it's good though. I'm thinking that later in life, when I get older, they'll be closer to me. And I like to be close to my kids. (Hood & Golden, 1979, p. 597)

Other couples intentionally select a lifestyle that enables both spouses to pursue careers and is based on the principle of role sharing. These couples carefully work out schedules so that one of them is always at home, or they put their children in day care when both are at work. Many of these men are committed to child rearing before their children are born (Kemper, 1979).

One other kind of fathering that is readily identifiable represents role reversal. The man becomes a "househusband" while the woman becomes the breadwinner. Few fathers choose such an arrangement, but because many unemployed men have wives who continue to work, this category is increasing. One man who had been forced to quit work because of health problems described his experience to us as follows:

At first it was real hard for me. I have always believed I proved my worth with my paycheck. And sometimes I resent it when my wife leaves me a list of things to do. But I've gotten so I enjoy dropping the kids off at school and look forward to hearing about their day in the afternoon. We are lots closer than we were—the whole family is—and I've learned something about myself I wouldn't have known. Of course, there are times when I'm depressed and fly off the handle. And I wish I wasn't sick. But on the whole I like getting to know my kids while they are little, and I like the closeness in our family.

Levine (1976) studied men who were involved in more active fathering. One of the men he interviewed said:

It sort of grew out of my wanting to change myself, the way I am. Also, I wanted to be with Tony. I didn't want him to have the same thing I had with my father. He was always off on business trips when I grew up. I grew up in a classic American home where the father makes all the decisions, and gets all the deference. I was just doing the same thing my father did. I get into this big-daddy thing, too, where I take all the responsibility of everything. I'd been aware of it before, but right then it seemed isolating to me. I wanted to open up, to loosen up. I don't feel that a lot of men ever have a chance to get into their feelings about their kid. Once I had a chance to get my hands in there, a whole lot of feelings started to come alive. I had cared about Tony, but it wasn't real personal and intimate. Once I started to spend time, I started to really love him and care about him a lot. Before it was more of an intellectual relationship: I'm the father, that's my son. . . . Being with him has opened up a side of me that I have trouble expressing otherwise. I started talking to my own father about how hard he was to communicate with and how I'd like to change that, how we never really had any personal communication at all. In the process of doing that, he told me a lot about his own childhood. I hadn't really had any person-to-person communication with my father since I was in junior high school.*

Househusbands typically go through a period of stress when they may feel overwhelmed and resentful of their wives' freedom. Trust usually begins to develop, and they learn to share their ideas and frustrations with their wives. The ability of a househusband to perform and integrate the roles of father, homemaker, and spouse and still maintain a sense of self varies with the ages and number of children, resources available to him, and other personality factors. The common coping problem, if there is any, is the "master-become-slave syndrome" (Levine, 1976, p. 139). The major ingredients for a success in such role reversals are that both spouses choose this arrangement and are able to link their personal choice to bring a sense of solidarity to this change (Levine, 1976).

Experimenting with innovative models of fatherhood also has negative consequences. Role reversals are seldom easy, and before encouraging men to participate more actively as fathers, it is important to examine some of the "costs" involved. Some men may make an intellectual commitment to role reversals but then experience an unexpected negative emotional reaction as they find themselves feeling isolated and having little in common with their male peers (Levine, 1976).

LaRossa and LaRossa (1981) interviewed a man who became a full-time father when his second child was born. He arranged his work so he could stay home until early afternoon to care for his daughter while his wife worked and his son was in nursery school. After 6 months he said:

> Well, I get pretty frustrated and pretty angry sometimes, sometimes at the baby, sometimes at myself, sometimes at Sharon [his wife], but for no particular reason other than just the fact that I want to be doing something else. . . . I suppose that's a small benefit that before at an intellectual level. . . . I suppose every man can empathize with the problems of a working mother and so forth, but before [but now] I have felt [what it's like] . . . changing diapers and doing all that stuff on a full time basis for four or five hours a day. So it's been something of an exercise in growth in that respect. I've seen exactly what my limits are. . . . (LaRossa & LaRossa, 1981, p. 187)

Men involved in child care risk having others question their masculinity, and they may often be overwhelmed by the unfamiliar demands

*Reprinted with permission from J. Levine, *Who Will Raise the Children? New Options for Fathers (and Mothers)*. New York, Lippincott, 1976, pp. 73-74.

of child care (Levine, 1976). Many men have been taught that house-work and child care are demeaning and are therefore uncertain about giving up their privileged position in the family (Lein, 1979). The great-est ambivalence comes from the pressures they face if they do assume a larger role. One father who took care of his son during the day overheard a woman say, "That poor little boy. His mother must be dead—it's always his father who brings him here" (Lein, 1979, p. 491).

There are few social networks providing support for fathers. Their families and friends usually offer little support (Berger, 1979). Men's peer groups are more apt to ridicule than to understand a caretaker father.

> Perhaps more difficult is the lack of genuine understanding and support from others. Few understand in the bone-deep way one learns from direct experience what it means to care for a child all day. Admiration is cold comfort when you have just discovered the light of your life has been sitting on a mess through lunch that has soaked its way down to her left shoe . . . and you are out of clean pants . . . and she kicks over the water bowl while you are trying to change her. All with a beatific smile. For most men, caring for a child is like the Amazon: a great place to visit but only women ought to live there. I have only felt genuine support once when a friend called from his office. I had been bouncing off the walls that day with Kate. "At least you are doing something worthwhile," he said. "I've been sitting at this desk all day and feel I've accomplished nothing." Rare words. (Daloz, 1981, p. 287)

Careers can be damaged if men spend too much time with their families (DeFrain, 1979; Lein, 1979). Pressures on men to value work over their personal lives are a constant struggle for fathers who want to spend time with their children. Certainly, the structure of men's work generally is not built around their children's schedules (Bear, Berger, & Wright, 1979). The situation is so bad that one father com-mented, "I can think of nothing that our society does to help families who want to try something new" (DeFrain, 1979).

New father roles may also be difficult for women to accept. Some mothers push fathers away from involvement with their children out of fear that their territory has been invaded. Some of the traditional fathers we talked with mentioned that their wives had not told them about difficulties their children were having because their wives were afraid of "losing control of the situation" if the fathers were involved. Another father expresses this situation well:

> Although my wife and I wanted to make changes, we were still too bound up in the rewards and delusions of traditional role playing. Sure I said I wanted to participate more fully in the family, but I didn't know where to begin. There was little real incentive, and my wife ran the

house quite well. I was lazy and intimidated by her competence in the home. She wanted more from me but seemed vaguely threatened by loss of control in "her" areas. She did not like my buying the "wrong" brands. We just never worked it out. (Danzig, 1981, p. 176)

## CONCLUSION

The ideal father has been described as affectionate, emotionally involved, and willing to play with his children (Heath, 1976). To date, however, researchers have not determined which type of fathering is best, and there is little data indicating men's preferences (Flake-Hobson, Robinson, & Skeen, 1983). Research shows that when time is considered, the father's involvement with children is equal to the mother's, and even among dual-career couples, the time spent in fathering is almost the same as mother's (Booth & Edwards, 1980). Husbands of working women, however, generally tend to maintain the traditional instrumental role as a parent (Bernard, 1975).

It is unlikely that a single "ideal" father model will be identified; what is important that men be allowed to choose their own style of fathering. Professionals should not impose either an instrumental or a contemporary model of fatherhood, but should encourage men to become the kind of father that works best for them and their families. The instrumental model continues to predominate, but a growing number of men have realized that they are often limited by the father role assigned to them (Josselyn, 1956).

Recently, the Fatherhood Project was launched in New York City to critically examine innovative policies and programs that encourage more involved fathering. This project may point the way to the future. It has already developed educational programs about child care for elementary and high school age boys as well as postpartum father support groups, and encouraged employer-sponsored leave policies for fathers and divorce/custody mediation services based on the belief that fathers are more than adequate as custodial parents (Levine, Pleck, & Lamb, 1983). As this organization gathers information, conducts research on innovative programs, and publishes *The Future of Fatherhood*, men will become more aware of alternatives, and will be better able to make informed choices for themselves.

The fathering research that appeared during the late 1970s and early 1980s has shown that fathers are not social accidents. We now know that fathers make important contributions to the social and intellectual development of their children, and can be just as skillful and gentle as mothers in handling their babies and in responding to their needs. Men are rethinking their fatherhood role and more options are available to them today. The nurturing ability of men has been established as important in quality if not in quantity (Lamb, 1977, 1979, 1980, 1981; Lamb & Stevenson, 1978), imitative of women (Reiber, 1976), significant for their children (Kotelchuck, 1976; Parke & O'Leary, 1976; Flake-Hobson, Robinson, & Skeen, 1983), and a meaningful experience for men (Cordell et al., 1980). Fathers and mothers are more similar than different in their ability to parent (Parke, 1981). In so far as parenting is concerned, men are excluded only from gestation and breastfeeding (Fein, 1978). No longer is the father's role merely to pass on a sex-role identity to his children (Pleck, 1981), and the supposed biological superiority of mothers as nurturers is no longer readily and universally accepted (Frodi et al., 1978). There is strength in the diversity of fathering models. It is clear that more and more men are aware that being a father is a rewarding and meaningful life experience.

## SUGGESTIONS TO PROFESSIONALS

Professionals can be especially useful in sensitizing families to choices in fathering. The following suggestions, drawn from the literature and our interviews, are offered in the hope that men will gain fuller meaning from their fathering experiences.

1. We emphasize the need for professionals involved with family life to be aware of their own biases about fatherhood. Support groups led by empathic individuals who understand their own views could provide badly needed assistance to fathers. Men who are more traditionally inclined could become aware of more ways to fulfill the father role that do not violate their sense of propriety. Fathers who are more involved could find a kinship that would reduce the isolation reported by many men who are active in parenting.

2. Rigidity, whether in the instrumental or expressive ends of the fatherhood spectrum, is probably far more damaging than any one model of parenting. Where rigidity is identified in the parent, attempts should be made to enhance flexibility. Flexibility will be encouraged by making available information about different kinds of fathering and emphasizing the individual's right to choose the behavior that suits him best.

3. There is a need for empirical studies of all kinds of fathers. Professionals with access to populations of fathers can cooperate with

researchers or, after consulting with researchers, could develop their own studies. A topic needing study is the influence of the structure of the workplace on the options of both fathers and mothers. In many instances, stress originating at work is mistakenly attributed to the family (Pleck, 1981). Studies of men's reasons for reluctance to become involved are also needed. A Swedish experiment that encouraged more father participation in child care attracted only 10.7% of fathers to take leave in 1979 (Lamb & Levine, 1983). In addition, the specific ways in which traditional roles restrict the lives of some men should be studied.

4. Some men tend to blame their wives, children, and employers when times are rough. This blaming tendency could be especially active when men are being pushed into a father mold, whether instrumental or expressive, that does not suit their needs. The effective counselor will probe symptoms of blame to determine whether the man may feel pushed into more fathering responsibilities than he can handle. It is hoped that as these men become aware of the choices they have made, their stress will abate and attention can be directed toward ways to fill the selected role more fully.

5. It is obvious that courses in family life education and parenting manuals need to emphasize a variety of fathering models. Classes could be offered at churches and YMCAs for fathers and their babies (Resnick, Resnick, Packer, & Wilson, 1978; Rypma & Kolarik, 1981). These courses could also be offered to teenage boys and might include information on nutrition, communication, primary care, and health tips. The topic of fathering in most family life programs needs to be expanded.

6. There are indications that positive nonsexist influencing by fathers has the greatest positive impact on children before the age of 4 (Thornburg, 1979). In general, by that age children have adopted the roles modeled by their parents. Men with older children who attempt to become more involved will probably be addressed by their children with comments such as, "Why are you doing women's work?" Professionals can help fathers to anticipate such comments and to view them as opportunities for dialogue and as paths to change their children's attitudes so these men will feel more successful in their fathering role. As leisure time increases, all workers are given opportunities to spend more time with their children. Because some traditional fathers may not be skilled in creating expanded relationships with their children, they may need special help to learn how to play, talk, and listen.

7. Employers could respond to fathers' needs by developing policies that acknowledge the appropriateness of men being more involved with their families (Lamb & Sagi, 1983). Employment policies gener-

ally encourage female employees to become "superwomen" who excel at home and at work, usually at a high cost. On the other hand, men who attempt to become "supermen" are often regarded suspiciously and may even be denied promotion (Berger, 1979). Unfortunately, high unemployment during the early 1980s enabled some employers to reduce benefits for workers, such as more flexibility in working hours and possibilities for job sharing. It is hoped that more concerned and progressive employers will begin to value men who indicate they value their families. Paternity leave, work-based parent education, and alternative work schedules are methods that employers could implement to increase father involvement (Pleck, 1984).

8. More men are needed in day care, kindergartens, and elementary schools (Robinson, 1979). These men need to be present not as models of masculine traits but as surrogate fathers to children whose own fathers may be totally uninvolved. Perhaps some of the low academic achievement of boys who have been rejected by their fathers could be overcome by more natural involvement with other men (Lynn, 1974). Practitioners can be aware of this need and encourage men to model both traditional and nontraditional fathering behaviors. They can also encourage these men to withstand the subtle and not-so-subtle societal pressures to abandon child care as a non–gender-appropriate activity.

As more becomes known about all types of fathers, a clearer picture of fathering will emerge, which will allow professionals to be more helpful to men and their children. It may be that one day the term "working father" will evoke the same concerns about child development as "working mother" does.


## PROFESSIONAL RESOURCES FOR WORKING WITH FATHERS IN CHANGING ROLES

### Books and Articles

Adams, S. *The father almanac.* New York: Doubleday, 1980.

Atkin, E., & Rubin, E. *Part-time father.* New York: New American Library, 1976.

Bell, D. H. *Being a man: The paradox of masculinity.* Brattleboro, Vt.: Lewis, 1982.

Bird, C. *The two-paycheck marriage.* New York: Simon & Schuster, 1979.

Bohen, H., & Viveros-Long, A. *Balancing jobs and family life: Do flexible work schedules help?* Philadelphia: Temple University Press, 1981.

Bozett, F., & Hanson, S. (Eds.). *Dimensions of fatherhood.* Beverly Hills, CA: Sage Publications, 1985.

Brancet, A. Father love. *Esquire.* 1982, *100,* 11, 80.

Caplan, F. (Ed.). *Parents' yellow pages.* Garden City. N.Y.: Anchor Press/Doubleday, 1978.

David, D. S., & Brannon, R. *The 49% majority, the male sex role.* Addison-Wesley, 1976.

Firestone, Ross (Ed.). *A book of men.* New York: Stonehill, 1978.

Franklin, J. B. Conscious fathering: Developing new roles. *Genesis,* 1983, *3,*(4), 24–29.

Gerzon, M. *A choice of heroes: The changing faces of American manhood.* Boston: Houghton Mifflin, 1982.

Gilbert, S. D. *What's a father for?* New York: Parents' Magazine Press, 1975.

Grad, R., Bash, D., Guyer, R., Acevedo, Z., Trause, M. A., & Reukauf, D. *The father book: Pregnancy and beyond.* Washington, D.C.: Acropolis, 1981.

Gresh, S. *Becoming a father.* New York: Bantam, 1982.

Gresh, S. Fathers: Strategies for changing roles. *Genesis,* 1983, *3,*(4), 20–21.

Haddad, W., & Roman, M. *The disposable parent.* New York: Holt, Reinhart & Winston, 1978.

Hamilton, K., & Hamilton, A. *To be a man—To be a woman.* Nashville: Abingdon Press, 1975.

Johnson, Spencer. *The one minute father.* New York: William Morrow, 1983.

Klinman, D., & Kohl, R. *Fatherhood U.S.A.* New York: Garland, 1984.

Kohn, H. *Growing with your children.* Boston: Little, Brown, 1978.

Lamb, M. E., & Sagi, B. *Fatherhood and family policy.* Hilldale, N.J.: Lawrence Erlbaum, 1983.

LeMasters, E. E., & DeFrain, J. *Parents in contemporary America: A sympathetic approach* (4th ed.). Homewood, Ill.: Dorsey, 1983.

Levine, J. *Who will raise the children? New options for fathers and mothers.* New York: Lippincott, 1976.

Lewis, R. A. *Men in difficult times.* Englewood Cliffs, N.J.: Prentice-Hall, 1981.

Lewis, R. A., & Pleck, J. H. Men's roles in the family. Special issue of the *Family Coordinator,* 1979, *28,* 4. National Council on Family Relations, 1219 University Avenue SE, Minneapolis, Minn. 55414.

Lewis, R. A., & Sussman, M. B. (Eds.). *Men's changing roles in the family.* New York: Haworth Press, 1985.

McGinnis, T. C., & Ayres, J. H. *Open family living: A new approach for enriching your life together.* Garden City, N.Y.: Doubleday, 1976.

Phelan, G. K. *Family relationships.* Minneapolis: Burgers, 1979.

Pleck, J. H. *The myth of masculinity.* Cambridge, Mass.: The MIT Press, 1982.

Pleck, J. H. *The impact of work schedules on the family.* Ann Arbor, Mich.: Institute of Social Research, 1983.

Pogrebin, L. C. *Growing up free: Raising your child in the 80s.* New York: McGraw-Hill, 1980.

Reynolds, W. *The American father.* New York: Grosset & Dunlop, 1978.

Russell, G. *The changing role of fathers.* St. Lucia, Queensland, Australia: University of Queensland Press, 1982.

Sayers, Robert (Ed.). *Fathering: It's not the same. Anthology of issues.* Larkspur, Calif.: The Nurtury Family School, 1981.

Sifford, D. *Father & son.* Philadelphia: Westminister/Bridgebooks, 1982.

Singer, M. *Real men enjoy their kids!* Nashville, Tenn.: Abingdon, 1983.

Stafford, L. M. *One man's family.* New York: Random House, 1978.

Stanley, H. P. *The challenge of fatherhood in today's world.* St. Meinrad, Ind.: Abbey Press, 1982.

Stein, Edward V. *Fathering: Fact or fable?* Nashville, Tenn.: Abingdon, 1977.

Steinberg, D. *Father journal: Five years of awakening to fatherhood.* New York: Times Change, 1977.

Stevens, J., & Stevens, M. *Mother/child, father/child relationships.* Washington, D.C.: The National Association for the Education of Young Children, 1978.

Sullivan, S. A. *The father's almanac.* Garden City, N.Y.: Doubleday/Dolphin, 1980.

Torjensen, J. *The house-husband's world: Reflections of a former diplomat at home.* Unpublished manuscript. Available from P.O. Box 844, Eden Prairie, MN 55344.

Walters, J. (Ed.). Fatherhood. Special Issue. *The Family Coordinator,* 1976, *25*(4), 335–520.

Yablonsky, L. *Fathers and sons.* New York: Simon & Schuster, 1982.

## Periodicals

*Co-Parent: The Survival of the Post-nuclear Family. Co-Parent* is for and about the next generation and those who care for them: parents and their partners, teachers—especially of the very young. *Co-Parent* is also for and about men who are finding themselves in a more active fathering role— sometimes as the "fission" products of the exploded nuclear families of the past recombine with new elements in new ways. P.O. Box 92262, Milwaukee, WI 53202. Published five times a year.

*Dad's Only* (monthly), P.O. Box 340, Julian, Calif. 92036.

*Family Life Educator.* This quarterly magazine offers up-to-date information and practical teaching techniques to help ensure continuing quality educational efforts. National Family Life Education Network, 1700 Mission Street, Suite 203-204, Santa Cruz, Calif. 95060.

*Gentlemen for Gender Justice.* The only nationwide feminist journal about men and the men's movement. 306 North Brooks, Madison, Wisc. 53715.

*Nurturing News.* A national newsletter providing a forum for nurturing men, now in its third year of publication. 187 Caselli Avenue, San Francisco, Calif. 94114.

*Papa's News.* Published by the Parents as Partners Association. Lists training (groups, discussions, workshops, counseling) opportunities for fathers (and mothers) in the San Diego area. 1227 Fort Stockton Drive, San Diego, Calif. 92103.

*Parenting Studies.* An international quarterly journal designed to be a forum for professionals and scholars interested in issues for parenting and related research. Dr. Sedahlia J. Crase, Department of Child Development, Iowa State University, Ames, Ia. 50011.

*Pediatrics for Parents.* A monthly newsletter providing recent, practical, and important information about children's health. 176 Mt. Hope Avenue, Bangor, Me. 04401.

## Audiovisuals

*American man: Traditional and change.* A documentary, this film provides insight into changing attitudes toward work and family. Butterick Publishing, 161 Avenue of the Americas, New York, N.Y. 10013. 23 minutes.

*The fable of he and she.* A mythical tale in which an event causes both sexes to assume new roles to survive is presented in this film. Learning Corporation of America, 1350 Avenue of the Americas, New York, N.Y. 10019. 12 minutes.

*Fathers.* Contemporary American men share their innermost feelings about childbirth and parenthood. A warm, revealing, and sometimes astonishing film portrait of men breaking down the barriers to love, affection, and satisfaction in their lives. American Society for Psychoprophylaxis in Obstetrics, 1411 K Street, NW, Suite 200, Washington, D.C. 20005. 26 minutes, color, 1980.

*Fathers.* A film about being a father in our culture and some difficulties in being a good one. Filmed with three families: the busy-at-work father, the authoritarian, and a father sharing child care. Churchill Films, 622 North Robertson Bvd., Los Angeles, Calif. 90069. 16 mm, 23 minutes.

*A man's place.* A documentary film depicting new and expanding roles of five men: a homemaker, a nurse, a father who has taken paternity leave to care for an infant, a husband sharing responsibilities with a working wife, and a couple with an equal partnership at work and home. Center for Advanced Study in Education, Institute for Research and Development in Occupational Education, 33 West 42nd St., New York, N.Y. 10036. 16 mm, 30 minutes, color.

*Marriage is getting harder, but better.* Discusses how the idea of sexual equality has led to major changes in goals and expectations. Suggests that happiness as the primary aim of marriage is a new aspiration. Sunburst Communications, 39 Washington Avenue, Pleasantville, N.Y. 10570. Filmstrip and cassette.

*Men's lives.* A documentary film about masculinity in America by Josh Hanig and Will Roberts. New Day Films, P.O. Box 315, Franklin Lakes, N.J. 07417. 43 minutes, 1975.

*Mother/father roles.* This film depicts mother–father role reversal and the effects on the child. Parent's Magazine Films, 52 Vanderbilt Avenue, New York, N.Y. 10017. PFM Films, Inc., Box 500, Communications Park, Mount Kisco, N.Y. 10549. Filmstrip, 40 minutes, 1977.

*New relations: A film about fathers and sons.* As his son's first birthday approaches, the filmmaker explores the economic and emotional costs as well as the rewards of having decided to become a father in his mid-30s and of choosing to share child care equally with his wife, who also has a career. Plainsong Productions, 47 Halifax Street, Jamaica Plain, N.Y. 02130. 16 mm, 34 minutes, color.

*Nicholas and the baby.* Centre Productions, Inc., 1327 Spruce Street, Suite 3, Boulder, Co. 80302. 16 mm and video, 23 minutes, color.

*The nurturing father.* This film shows the validity of a nurturing role for fathers and how father nurturance greatly enhances the intellectual and moral development of children. Media for Childbirth Education, P.O. Box 2092, Castro Valley, Calif. 94546. Available in slide/tape program or filmstrip/tape program. 11 minutes.

*Parental roles.* This film shows a mother and father with different parenting styles and the ways their differences generate tension within their children. Encyclopedia Brittanica Educational Corp., 425 N. Michigan Avenue, Chicago, Ill. 60611. 29 minutes.

## Organizations

*The Fatherhood Project,* Bank Street College, 610 West 112 Street, New York, N.Y. 10025, operates a national clearinghouse for information about men in various fathering roles.

National Council on Family Relations, 1219 University Avenue SE, Minneapolis, MN 55414. Publishes *Family Relations,* formerly *The Family Coordinator.*

## Support Groups

American Academy of Husband-Coached Childbirth, Box 5224 Sherman Oaks, Sherman Oaks, Calif. 91413; (213) 788-6662.

Eastside Parent Center, 520 East 81 Street, New York, N.Y. 10028; (212) 988-7806.

The Fathers' Center, 120 West Lancaster Avenue, Ardmore, Pa. 19003; (215) 644-6400.

The Fathers' Forum, The Elisabeth Bing Center for Parents, 164 West 679th Street, New York, N.Y. 10024.

## REFERENCES

A new kind of life with father. *Newsweek,* November 30, 1981, pp. 93–98.

Abt, B. Styles of fathering. *Nurturing News,* 1979, *1,* 1–6.

Baruch, G. K., & Barnett, R. C. Father's participation in the care of their preschool children. *Sex Roles,* 7(10), 1981, 104–108.

Baumrind, D. Are androgynous individuals more effective persons and parents? *Child Development,* 1982, *53,* 44–75.

Bear, S., Berger, M., & Wright, L. Even cowboys sing the blues: Difficulties experienced by men trying to adopt nontraditional sex roles and how clinicians can be useful to them. *Sex Roles: A Journal of Research,* 1979, *2,* 191–197.

Bem, S. The measurement of psychological androgyny. *Journal of Consulting and Clinical Psychology,* 1974, *42,* 155–162.

Bem, S. Androgyny vs. the tight little lives of fluffy women and chesty men. *Psychology Today,* 1975, *9,* 58–62.

Bem, S. L., & Lenney, E. Sex typing and the avoidance of cross-sex behavior. *Journal of Personality and Social Psychology,* 1976, *33,* 48–54.

Bem, S. L., Martyna, W., & Watson, C. Sex typing and androgyny: Further exploration of the expressive domain. *Journal of Personality and Social Psychology,* 1978, *34,* 1016–1923.

Benson, L. *Fatherhood: A sociological perspective.* New York: Random House, 1968.

Berger, M. Men's new family roles—some implications for therapists. *The Family Coordinator,* 1979, *28,* 638–646.

Bernard, J. *The future of motherhood.* Baltimore: Penguin, 1975.

Booth, A., & Edwards, J. Fathers: The invisible parent. *Sex Roles,* 1980, *6,* 445–456.

Bozett, F., & Hanson, S. *Dimensions of fatherhood.* Beverly Hills, California: Sage Publications, 1985.

Carro, G. Stay-home fathers' superkids. *Psychology Today,* 1983, *17,* 71.

Colman, A., & Colman, L. *Earth father/sky father: The changing concept of fathering.* Englewood Cliffs, N.J.: Prentice-Hall, 1981.

Cordell, A., Parke, R., & Sawin, D. Fathers views of fatherhood with special reference to infancy. *Family Relations,* 1980, *29,* 331–338.

Daloz, L. Shared parenting: The male perspective. In R. A. Lewis (Ed.), *Men in difficult times,* Englewood Cliffs, N.J.: Prentice-Hall, 1981.

Danzig, P. Fatherhood and my rebirth as a man. In R. A. Lewis (Ed.), *Men in difficult times,* Englewood Cliffs, N.J.: Prentice-Hall, 1981.

DeFrain, J. Androgynous parents tell who they are and what they need. *The Family coordinator,* 1979, *28,* 237–244.

DuBrin, A. *The new husbands and how to become one.* Chicago: Nelson-Hall, 1976.

Elliot, F. Occupational commitments and paternal deprivation. *Child: Care, Health, and Development,* 1978, *4,* 305–315.

Erikson, E. *Ghandi's truth.* New York: Norton, 1969.

Eversoll, D. The changing father role: Implications for parent education programs for today's youth. *Adolescence,* 1979, *14,* 535–544.

Feigen-Fasteau, M. *The male machine.* New York: McGraw-Hill, 1974.

Fein, R. A. Research on fathering: Social policy and an emergent perspective. *Journal of Social Issues,* 1978, *34,* 1, 122–135.

Field, T. Interaction patterns of primary versus secondary caretaker fathers. *Developmental Psychology*, 1978, *14*, 183–185.

Flake-Hobson, C., Robinson, B. E., & Skeen, P. *Child development and relationships.* Reading, Mass.: Addison-Wesley, 1983.

Flake-Hobson, C., Robinson, B., & Skeen, P. The relationship between parental androgyny and early child-rearing attitudes and practices. *Psychological Reports*, 1981, *49*, 667–675.

Frodi, A., Lamb, M., Leavit, L., Donovan, W., Neff, C., & Sherry, D. Fathers' and mothers' responses to the faces of normal and premature infants. *Developmental Psychology*, 1978, *14*, 490–498.

Gilbert, L., Hanson, G., & Davis, B. Perceptions of parental role responsibilities: Differences between mothers and fathers. *Family Relations*, 1982, *31*, 261–268.

Grossman, F. K. A longitudinal focus on fathers: Predicting toddler adaptation. Paper presented at the meeting of the Society for Research in Child Development, Boston, March, 1981.

Heath, D. Competent fathers: Their personalities and marriages. *Human Development*, 1976, *19*, 26–39.

Heath, D. What meaning and effects does fatherhood have for the maturing of professional men? *Merrill-Palmer Quarterly*, 1978, *24*, 265–278.

Hood, J., & Golden, S. Beating time/making time: The impact of work scheduling of men's family roles. *The Family Coordinator*, 1979, *28*, 575–582.

Hopkins, J., & White, P. The dual-career couple: Constraints and supports. *The Family Coordinator*, 1978, *27*, 253–259.

Josselyn, I. Cultural forces, motherliness and fatherliness. *American Journal of Orthopsychiatry*, 1956, *26*, 264–271.

Kemper, R. *Childrearing fathers: Conflict and adaptation.* Unpublished doctoral dissertation, University of Michigan, 1979.

Kotelchuck, M. The infant's relationship to the father: Experimental evidence. In M. E. Lamb (Ed.), *The role of the father in child development.* New York: Wiley, 1976.

Lamb, M. Father–infant and mother–infant interaction in the first year of life. *Child Development*, 1977, *48*, 167–181.

Lamb, M. Paternal influences and the father's role: A personal perspective. *The American Psychologist*, 1979, *34*, 938–943.

Lamb, M. The father's role in the facilitation of infant mental health. *Infant Mental Health Journal*, 1980, *1*, 140–149.

Lamb, M. *The role of the father in child development* (2nd. ed.). New York: Wiley, 1981.

Lamb, M. Why Swedish fathers aren't liberated. *Psychology Today*, October, 1982, 74–77.

Lamb, M., & Levine, J. The Swedish parental insurance policy: An experiment in social engineering. In M. Lamb & A. Sagi (Eds.), *Fatherhood and family policy.* Hillsdale, N.J.: Erlbaum, 1983.

Lamb, M., & Sagi, A. (Eds.). *Fatherhood and family policy.* Hillsdale, N.J.: Erlbaum, 1983.

Lamb, M., & Stevenson, M. Father–infant relationships: Their nature and importance. *Youth and Society,* 1978, *9,* 277–298.

LaRossa, R., & LaRossa, M. *Transition to parenthood.* Beverly Hills, Calif.: Sage, 1981.

Lein, L. Male participation in home life: Impact of social supports and breadwinner responsibilities on the allocation of tasks. *The Family Coordinator,* 1979, *28,* 489–495.

Levine, J. *Who will raise the children? New options for fathers (and mothers).* New York: Lippincott, 1976.

Levine, J., Pleck, J., & Lamb, M. The fatherhood project. In M. Lamb & A. Sagi ( Eds.), *Fatherhood and family policy.* Hillsdale, N.J.: Erlbaum, 1983.

Liss-Levinson, W. Men without playfulness. In R. A. Lewis (Ed.), *Men in difficult times: Masculinity today and tomorrow.* Englewood Cliffs, N.J.: Prentice-Hall, 1981.

Lynn, D. *The father: His role in child development.* Monterey, Calif.: Brooks/ Cole, 1974.

Macklin, E. Nontraditional family forms: A decade of research. *Journal of Marriage and the Family,* 1980, *42,* 905–922.

Maxwell, J. The keeping fathers of America. *The Family Coordinator,* 1976, *25,* 387–392.

Nash, J. The father in contemporary culture and current psychological literature. *Child Development,* 1965, *36,* 261–297.

O'Neill, N., & O'Neill, G. *Open marriage: A new lifestyle for couples.* New York: Evans, 1972.

Parke, R. *Fathering.* Cambridge, Mass.: Harvard University Press, 1981.

Parke, R. Perspectives on father–infant interaction. In J. Osofosky (Ed.), *Handbook of infant development.* New York: Wiley, 1979.

Parke, R., Hymel, S., Power, T., & Tinsley, B. Fathers and risk: A hospital based model of intervention. In D. Sawin, R. Hawkins, L. Walker, & J. Penticuff (Eds.), *Psychological risks during pregnancy and early infancy.* New York: Brunner/Mazel, 1979.

Parke, R., & O'Leary, S. Father–mother–infant interaction in the newborn period. In K. Riegel & J. Mechan (Eds.), *The developing individual in a changing world.* The Hague: Mouton, 1976.

Parsons, T. The family symbol. An appraisal in the light of psychoanalytic and sociological theory. In L. Bryson, L. Kinkelstein, R. MacIver, & R. McKeon (Eds.), *Symbols and values.* New York: Harper & Row, 1954.

Pleck, J. Men's family work: Three perspectives and some new data. *The Family Coordinator,* 1979, *28,* 481–488.

Pleck, J. Men's power with women, other men, and society. In Pleck, J., & Pleck, E. (Eds.), *The American Man.* Englewood Cliffs, N.J.: Prentice-Hall, 1980.

Pleck, J. Prisoners of manliness. *Psychology Today,* 1981, *15,* 69.

Pleck, J. The workplace: A new focus for fatherhood activists. *Nurturing News,* 1984, *6,2,* 2–10.

Reiber, V. Is the nurturing role natural for fathers? *The American Journal of Maternal Child Nursing,* 1976, *6,* 366–371.

Resnick, J., Resnick, M., Packer, A., & Wilson, J. Fathering classes: A psychoeducational model. *The Counseling Psychologist,* 1978, *7,* 56–60.

Robinson, B. Men caring for the young: An androgynous perspective. *The Family Coordinator,* 1979, *28,* 553–560.

Ross, J. The roots of fatherhood: Excursion into a lost literature. In S. Cath, A. Gurwitt, & J. Ross (Eds.), *Father and child: Developmental and clinical perspectives.* Boston: Little, Brown, 1982.

Russell, G. The father role and its relation to masculinity, femininity, and androgyny. *Child Development,* 1978, *49,* 1174–1181.

Rypma, C., & Kolarik, G. A training project for fathers. In R. A. Lewis (Ed.), *Men in difficult times.* Englewood Cliffs, N.J.: Prentice-Hall, 1981.

Spence, J., & Helmrich, R. *Masculinity and femininity: Their psychological dimensions, correlates, and antecedents.* Austin, Tex.: University of Texas Press, 1978.

Tognoli, J. The flight from domestic space: Men's roles in the household. *The Family Coordinator,* 1979, *28,* 599–607.

Thornburg, H. The male as a family role model. *Family Therapy,* 1979, *6,* 185–194.

Yankelovich, D. *The new morality: A profile of American youth in the 1970's.* New York: McGraw-Hill, 1974.

# CHAPTER FOUR

# *Fathering Across the Life Span*

## THE CASE OF A FATHER LETTING GO

When I first became a father almost 20 years ago, I knew that I wanted to be deeply involved in raising my children. Sometimes I even wonder if maybe the main reason I left a promising business career for teaching wasn't because as a teacher I would have more time for my kids. Whatever, over the years I have loved being a father and have lots of happy memories I still enjoy today.

When the kids were little, we went camping for the first time on a weekend early in October. Our cousins were not arriving until late, so we had our first meal alone, and for several hours afterward, we were alone in a deserted campground in the Virginia mountains. As dark and an unexpected cold front descended, we gathered closely around the campfire, singing and telling stories to help the kids forget the cold and feel safe in the dark. I felt so complete in that moment; it seemed that all of my dreams of family life were being met. It just felt so *right* for the four of us to be together—nothing else really mattered.

I loved bringing our third baby home and watching the look of wonder and tenderness in her sisters' eyes as they first looked, and then, so gently, reached out to touch our baby. I have enjoyed teaching them to ride bicycles, watching them learn about people and relationships, laughing at silly times together, and dreaming about the times ahead of us. When they were all teenagers we took some extra money I had earned and blew it on a weekend in New York City. I was fascinated watching their amazement, excitement, and puzzlement as we explored the city. I am so glad I was there to be a part of their growing awareness of the world.

Lately I have been involved in the biggest struggle of my fathering years. One daughter has gone off to college and the second is poised and ready to leave. I am having to accept that the time has come for them to move out on their own and have experiences with people and places that are uniquely theirs. I am so sad to give up being a central person in their daily activities, and I guess there's a part of me that is afraid they may discover they can get along without my advice and counsel. The truth is that they can get along fine and that I want them to move on to whatever is next for them. But, at the same time, I am unsettled about what is next for me with them. Right now they mostly seem to need money (and lots of it) and I am not sure what other ways I can be a father to them. Letting them go gracefully is what I want to do, but what then? I don't know how to be a father to adults, and I am not sure how I am going to like being an occasional father.

I know I will always love them, and I hope I will never let my own needs burden them too much. It's just that this dream I have had about fathering after the high school years did not include dreading their leaving and sadness about not being needed so much any more. The time has come when other things will take a more central role in my life, and my task, one that seems so different from other tasks of adult life, is to figure out what those activities will be and get on with them.

*Anonymous*
*Atlanta, Georgia*

As babies become toddlers, school-aged children, adolescents, and finally adults, the role of the father shifts, just as it does when he recognizes transitions in his life—the movement from young adulthood to middle life and finally to old age. Fathers need to adjust to the constantly changing interplay of their own needs and the needs of the family. Most men develop a natural rhythm of parenting over the years. But some, like the father in this chapter's case example, find themselves suddenly aware that their roles as fathers are undergoing rapid and permanent change.

## THE TIMING OF FATHERHOOD

Is there a "best" age to become a father? The answer is no, with qualifications. The timing of fatherhood obviously plays a role in the quality of parenting. Many couples today are delaying parenthood until their careers are solidly launched and they have acquired a firm financial base. Delaying too long, however, can pose health problems for both the mother and child and may even result in parents' having to face their children's adolescent upheavals during their preretirement years.

In their 20s, young fathers bring a freshness and openness to parenting that can significantly enrich the quality of parenting. Many young fathers, however, are also deeply involved in establishing their careers and have less time for parenting than do older fathers whose careers are secure (Moreland & Schwebel, 1981). A typical response to first-time fatherhood is to invest even more energy in work, sometimes taking a second job, to provide extra money for the growing family's needs (Daniels & Weingarten, 1982). Men who have their families when they are young will be relatively young as their children mature, and consequently it may be easier for them to relate to children's activities. These men are in midlife when the children leave home, and the economic consequences of this are obvious:

> I was 48 when I paid my last college tuition. We're young enough so that we can enjoy the money I'm making now and I don't have to be worrying about retirement yet either. I'm glad we have the money now, rather than when we were 20, because we wouldn't have appreciated it half as much then. Now we know what we want to do with it. (Daniels & Weingarten, 1982, p. 138)

On the other hand, there are advantages to delaying parenthood. A more mature man has a better sense of his personal identity and may feel surer about choosing parenthood. Because his career is well underway, he may have more time to spend with his children, and his marriage may have a stability and intimacy not yet established by younger parents. However, older parents may be less tolerant of the confusion children create and may face college tuitions when they are burdened with increasing medical costs from their own illnesses or from their aging parents' need for care. Further, if parenthood is delayed too long, grandchildren may never know their grandparents. In addition, men who delay parenthood risk trading off financial security for decreased fertility (Wilkie, 1981). Men who delay fatherhood appear to be using more information from parenting literature to make decisions about the timing of their first children (Schlossberg, 1981).

Daniels and Weingarten (1982) studied 86 couples who had children at different ages. "Early-timing parents" began their families in their teens or early 20s, "late-timing parents" had their first child in their late 20s or 30s, and "midlife parents" waited until their late 30s or early 40s to become parents. Table 1 shows some of the advantages and disadvantages for younger versus older parents.

Daniels and Weingarten (1982) point out that there is no single "right" time for fatherhood. Others claim that parents who have children when they are too young or too old suffer negative psychological consequences (McLaughlin & Micklin, 1983). Major factors in a man's readiness for fatherhood are the extent to which he has separated himself from his own parents and his willingness to nurture his partner. A strong marriage as well as a clear personal identity are also good predictions for involved fathering (Daniels & Weingarten, 1982).

Although the timing of the first child is important, spacing of subsequent children also plays a major role in family dynamics. Some of the older fathers we interviewed were overwhelmed by the advent of children spaced over periods of 5-12 years. They spoke of being constantly tired from the demands of their infants. Like younger parents they were eager to get on with parenting older children. And obviously

**Table 1.**
*Advantages and Disadvantages Related to the Timing of Parenthood*

| ADVANTAGES | DISADVANTAGES |
|---|---|
| Younger Parents (20–35 years) | |
| More flexible, adaptable | Uncertain personal identity |
| Identification as parent becomes strong part of self-identify | Few years of freedom as single person |
| Fresh, open approach to parenthood | Early stress on marriage |
| | Meager economic resources |
| Freed from demands of children while still young | Neophyte in challenges of adult life |
| Enjoyment of grandchildren | Less likely to develop equal sharing of child care |
| Older Parents (36–50 years) | |
| Personal identity more secure | Impatience due to a lack of privacy, solitude |
| Time to appreciate children | |
| Eager for children | Difficult to give up sense of freedom |
| Sense of regeneration is keen | |
| Financially secure | Children may be burdened with aging parents at a young age |
| Marital intimacy established | |
| More parenting resources available | May not live to enjoy grandchildren |
| More equal sharing of parental responsibilities | Marital intimacy curtailed |

Adapted from P. Daniels & K. Weingarten, *Sooner or Later: The Timing of Parenthood in Adult Lives.* New York: Norton, 1982.

the spacing of children influences the family's mobility. Some men never feel comfortable with babies but relate to more verbal and independent children well. And others show a definite preference for involvement with their sons (Bronfenbrenner, 1960). Some men are involved fathers from birth; others may not spend much time fathering until the teenage years. One father we interviewed said:

> I didn't know how to relate to my kids when they were small. So by the time they became teenagers I was eager to spend time with them. Now we play golf and tennis together and can talk about books and movies on a more equal basis. Before I would sometimes read them a story or put them to bed, but now I actually look forward to being with them.

There are endless timing patterns, from "stairstep" families, where children come one after another, to "recycled fathers," who have two or more "sets" of children (see box entitled Recycled Fathers). The chronological gap in some families may span two or even three generations.

### RECYCLED FATHERS*

LINCOLN, Neb. (AP) Recycled fathers, as defined by Kathryn Weil Simon, are older men who became fathers for the first time between the ages of 20 and 24 and again became fathers between the ages of 45 and 60.

Mrs. Simon . . . studied recycled fathers for her master's thesis from the Department of Human Development and the Family at University of Nebraska in Lincoln. . . . The 373 men who participated are from 47 states. The average recycled father in the study is a white Catholic between the ages of 47 and 49 who was a first-time father between the ages of 20 and 24. Most of them are in their second marriages (92 percent of those studied are divorced) and their wives are full-time homemakers. Most are college graduates and work or own a medium-size business.

Some of the men objected to the term "recycled fathers" because they viewed parenting as a continuum. . . . Overall, the study indicated that older fathers may make better fathers, she says. "Even though they (older fathers) are off-time with most other men (in terms of parenting) . . . the maturity factor is a plus."

For some men, being a recycled father is advantageous because they have had experience as a parent before; their careers are established; they have more leisure time; and they seem to be in a happier marriage, Mrs. Simon says. In addition, she says, men who regard their first marriage

*Reprinted with permission from Associated Press, "Dear Old Dad, the Second Time Around." *The Gastonia Gazette*, Gastonia, N.C., March 13, 1983, p. 1-E.

as a failure may want to prove they can be a good parent, and this represents what may be their last chance to do so. Perhaps the study's most surprising finding, Mrs. Simon says, was that 2-1/2 times as many recycled fathers preferred girls compared with when they were first-time fathers. Some of the older fathers indicated they were tired of participating in activities such as Little League and basketball. "Most thought it would be nice to go to a dance recital and watch this time," Mrs. Simon says. "They also seemed to have the feeling that little girls would do more hugging and kissing and be more dependent. And some felt a girl would be a better companion for the mother if they were no longer around."

A summary of the research results also showed:

- Three times as many recycled fathers indicated that they attended childbirth preparation classes and were present in the delivery room at the birth of their infant, as first-time fathers.
- Statistically a higher proportion indicated that they felt very close in their relationship with their wives during the first six months after the birth of their child and as their child got older compared with their first experience as fathers.
- A statistically significant number of recycled fathers stated that their ability to communicate, use compliments and express affection improved.
- A statistically significant number of recycled fathers indicated that they were more willing to be flexible and share child-care responsibilities with their wives than as first-time fathers.
- Most recycled fathers take time to participate in recreational and other kinds of activities with their children.
- Recycled fathers feel more confident in their parenting skills than they did as first-time fathers.

Their problems and concerns included: the discomfort that occurs if the recycled father is mistaken for a grandfather; being uncomfortable at PTA or other meetings where the majority of fathers are younger; not being able to call on grandparents for support, because they are dead or too old to be of assistance; and resentments older children may have toward the younger siblings.

## FATHERHOOD AND MARITAL SATISFACTION

Most research shows that marital satisfation is lowest during the childbearing years (Glenn & McLanahan, 1982; Glenn & Weaver, 1978; Kimmel, 1974; LeMasters, 1957; Miller & Sollie, 1980; Rollins & Feldman, 1970; Ryder, 1973; Waldron & Routh, 1983). Graphs of marital satisfaction are usually U shaped, reflecting the high levels of marital comfort before children are born and after they leave home. This does not suggest that children destroy marriages (although in some cases they may be allowed to do so). Instead, children frequently place such abundant demands on the couple that there is little time or energy left to fuel the marriage relationship. This situation is often more critical when a child is ill, or dying, or when both spouses are career-oriented (Alpert, 1981). One father in a dual-career marriage told us: "By the time we get the housework done, the kids' needs covered, and all the other things that go into running a family done, we are both exhausted. There seems no choice but to put our needs last."

This lack of energy is especially crucial during the early years when children so often seem in control. Miller (1971) tells of his struggle while his children were small:

> Probably the most important factor which accounts for the direction we took was our naiveté about the impact of having children. A naiveté incidentally which I see today having a similarly devastating effect on many young parents. We just had no idea how much time and emotion children captured and how they simply changed our lives. . . . Our first son was superactive and did not sleep through the night. We were both exhausted. My wife insisted that I not leave everything to her; she fought with me to participate in the care of our son and apartment. I took the 2 a.m. and 6 a.m. feedings and changings, for my ideology did not allow me to just help out; I had to "share" and really participate in the whole thing. I resented the degree of involvement; it seemed to interfere terribly with the work I wanted to achieve. (p. 247)

During the middle years of parenting (when the children are ages 4–14), marital satisfaction is low and relatively flat (Rossi, 1968). Early in this "plateau phase" the family is typically under financial strain and is further stressed by attempting to maintain a sense of order in the midst of confusion created by children's activities (Rapoport, Rapoport, & Strelitz, 1977). Marriage during these years is often "better" for fathers than mothers, who usually have more negative experiences with their children, are more tired, feel more isolated, and are more vulnerable to psychosomatic stress ailments (Rapoport *et al.,* 1977). Negative feelings between couples are frequently highest at this stage (Bernard, 1975). Galinsky (1981) quotes a father who spoke about some of the ambivalence he felt at this point in his life:

> At first it was strange to have children. Lauren [his wife] took right over. I was not used to her as a mother, and I felt slighted. I didn't really understand what had happened to me. I didn't become interested in the

children until they were two-year-olds, until they developed a personality that I could respond to. Increasingly, I've become sorry that I missed those early years. What scares me now is that I'm so attached that I'm afraid of what I'll be like without my children. We're a family. Everybody that's included in our children's lives is included in our lives. And I feel that we [he and his wife] don't really have an identity of our own. Not a strong identity. Not as strong as our identity as a family. . . . But I also go through times when I wish they would be gone, when I say to myself, "This is enough." I would like to experience a little more of myself without them. (Galinsky, 1981, p. 285)

Marital satisfaction usually reaches its lowest point when the children reach school age and rises as children get older and more independent (Anderson, Russell, & Schumm, 1983). Many studies indicate the postparental years are a time of marital renewal—a "second honeymoon" (Lewis & Roberts, 1982).

## TASKS OF FATHERHOOD OVER TIME

The tasks of fathering are complex during the middle years of childhood. During the preschool years fathers mainly interact with their children through play. Simultaneously, however, through modeling the father provides the tools for children to build positive self-esteem (Sarnoff, 1982). Benson (1968) suggests that as children age, the disciplinary role of the father must increase. During these middle years the father can be a teacher, coach, confidant, and pal as well as an authority figure. Ideally, he will respond in ways that are both encouraging and controlling. Men are learning that both parents are responsible for their children, and men are tending to share child-care tasks more frequently (see Chapter 3). When parenting tasks are assigned on a more equal basis, the couple may attain a new sense of vitality because they have more time to spend together.

Galinsky (1981) suggests that parenthood is a personal "saga" in which men and women continually modify their images of good parents to conform with the real constraints in their lives. Tension often arises because many men find that meeting the demands of their work conflicts with their desire to be with their families. Some men feel forced to put their jobs first because of the need for more financial security. Or some put work first because they lack the flexibility to grow and change with their children (Benson, 1968). Many men learn that family life offers greater rewards than the work world and become even more involved with their children (Rapoport et al., 1977).

Parents are constantly changing as they create and destroy bonds with their children. At midlife, when the changes created by the need to begin letting go of adolescent children may seem threatening, fathers may begin to have feelings of envy, hostility, pride, and perhaps regret as they realize they are needed less. In the trials of the children's adolescence, the father's new relationship is formed:

> You know, it was easier when she was a baby. I just left it all to my wife and went to work. But I can't do that now. My wife won't let me walk away; she needs me to help her deal with Amy; she insists on my help. Amy won't let me off the hook either. She comes to me more often than her mother. You know, I like it this way, but it sure as hell isn't easy. (Colarusso & Nemiroff, 1982, pp. 325–326)

Some families experience extreme stress during the children's adolescence, if fathers and mothers refuse to let go of children and do not want to acknowledge that the relationship has changed (Lewis & Roberts, 1982). These are the fathers who become more strident in enforcing the family rules, almost as if they are determined to hold on to a relationship that they know is gone (Farrell & Rosenberg, 1981). Happily for most, once the separation has been completed, the new relationship has its own rewards. As one father told us:

> Looking back I'm not sure how we made it through the teenage years. I learned that I did need to be clear about the rules, but that sometimes the rules would have to bend, and I learned that all of us would have to begin to trust each other in new ways. My sons were no longer content being the persons I wanted them to be. Once I began to try to get to know them as the unique young men they were, and to acknowledge that in many instances they were different from me, we began to get along better. Sometimes I wonder if all my strictness didn't make the situation worse. Sure my kids do things that I cannot approve. But they are also very fine people in lots of other, and maybe more important, ways.

Although many men grieve the loss of daily contact with their children, they continue to be important figures throughout their children's lives (Pearson, 1958). A father whose children left home told us:

> When they left home I realized how much they meant to me. I found myself looking for ways to keep them around, and sometimes I would resent the carefree times they were having in college. It seemed that I was the only one feeling this way, and that I was the one who had to change if I wanted to maintain my relationship with them. Now that they are both married and out on their own they still come to me for advice and sometimes for money. I help them out when I can, and I like the more equal relationships we have now. Sometimes we can take a trip together, and I really have a good time with them.

Parenting at midlife is characterized by intensified change. Wives may find rewarding activities outside the home, and children leave. There is often a keen sense of regret because fathering is over and the grown child appears to no longer need a father. The task at this point is to accept the child as an adult who has a life and individuality separate from the parents. There may also be a need to evaluate the success of the stage of active parenting—to see how well one has lived up to the idea of a good father (Galinsky, 1981). Fortunately, this separation is gradual. The adolescent slowly moves away, unleashed by a driver's license and the possibility of leaving home for college while still being financially supported. The father must now forge a new identity as an individual and as a spouse, a task that is not easy for all men. Some fathers' reactions to the departure of their children are so strong, they are diagnosed as suffering from postparental distress syndrome (Lewis & Roberts, 1982). Symptoms of the syndrome are an inability to acknowledge that the relationship must change when children depart, feelings of powerlessness and not being needed in the marriage, and frustration because the breadwinner role no longer has the same importance in the family. Husbands experiencing such discomfort typically shift from alarm to anger and entreat their wives and children to come back to them by promising gifts. When the elements generating these feelings are misunderstood, some men become afraid of being out of control in an unfamiliar world. Many of them fantasize that their relationships with their children had been perfect (Galinsky, 1981). The successful midlife father accepts his children's separateness and individuality but maintains regular contact with them.

There are, of course, mediating events that ease this transition. Aging parents often begin to demand more attention. A new sense of freedom, especially when coupled with an enriched marriage, leads many men to a finer appreciation of life (Cohen & Gans, 1978). Many men become more sensual and develop better peer relationships. They typically "mellow" and seek more companionship than previously (Zube, 1982).

When the children leave home, fatherhood is not over; new and less dependent relationships between fathers and children are important for both (Fogarty, 1975). One father expressed some of the conflict in this period:

Our daughter, Betty, recently moved back home after flunking out of college for the second time. I was glad to have her around at first and proud when she got a job. But Marian and I have come to really enjoy being at home together. Being able to eat later, to have our own schedule, and to have a freer sex life ended when Betty moved back in. Finally both of us got so fed up with planning our lives around her activities that I told her she needed to move out. We deserve some time alone after all those years with kids around. Betty understood even though she had to take a second job to be able to afford an apartment.

Midlife is a critical time for fathers to find new and more satisfying but less dependent relationships with their children (Colarusso & Nemiroff, 1982).

## GRANDFATHERHOOD

For many men grandfathering generates a renewed sense of excitement about life (Benedek, 1970). Grandchildren ensure the continuation of the family as "past and future merge into the present" (Mead, 1972, p. 311). This new parental relationship is usually not complicated by the responsibilities, obligations, and conflicts of the father–child relationship. Grandchildren also often fill the activities gap that occurs at retirement (Cath, 1982; Group for the Advancement of Psychiatry, 1973; Kivnick, 1981; McCullough, 1980).

Neugarten and Weinstein (1975) suggest there are four styles of grandparenting: the patriarch, who is wise; the substitute parent, who provides regular care; the formal grandfather, who loves to play; and the distant grandfather, who is benevolent but rarely involved. Maas and Kuypers (1974) suggest that family-centered fathers who are rated high on marital adjustment, center their activities around their children, and have stable occupations enjoy seeing their grandchildren often and like to have their children living nearby. These grandfathers like to help married children and grandchildren with gifts, money, advice, and so on (Sussman, 1965).

In some families the grandparents and grandchildren seem to form an alliance against their common enemy—the parents (Group for the Advancement of Psychiatry, 1973). In other families there is a strong sense of union as three generations come together. Haggerson (1981) witnessed his grandson's birth:

At one time during the birth I had looked around the room and noticed the plants seemed to be smiling along with us. The next day I began to reconstruct the experience . . . the notion I had carried for many years that pain was necessary was dispelled. . . . Seeing my son deliver his own child with skill, courage, patience, tenderness relieved me of wondering how in the world I would ever teach my sons how not to be fearful and flee from birth. . . . Being an integral part of the birth, in view of my earlier fears, is one of the highlights of my life. I learned so much; I felt such joy, experiencing such beauty. This experience at once took much of the mystery out of birth and added infinity to the mystery of life! My grandson's birth was in some sense my own rebirth. (pp. 182–183)

Just as there are stereotypes of all kinds of parents, there is a stereotype of the kindly, aging grandfather who has little to do other than go on walks with his grandchildren. The reality is much more diverse. Today many men become grandfathers while in the prime of life and may be more interested in playing golf than babysitting. Many others become stepgrandparents when their children choose a spouse who already has a family. Some men are so busy that they refuse to allow their grandchildren to complicate their lives (Troll, 1971). For others, grandfatherhood provides an outlet for long-suppressed nurturing instincts. The grandfather often assumes a more maternal role, since the father role is not viewed as sharable (Cath 1982; Neugarten & Weinstein, 1975; Troll, 1971).

As a nurturer, the grandfather can indulge in his grandchildren many behaviors he would have discouraged in his own children. One man watched with amazement at this kind of relationship develop between his father and his own son. His militaristic father had taught him that a man could never cry or show emotional distress. He was astonished to find that his father no longer expected from his grandson the stoicism he had demanded 20 years earlier from his son (Cath, 1982).

To some extent grandfathering is influenced by the relationship between the grandfather and his adult children. Research suggests that parents continue to "give" more to their children than is given back and that among blue-collar workers there is more assistance from parents to adult children than from children to parents (Robertson, 1976; Watson & Kivett, 1976). Aging parents tend to prize their independence and do not want to be dependent on their children, but in times of emergency or grief they turn to them first. In a 1968 survey Shanas, Townsend, Wedderburn, Friis, Milkhoy, and Stehouwer reported that 84% of the elderly live less than an hour from one of their adult children. This proximity to children and grandchildren increases the benefits of grandfathering (Maas & Kuypers, 1974; Sussman, 1965; Troll, 1971).

Kivnick (1982) interviewed 30 grandparents and found that they valued most the following aspects of grandparenting: (1) *centrality* in life through increased identity and feelings of personal meaning; (2) *being a valued elder* who is a source person for his children and identifies with his grandchildren; (3) *immortality* assured as his patriarchial responsibility has been assured; (4) *reinvolvement with personal past* as his grandchildren evoke memories of his own early years and he recalls experiences with his own grandparents; and (5) *the opportunity to indulge grandchildren* allows him to be lenient without worrying about spoiling their behavior. Colarusso and Nemiroff (1982) suggest similar values for grandparents. Although for some of the men they studied, grandfatherhood evoked fears of approaching death, in healthy fathers, grandchildren become "psychic organizers" who infuse new meaning to life. Grandchildren ensure the grandfather's genetic immortality and offer the promise of recapturing the unquestioning love that children give. The grandfather's own sexuality is reaffirmed, and the child provides a new focus and an outlet for nurturing at a time of frustration and fears over loss of his children and awareness of physical decline. One grandfather told us:

> Three years ago I became a grandfather, and that's been lots more fun than I had ever imagined. When my grandson comes over I find myself sprawled out on the floor playing games again. And I love the way he crawls up into my lap just to snuggle. He loves to go around the house and remove all the knobs, buttons, and switches that are not glued down. Whenever he leaves we have to search around in his hiding places to see if we can find those missing items. And I think it is a riot! When my own kids were little I would have been angry and yelled at them. But with Tad, I mostly just laugh. I never thought I could enjoy a grandson as much as I do.

Grandparenthood can add to the overall quality of life and thereby increase mental health. It can be an experience of daily delight and long-term enrichment. Quinn (1983) suggests that health and the quality of relationship with one's children are the two major factors in adjustment to old age. Although grandfathers have been shown to be less involved than grandmothers, overall the experience is powerful (Langford, 1972). Indeed, being a grandfather may be the most powerful aspect of fatherhood.

## CONCLUSION

Although the developmental changes of children may be more evident, the role of the father also undergoes a constant evolution with potential for added meaning. Fatherhood is experienced by persons who are maturing and changing, whose lives are filled with other activities, whose marriages evolve into complex and often highly controlling systems, and whose work must sometimes take priority over the needs of their families. The changing demands and needs of their children push men into new and perhaps unanticipated kinds of parenting and grandparenting. It is evident that being a father is a central role in many men's lives, and because fathers are more reluctant to abandon their children than their spouses, it may be that fatherhood offers the most constant source of meaning in life (Quinn, 1983).

In the remaining chapters different kinds of fathers are discussed. Their lifestyles vary, but each must decide how involved he will be, and he must also learn how to let go as his children become adults and need him less. Time forces all fathers into new ways of interacting with their children.

## SUGGESTIONS TO PROFESSIONALS

*1.* Professionals who routinely interact with or study families need to constantly seek the highly complex and often obscure interactions that may underlie observed behavior. For example, some men seem so preoccupied with their careers they have no time left to serve as fathers; however, these same men may have been closed out of a fathering role by wives who do not want them to interfere, by developmental issues (Chapter 1) that demand attention, or by lack of knowledge about how to father. It may appear that family stress results from infrequent father contact when in fact the stress is generated by a poor marital relationship that has dictated a limited role for the father. More knowledge about adult development and family systems (see Chapter 1) will strengthen interventions with fathers.

*2.* There is a tendency for myths about fathers to govern expectations. Farrell (1975) suggests that the following myths limit the development of both sexes:

- Women have instinctual drives and needs to nurture children; men do not.
- Women innately know more about children than men.
- Women cannot be fulfilled without children.
- A mother's constant attention to her child cannot be replaced by a man's constant attention.
- Fathering is important to children but impractical because of men's primary role as breadwinner.

It is important for professionals to dispel these myths. This can be accomplished by examining one's own beliefs and evaluating curriculum materials, lesson plans, sermons, and other instructional materials to ascertain that fathers are not being depicted stereotypically. By offering more fatherhood options, men and women may become more aware of choices they can make in their families.

3. Professionals need to be able to value many models of family life and to realize that there is no one "best" time for parenthood. It is important to remember that contrary to expectations, many midlife couples make extremely successful transitions to parenthood. Recent medical advances enable more couples to choose when they want to become parents. Couples considering first-time parenthood at midlife need to be aware of the associated health risks and medical procedures such as amniocentesis that indicate the physical health of the unborn (DeCherney & Berkowitz, 1982).

4. In interactions with men who have young adult children, indications of postparental father distress should be anticipated. Focusing on the feelings surrounding the departure of their children might help them more fully understand their experiences. Some men know they are upset but do not understand that giving up children normally creates distress. By receiving information about fathering, they are better able to attribute their feelings to events they had been unaware of, which may be reassuring. More "empty nest" fathers are seeking treatment (Lewis, Freneau, & Roberts, 1979). Practitioners could develop structured groups for these men that provide information and emotional support. These groups could follow up courses in fathering for men with school-age children (Moreland & Schwebel, 1981). Many men attempt to repress midlife issues because the stereotype of the "midlife fling" seems so trite and demeaning (Cohen, 1979), and they tend to idealize their past relationships with their children. For many men, transversing the midlife transition and developing a sense of personal identity that does not include an active fathering role may be difficult. Helping men to develop more realistic views of their past relationships as well as to become aware of the potential for new kinds of relationships with their children will ease the transition to middle age.

6. Closely parallel with the issue of letting go of the children is the issue of creating a new relationship with one's own parents. There is a need for programs that help aging parents and their children to communicate better. Johnson and Spence (1982) developed a format that includes information, education, and instruction in communication skills for the elderly and their children. Such programs will be more successful if they draw from and overtly value the rich experience of the elderly (Zube, 1982). Today's middle-aged population is the first group to be concerned with large numbers of parents in their 70s and

80s. Both generations need more information and perhaps a new definition of parent–child relationships in later life (Cohen & Gans, 1978).

7. The role of effective grandparenting (and stepgrandparenting) needs more emphasis, especially as it adds to the quality of life for all three generations. Grandfatherhood can become a healthy focus as men approaching death find self-renewal in the birth of grandchildren. The grandchild evokes memories of the past and may become a source of unwavering acceptance and love. Programs in churches, schools, nursing homes, senior citizens centers, and the like that allow grandfathers to discuss this role may help reduce some of the social isolation elderly men experience (Kivnick, 1982). Treatment plans that include regular contact with grandchildren, even if only by mail or phone, can add a new sense of vitality.

## PROFESSIONAL RESOURCES FOR WORKING WITH FATHERS ACROSS THE LIFE SPAN

### Books

Baranowski, M. D. Men as grandfathers. In F. Bozett and S. Hanson (Eds.), *Dimensions of fatherhood.* Beverly Hills, Calif.: Sage Publications, 1985.

Biller, H. *Father power.* New York: Anchor Books, 1975.

Carter, E., & McGoldrich, M. (Eds.). *The family life cycle: A framework for family therapy.* New York: Gardner, 1980.

Daniels, P., & Weingarten, K. *Sooner or later: The timing of parenthood in adult lives.* New York: Norton, 1982.

Kohl, H. *Growing with your children.* Boston: Little, Brown, 1978.

Kornhaber, A., & Woodward, K. L. *Grandparents/grandchildren: The vital connection.* Garden City, N.J.: Anchor, 1981.

Rapoport, R., Rapoport, R., Strelitz, Z. *Fathers, mothers and society.* New York: Basic Books, 1977.

Scott, Lucy. *Parenthood after 30: Resource manual.* Santa Cruz, Calif.: Network Publications, 1981.

Scott, Lucy. *Parenthood after 30? Questions and answers.* Santa Cruz, Calif.: Network Publications, 1983.

Yablonsky, L. *Fathers and sons.* New York: Simon & Schuster, 1982.

### Audiovisuals

*Adolescent conflict: Parents vs. teens.* This film provokes a response to a major problem of growing up—conflict between parents and teens. It shows teen–parent conflicts as almost inevitably due to the adolescent's search for independence and parental fears of "letting go." Sunburst Communications, 39 Washington Avenue, Pleasantville, N.Y. 10570. Two filmstrips, two cassettes.

*Leaving home: A family in transition.* This autobiographical film shows one family's struggles with change as their four daughters reach adulthood and prepare to leave the nest. Direct Cinema Ltd., P.O. Box 69589, Los Angeles, Calif. 90069. 28 minutes.

## Organizations

The Family Resource Coalition, Suite 1625, 230 North Michigan Avenue, Chicago, Ill. 60601, is an organization that publicizes new parenting styles and provides general family resource material.

Grandparents–Childrens Rights, Inc., P.O. Box 444, Haslett, Mich. 43840, provides information to grandparents facing loss of contact with their grandchildren because of divorce or remarriage.

## REFERENCES

Alpert, J. Theoretical perspectives on the family life cycle. *The Counseling Psychologist*, 1981, *9*, 25–34.

Anderson, S., Russell, C., Schumm, W. Perceived marital quality and family life cycle categories; A further analysis. *Journal of Marriage and the Family*, 1983, *45*, 127–139.

Associated Press. Dear old dad, the second time around. *The Gastonia Gazette*, Gastonia, N.C., March 13, 1983, p. 1-E.

Benedek, T. Parenthood during the life cycle. In E. J. Anthony & T. Benedick (Eds.), *Parenthood: Its psychology and psychopathology*. Boston: Little, Brown, 1970.

Benson, L. *Fatherhood: A sociological perspective*. New York: Random House, 1968.

Bernard, J. *The future of motherhood*. Baltimore: Penguin, 1975.

Bronfenbrenner, H. *Freudian theories of identification and their derivatives. Child Development*, 1961, *31*, 15–40.

Cath, S. Vicissitudes of grandfatherhood: A miracle of revitalization? In S. Cath, A. Gurwitt, & J. Ross (Eds.), *Father and child: Developmental and clinical perspectives*. Boston: Little, Brown, 1982.

Cohen, J. Male roles in midlife. *The Family Coordinator*, 1979, *28*, 465–471.

Cohen, S. Z., & Gans, B. M. *The other generation gap: The middle aged and their aging parents*. Chicago: Follett, 1978.

Colarusso, C., & Nemiroff, R. The father in midlife: Crisis and the growth of paternal identity. In S. Cath, A. Gurwitt, & J. Ron (Eds.), *Father and child: Developmental and clinical perspectives*. Boston: Little, Brown, 1982.

Daniels, P., & Weingarten, K. *Sooner or later: The timing of parenthood in adult lives*. New York: Norton, 1982.

DeCherney, A. H., & Berkowitz, G. S. Female fecundity and age. *New England Journal of Medicine*, 1982, *306*, 424–426.

Farrell, M. *The liberated man.* New York: Bantam, 1975.

Farrell, M., & Rosenberg, S. *Men at midlife.* Boston: Auburn House, 1981.

Fogarty, M. *40 to 60: How we waste the middle aged.* London: Bedford Square Press, 1975.

Galinsky, E. *Between generation: The six stages of parenthood.* New York: Times Books, 1981.

Glenn, N., & McLanahan, S. Children and marital happiness: A further specification of the relationship. *Journal of Marriage and the Family*, 1982, *44*, 63–72.

Glenn, N., & Weaver, C. A multivariate, multistudy of marital happiness. *Journal of Marriage and the Family*, 1978, *40*, 269–282.

Group for the Advancement of Psychiatry. *The joys and sorrows of parenthood.* New York: Scribner's, 1973.

Haggerson, N. Birth rites: Grandson and grandfather. In R. A. Lewis (Ed.), *Men in difficult times: Masculinity today and tomorrow.* Englewood Cliffs, N.J.: Prentice-Hall, 1981.

Johnson, E., & Spence, D. Adult children and their aging parents. *Family Relations*, 1982, *31*, 115–122.

Kimmel, D. *Adulthood and aging.* New York: Wiley, 1974.

Kivnick, H. Grandparenthood and the mental health of grandparents. *Aging and Society*, 1981, *1*, 365–391.

Kivnick, H. Grandparenthood: An overview of meaning and mental health. *Gerontologist*, 1982, *22*, 59–66.

Langford, M. Community aspects of housing for the aged. Research report No. 5, *14*, New York: Center for Housing and Environmental Studies, Cornell University, 1972.

LeMasters, E. Parenthood as crisis. *Marriage and Family Living*, 1957, *19*, 352–355.

Levinson, D. J. *The seasons of a man's life.* New York: Ballantine, 1978.

Lewis, R., Freneau, P., & Roberts, C. Fathers and the postparental transition, *Family Coordinator*, 1979, *28*, 514–520.

Lewis, R., & Roberts, C. Postparental fathers in distress. In K. Soloman & N. Levy (Eds.), *Men in transition.* New York: Plenum, 1982.

Maas, H., & Kuypers, J. *From thirty and seventy.* San Francisco: Jossey-Bass, 1974.

McCullough, P. Launching children and moving on. In E. Carter & M. McGoldrick (Eds.), *The family life cycle: A framework for family therapy.* New York: Garden, 1980.

McLaughlin, S., & Micklin, M. The timing of the first birth and changes in personal efficacy. *Journal of Marriage and the Family*, 1983, *45*, 47–55.

Mead, M. *Blackberry winter.* New York: William Morrow, 1972.

Miller, B., & Sollie, D. Normal stresses during the transition to parenthood. *Family Relations*, 1980, *29*, 459–465.

Miller, S. The making of a confused middle aged husband. *Social Policy*, 1971, *2*, 2.

Moreland, J., & Schwebel, A. A gender role transcendent perspective on fathering. *The Counseling Psychologist*, 1981, *9*, 45–54.

Neugarten, B., & Weinstein, K. The changing American grandparent. In B. Neugarten (Ed.), *Middle age and aging*, Chicago: University of Chicago Press, 1975.

Pearson, G. *Adolescence and the conflict of generations*. New York: Norton, 1958.

Quinn, W. Personal and family adjustment in later life. *Journal of Marriage and the Family*, 1983, *45*, 57–73.

Rapoport, R., Rapoport, R., & Strelitz, Z. *Fathers, mothers, and society*. New York: Basic Books, 1977.

Robertson, J. F. Interaction in three generation families. Parents as mediators: Toward a theoretical perspective. *International Journal of Aging and Human Development*, 1976, 103–109.

Rollins, B., & Feldman, H. Marital satisfaction over the family life cycle. *Journal of Marriage and the Family*, 1970, *32*, 20–28.

Rossi, A. Transition to parenthood. *Journal of Marriage and the Family*, 1968, *30*, 26–39.

Ryder, R. Longitudinal data relating marital satisfaction and having a child. *Journal of Marriage and the Family*, 1973, *5*, 604–606.

Sarnoff, C. The father's role in latency. In S. Cath, A. Gurwitt, & J. Ross (Eds.), *Father and child: Developmental and clinical perspectives*. Boston: Little, Brown, 1982.

Schlossberg, N. A model for analyzing human adaptation to transition. *The Counseling Psychologist*, 1981, *9*, 2–18.

Shanas, E., Townsend, P., Wedderburn, D., Friis, H., Milkhoy, P., & Stehouwer, J. *Older people in industrial societies*. New York: Atherton, 1968.

Sussman, M. Relationships of adult children with their parents in the United States. In E. Shanas & G. Stieib (Eds.), *Social structure and the family*, Englewood Cliffs, N.J.: Prentice-Hall, 1965.

Troll, L. The family of later life: A decade review. *Journal of Marriage and the Family*, 1971, *33*, 263–290.

Waldron, H., & Routh, D. The effect of the first child on the marital relationship. *Journal of Marriage and the Family*, 1981, *43*, 785–788.

Watson, J., & Kivett, V. Influences on the life satisfactions of older fathers. *The Family Coordinator*, 1976, *25*, 482–488.

Wilkie, J. The trend toward delayed parenthood. *The Journal of Marriage and the Family*, 1981, *43*, 583–591.

Zube, M. Changing behavior and outlook of aging men and women: Implications for marriage in the middle and later years. *Family Relations*, 1982, *31*, 147–156.

# II

# Types of
# Fathering Experiences

# CHAPTER FIVE

# Single Fathers

## THE CASE OF A SINGLE FATHER

Driving back from the small Southern town 14 years ago, I pulled to the side of the road and sobbed out of control. The marriage was over. "What would I do with three small sons, aged 3, 6, and 8? God, what would I do with them and myself and my life?" And what about my vocation? I didn't even know another divorced man taking care of his children. I wondered, "What do I do now?" The first thing I did was grieve—grieve a lot out of empathy for children whose parents were far away from each other and whose mother was geographically separated from them.

The next thing I did was to get on with looking after my kids. The first few months are the most difficult to recall in terms of feelings. Shock numbed my feelings. In those early days, the physical demands of my own work, and the added responsibility of providing 24-hour care for three young children, plus dealing with the trauma of an ending relationship zapped my energies. One of the anticipated pleasures of those days was an early-to-bed evening to sleep away the exhaustion.

Fortunately, during that 1st year, I had the inclination and determination to seek the aid of a trusted counselor to help me make my way. After many counseling sessions the numbness thawed for good and a renewed sensitivity returned. I knew I would survive. I learned that I had to work out my feelings, concerns about family and job, my recent doubts about my own personal adequacies, and my resolution to be the best father I knew how to be for my three sons. These issues had to be confronted, sorted, and resolved. I was *not* going to be mother *and* father, even though lots of my time was devoted to activities usually done by mothers. I could only be a *father*. My kids had a mother though she didn't live with them.

I have friends who remark, "I don't see how you did it"—meaning "raising" the children alone. That feels embarrassing. I did what I had to do. But I changed from feeling a victim in the situation, to feeling like a kind of "pioneer," though that word is much too noble. I began to feel in charge of both my life and this new chapter of solo parenting, and, the more I did it, the better I came to feel about *how* I did it. My boys weren't falling apart; they weren't losing weight or stamina or days, weeks, months of sleeping or eating. They were still surrounded by a degree of stability. Even months after we had begun to stabilize as a family of four, there were some terrible moments, remembrances that make anything ever read or seen in *Kramer vs. Kramer* mild by comparison.

My sons are beautiful young men today. One has just finished college and has acquired an exciting chemical laboratory job; the middle youth is beginning a 2nd year of college, and the youngest is finishing high school. Almost 15 years have gone by since I became a single father, a role I would never have chosen for myself; nonetheless, after the 1st year a role I began to celebrate everyday as the most exciting adventure of my adult years. The feeling about my sons that most characterizes those years is one of deep love, in holding them close enough, yet not so close as to smother them. As a result, I can let them go toward their own years of adulthood, and someday soon, the beginnings of their own roles of fatherhood. I would like to think that their roles as fathers would be one of a dual role out of the joy of sharing that role intimately with a spouse. But if that cannot be, and if they should become father–parents charged with the care of their children, I will not worry about them. They can do it; they know it can be done. They are the products of one man's attempts at trying, out of his loving and caring, to provide a place, a nurturing environment, a home.

**Ron Hall**
*Atlanta, Georgia*

The traditional American family has burst apart at the seams. The word "family" no longer automatically means father, mother, and children living together. The United States Bureau of the Census estimated in 1979 that 19% of all American households with children under 18 are single-parent families (U.S. Bureau of the Census, 1980). Single-parent families are rapidly increasing because of divorce, separation, death, desertion, and unmarried and adoptive parenthood (Flake-Hobson, Robinson, & Skeen, 1983). Between 1970 and 1979 the numbers of single fathers alone increased by 65% because of separation and divorce (U.S. Bureau of the Census, 1980). About 10% of the children of divorced parents lived with their fathers in 1979, and most of these children were school-age rather than preschoolers (Hetherington, 1979). It is estimated that there are 1.5 million single men rearing 3.5 million children for a total of 5 million single-father family members (Lewis, 1978).

Although the numbers of single fathers are increasing, single fathers are subject to misunderstanding, discrimination, and stereotypes by legal and helping professions.

## SINGLE FATHERS IN CUSTODY DISPUTES

Although the father in the opening case was awarded custody of his sons, this arrangement is exceptional. Typically, fathers have had nothing close to equal rights in child custody disputes (Bernstein, 1977). Between 1910 and 1960, for example, fathers were rarely granted child custody. Most courts adhere to the "tender years" doctrine, which has dominated divorce and custody proceedings. This principle suggests that the first five years are a critical time in the child's healthy personality development, and if separated from their mothers, children will be negatively and severely affected. Rooted in psychoanalytic theory (see Chapter 1), this doctrine exclusively favors the mother as the parent who can best provide the nurturance and love required for children's optimal development. This idea is so engrained in our culture that until recently, fathers were granted custody only in exceptional circumstances when the mother was shown to be grossly unfit.

In 1973 the case of *Watts v Watts* in the New York court system recommended that the "tender years" principle be discarded because "it is based on outdated social stereotypes rather than a rational up-to-date consideration of the welfare of the children involved" (*Watts v Watts*, 1973, p. 288).

Today the "tender years" guideline has been replaced with "the best interests of the child" doctrine, which provides more equal treatment for parents. This view has been supported by renewed interest in the study of the father and by findings that show his special contributions to the child's development (see Chapter 3). Because 45% of mothers with children under 6 years of age are wage earners (Hoffereth, 1979), full-time mothers in the home are no longer the typical family arrangement. This too has strengthened "the best interests of the child" guideline. But "best interests" is open to the subjective interpretation of a judge who in many instances continues to favor the mother (Thompson, 1983). Still, more custody decisions are emphasizing the rights of fathers as well as mothers. In the late 1970s only 10% of all single-parent families were single-father familes, although there is speculation that social changes would increase the percentage of single-father families to 30% by 1985 (LeMasters & DeFrain, 1983). This increase in the numbers of divorced single-parent fathers indicates that some of the stereotypes about solo parenting are breaking down (DeFrain & Eirick, 1981).

In 1980 California enacted one of the first innovative custody laws in the country. Instead of routinely entrusting children in the care of the mother, the law encourages close and continued contact with fathers and mothers and encourages both parents to share rights in their children's upbringing. Sharing these rights could take the form of joint custody, sole custody (in which one spouse has visitation rights), or split custody.

## JOINT CUSTODY

Although courts do not usually award fathers *joint or shared custody*—an arrangement in which children live an equal amount of time with each parent for a period of a week or month—indications are that shared arrangements are increasing (Abarbanel, 1979; Hanson, 1981). Even when courts do not decree joint custody, a growing number of couples work out a shared arrangement on their own. Joint custody is gaining increasing popularity. It is predicted that by 1990 joint custody will be the rule rather than the exception (Watson, 1981).

Experts disagree over the value of joint custody in which children have not only two homes, but also two sets of clothes, toys, and even in some cases two sets of friends (see Table 2). Some psychologists claim that such an arrangement only increases the child's problems (Goldstein, Freud, & Solnit, 1973; Spivey & Richards, 1976) by depriving him or her of permanency and stability. According to psychologist Jane Anderson, children need their own back yards where they can "secretly bury their turtle eggs" (Spivey & Richards, 1976, p. 81). Other professionals (Goldstein, Freud, & Solnit, 1973) maintain that although children have two biological parents in shared arrangements, they are prevented from forming a relationship with a "psychological parent" as a result of being shifted from one environment to another. An adult becomes a parent to the child in a psychological sense only from daily interaction, companionship, and shared experiences.

**Table 2.**

*Advantages and Disadvantages of Joint Custody From a Father's Perspective*

| ADVANTAGES | DISADVANTAGES |
| --- | --- |
| [b]Fathers can have more influence on the child's growth and development—a benefit for men and children alike. | [a]Children lack a stable and permanent environment, which can affect them emotionally. |
| 2[b]Fathers are more involved experience more self-satisfaction as parents. | [e]Children are prevented from having a relationship with a "psychological parent" as a result of being shifted from one environment to another. |
| [d]Parents experience less stress than sole-custody parents. | |
| [d]Parents do not feel as overburdened as sole-custody parents. | [e]Children have difficulty gaining control over and understanding of their lives. |
| [c]Generally, fathers and mothers report more friendly and cooperative interaction in joint-custody than in visitation arrangements, mostly because the time with children is evenly balanced, and agreement exists on the rules of the system. | [c]Children have trouble forming and maintaining peer relationships. |
| | [c]Long-term consequences of joint-custody arrangements have not been systematically studied. |
| [d]Joint custody provides more free social time for each single parent. Relationships with children are stronger and more meaningful for fathers. | |
| [d]Parental power and decision making are equally divided, so there is less need to use children to barter for more. | |

[a]Spivey & Richards, 1976, [b]Grief, 1979; [c]Abarbanel, 1979; [d]LeMasters & DeFrain, 1983; [e]Goldstein, Freud, & Solnit, 1973.

Many practitioners (e.g., Abarbanel, 1979) criticize parents with joint custody as being more concerned with their own welfare than that of their children—and in some cases, perhaps rightly so. An extreme case, although real nonetheless, is a single father we know who worked out a joint-custody arrangement with his 4-year-old son. Soon after the divorce the father moved 500 miles from his ex-wife's hometown. Every 2 weeks the child was put on an airplane and flown back and forth to honor the custody agreement, until certain behavior problems emerged. The problem resolved itself when the mother moved to be nearer the father. Continued joint custody involved the traverse of a city block for the child rather than the course of 1000 miles per month. Abarbanel (1979) argues that in more typical situations, when parents are committed to staying in close geographical proximity, joint custody works under certain conditions: when there is a commitment to the arrangement, when parents give their mutual support to each other and are flexible in sharing responsibilities (such as buying children's clothes or taking them to the doctor), and when everyone agrees on the implicit rules of the system.

Although opposition to joint custody is widespread, research indicates that such arrangements are more positive than when mothers are granted sole custody and fathers are granted simple visiting privileges (Greif, 1979; Keshet & Rosenthal, 1978; Thompson, 1983). Findings show, for example, that when fathers share custody, they are more likely to continue to have greater influence on their children's growth and development and to feel more self-satisfied as parents (Greif, 1979).

A major argument for joint custody is the research that shows the important effects that fathers have on their offspring's social and intellectual development. Personal adjustment, self-concept, maturity level, general social competence, and intellectual attainment of children in father-absent homes fall far below that of children living in father-present families (Parish & Dostal, 1980; Santrock & Warshak, 1979; Wallerstein & Kelly, 1980). Children living in father-present homes score higher on intelligence and achievement tests than children from father-absent households (Chapman, 1977; Santrock, 1972). In one study (Wallerstein & Kelly, 1980) 5 years after their parents' breakup, children who adjusted best were those who had full and continuous relationships with *both* father and mother. Intense and continued father contact after divorce was viewed as essential for children's adjustment. In contrast, children who did not have a consistent relationship with both parents displayed many behavioral problems.

Noted pediatrician Benjamin Spock believes the best answer for providing the continued contact children require from both parents is joint custody (Spock, 1979). Roman (1977), in his article, "The Disposable Parent," also argues that children without an active father in their lives are deeply troubled and feel abandoned by their father's absence. Sole-custody mothers, he suggests, sometimes shower attention and responsibility on young boys far beyond their maturity level. This overburdens children and compounds their problems. Success in joint custody arrangements, on the other hand, has been supported by clinical studies in which children living in two homes, after experiencing an initial period of adjustment, showed a renewed ability to function (Abarbanel, 1979). Teachers reported excellent school adjustment and the children said that they felt "at home" in both households. Other research has found that most children appear well adapted to both households with a minimum of conflict and confusion and are able to juggle complex schedules and to keep track of where they are supposed to be (Steinman, 1981). However, children were greatly affected by parents' conflicting child-rearing practices or major philosophical differences. The small portion of children in Steinman's study who had trouble living in two households and managing complicated schedules were usually the youngest, between 4 and 5 years of age, although there were also four boys 7–9 years old who were worried, frustrated, and generally unhappy because of their double living arrangement. Despite the inconvenience of going back and forth between two homes, most children preferred the joint custody arrangement because it gave them access to both parents and gave them a sense that both parents loved and wanted them, thereby enhancing their self-esteem (Steinman, 1981).

Fathers also derive benefits from joint custody. As a result of their continued and active involvement, single fathers in one study reported feeling more self-satisfaction as a parent (Greif, 1979). In another study joint custody permitted both parents to pursue their careers, to maintain active involvement with their children, and to be relieved from emotional stress and a sense of loss brought on by the divorce (Steinman, 1981). While they acknowledge a period of adjustment for children of joint custody, many fathers believe this is only temporary and that children are not negatively affected by the arrangement. In fact, one single father believes that consistency of the arrangement is the critical factor: "There is no shuttling back and forth, my son is shuttled every day to and from school. This is called consistency scheduling" (Greif, 1979, p. 317).

Another single father said, "We're a mobile society . . . some people move constantly during their lives, the rich often live in several homes . . . what makes a joint living arrangement so different?" (Greif, 1979, p. 318).

Based on their research, LeMasters and DeFrain (1983) cite the following advantages of joint custody for single parents over sole custody:

1. The happier parents are, regardless of the custody arrangement, the happier their children will be.
2. Parents with joint custody are less likely than sole-custody parents to feel overburdened by the children and are more likely to enjoy free social time from the setup.

3. Sole-custody parents say they have more stress in their lives than joint-custody parents, although children adjust equally well in both situations.

4. Joint-custody parents tend to live closer to their ex-spouse than sole-custody parents, feel more positively toward the ex-spouse, and say that the process of working out custody arrangements was mutual and friendly.

5. Although sole-custody parents more often wish the ex-spouse spent more time with the children, joint-custody parents are more satisfied with the time arrangements.

6. Children have stronger relationships with both parents in joint-custody households, compared with children in sole-custody situations, and joint-custody parents tend to value children's close contact with both parents.

## SOLE CUSTODY

Most experts agree that joint custody is preferable to the mother's *sole custody*, in which the father is granted mere visitation privileges. Silver and Silver (1981) recommend that the word "visitation" in terms of custody be eliminated from the family-law vocabulary. As they aptly describe, one "visits" inmates in prison or patients in hospitals; a father should not be in a position to "visit" his children. A father with visitation privileges often describes himself as a "Disneyland Dad" (Shepard & Goldman, 1979). Fearful of losing his children's love, he tries to win their affection through overindulgence rather than through a meaningful relationship. The focus of the interactions with his children is on material gifts and entertainment rather than expression of a natural, meaningful relationship. The important, daily things are missing— having time alone with his child in the evening, putting his child to bed, helping his children with homework or solve some personal problem, or cooking a meal together.

Partly out of guilt and partly out of trying to cram months of time into a day, the visiting father overindulges his children with material comforts. Some single fathers feel pressured to perform, to spend money, or to entertain so that their children will want to see them again. One father said, "I feel like a grandfather, always asking the kids, 'What did you do this week?' I plan activities for them which I don't want to do, but I want to keep them happy. I'm a good-time Charlie, which I resent" (Greif, 1979, p. 315).

A noncustodial father we know shrugged his shoulders and told us how he manufactured a relationship with his children:

One of the first realities I had to accept as a noncustodial father was the realization that children are basically hedonists. Though in an ideal world, we would like children to want to be with us because they love and enjoy our company, in fact, they require incentives—treats, fun events, a relaxed atmosphere. Also, in an ideal world, children would initiate contact. In fact, they rarely will. I quickly learned that, as a noncustodial parent, I would have to be prompting and planning visits and events. I would have to be the one to pick up the phone each day to initiate contact and carry the ball through these new and awkward telephone chats. Previously such contact was built in and readily available. Now it had to be produced.

When fathers are permitted only periodic visitation rights, they often feel cut off—divorced—from their children. "I had to adjust to the loss of control," the noncustodial father told us. "Not that I had been an authoritarian father at home, although I did exert a daily influence over their experience and their behavior. Now that influence became less frequent and more subtle, I had to bite my tongue over many decisions made outside of my domain. I had to use our visits to subtly communicate my values, being careful not to undermine their mother's authority." Fathers with visitation privileges react in different ways. Some accept the role assigned to them. Others give up and walk away from their children and put more time and psychological distance between them. According to Greif (1979), "More and more men currently find themselves separated from their children at the same time that they are being urged to take a more active and affective role in their child's growth and development" (p. 311). When a father is "divorced" from his children, he faces a serious crisis that can lead to frustration, depression, and to other emotional and physical complaints that are discussed later in this chapter.

Occasionally fathers receive sole custody of their children. This usually happens when former wives do not want custody or are unable to assume custody because of desertion, death, mental illness, or drug and alcohol dependence (Orthner, Brown, & Ferguson, 1976). Increasing numbers of unmarried single men are also being granted sole custody through adoption, as discussed in the box entitled Single Adoptive Fathers.

## SPLIT CUSTODY

An alternative to shared and sole custody, and perhaps the least desirable arrangement, is that of *split custody*—in which the mother receives custody of one or more children and the father receives custody of the remaining child or children. This arrangement usually results in boys living with Father, and girls living with Mother. In contested cases, courts typically award boys to fathers more often than girls (Chang & Deinard, 1982). Mothers, on the other hand, receive an equal proportion of boys and girls. Parents themselves usually decide that younger boys go with the father and younger girls with the mother (Smith & Smith, 1981). It appears that the historical assumption that the very young need a mother and the prohibitions regarding daughters being raised solely by fathers still have influence (Smith & Smith, 1981). Some research has shown that split custody is preferable to sole custody by the mother (Santrock & Warshak, 1979). Experimental observations of children in father-custody families showed that boys were more mature, independent, and socially competent than girls (Santrock, Warshak, Elliott, 1982). In contrast, girls in mother-custody families fared better than boys. It appears, then, that a

## SINGLE ADOPTIVE FATHERS

Despite the fact that they are increasing in large numbers, single-parent families—whether headed by men or women—are commonly regarded as deviant, which has led to discrimination against single-parent adoption. Practitioners and researchers (Hetherington, Cox, & Cox, 1976; Wallerstein & Kelly, 1980) have stressed the deficits experienced by children in single-parent families rather than the possible benefits. According to Levine (1976), ". . . for a child welfare agency to deliberately place a child with a single person was to challenge the sanctity of the two-parent family as an American norm" (p. 101). Thirty-eight-year-old Tony Piazza made history in 1965 when he became the first single man in the United States to adopt a child—an 18-month-old boy.

Adoptions by single men have been especially difficult, because practitioners and society generally do not approve of a single man rearing children. The desire of a man to become a parent without a wife to nurture the children has been viewed as unnatural. After all, the argument goes, women are by nature better equipped than men to nurture the young. Therefore, never-married men who wish to adopt are especially closely scrutinized. Their sexual orientation becomes a major concern: Are they unmarried because they are homosexual? Or if they are heterosexual, how will their sexual habits affect the children in their care? Although single women can adopt children of either sex, social workers are reluctant to place girls with men, because of a widespread fear that it is risky to place girls with men because of sexual attraction (Levine, 1976).

If a man is fortunate enough to become a single adoptive father, his choices are typically limited to school-age boys who are black, handicapped, or otherwise "hard to place" (Lewis, 1978). The typical adoptive fathering experience is with a child who has already had a life of inconsistency and abandonment and who has been shuffled from one home or single-parent custodial arrangement functions better when the child is the same sex as the custodial parent. These findings should not be used automatically as a rationale in split custody decisions of awarding girls to mothers and boys to fathers. Yet, the fact that boys thrive more in father-custody arrangements suggests that an a priori decision to award the child to the mother is unwise (Santrock *et al*, 1982).

Separating children, no matter how they are split, can be a shattering experience that further complicates their adjustment to divorce. The single father in the opening case told us of the devastation of separating his three sons:

> One night I was to return my youngest son to his mother. The judge granted her his custody and [granted me] the custody of the other two boys. I had to take him from his brothers and from my home to go live

institution to another. The adopted child often feels unworthy of anyone's lasting love. The single adoptive father is faced with the difficult responsibility of providing patient, consistent, and reassuring care. As Levine (1976) graphically describes, the child constantly rejects the love and attention from his new father until he ultimately becomes convinced that this relationship is truly permanent: ". . . after a hell-bent period of trying to be rejected, school-age children often become passive, totally dependent, then even out emotionally and begin to feel secure" (p. 118).

Levine (1976) describes single men who seek adoption as a self-selected group who have special patience and understanding of the children whom they adopt and a strong personal identification with these children's needs. As schoolteachers, therapists, Big Brother volunteers, or scout leaders, these men seek greater self-fulfillment and continuous involvement with children than their jobs or volunteer work affords. They are usually in their mid-30s and have established themselves in a career or business (Lewis, 1978).

Within 4 years after Tony Piazza paved the way in Oregon, adoption agencies in other states began taking applications from single men and women because good two-parent homes for children were hard to find. The practice of single-parent adoptions became more widespread and showed promise of being a positive alternative to foster homes and institutionalization. In 1975 eleven other states in addition to Oregon reported single-father placements, usually in urban centers (Levine, 1976). Today, there are approximately 52,000 never-married single adoptive fathers nationwide, compared to 704,000 separated or divorced single fathers and 569,000 widowed single fathers (U.S. Bureau of the Census, 1980). It is predicted that by 2000 half of all single-parent adoptions will be men (Lewis, 1978). Although most adoption agencies still prefer two-parent families for placement, acceptance of single adoptive fathers has increased because many men have proved it can work well.

with his mother. As I carried him in my arms through the door, he suddenly lunged for the door. I was holding him as he clung with both small clenched hands to the door facing, begging, crying not to leave us, not be carried away. Moments like that are so indelibly stamped on my mind that it is difficult to think or talk about them even now. But some things had to be done, though our feelings of sadness and terror and helplessness seemed overwhelming.

The long-term effects of splitting up the children may take from them the most important stabilizing source in their lives—their siblings. Judith Wallerstein (1982) discovered that 10 years after divorce many children survived the ordeal because they had brothers and sisters for support during the crisis:

> It seems that when the relationship between the parents weakens and disrupts that siblings turn towards each other to huddle together, to protect each other, to love each other, to remain intimate with each other, and perhaps most of all to remain faithful to each other. In a significant number of families, it seemed quite clear that the strongest, the most enduring, and the richest relationship during the childhood and adolescent years was that among the siblings, and that this relationship had survived the centrifugal pulls of adolescence and young adulthood. Considering the contemporary trend towards the one-child family, these findings regarding the social and psychological importance of siblings in providing comfort and reassurance to each other within the divorced family take on sobering implications. (p. 25)

## SETTLING CUSTODY DISPUTES

The road to settling custody disputes is ugly, and some believe that the court system, because of its favor to the mother, fosters this ugliness. One single father shared his experience in an article by Wright (1983):

> Under the present adversary system, where the parent desiring custody has to prove the "unfitness" of the other parent, the one who will stoop to the lowest in mudslinging, slander, character defamation, perjury, and vilification of the other is the one who has the best chance of gaining custody, or in the eyes of the law, being declared the most "fit" parent. . . . I wouldn't make my ex-wife out to be the cheap, trashy person the court demands that I must in petitioning for custody, so custody was not granted. (p. 4B)

In embittered custody battles children sometimes become unintentional targets. An angry mother with sole custody may use the child as a weapon against her husband. Visitation privileges may be suspended until the father concedes to the mother's wishes for alimony or child support. Or children may be interrogated after visiting with either parent.

There is no pat formula for settling custody disputes. Sometimes joint custody works best, and other times sole custody or split custody may be the answer. The best arrangement must be suited to the personalities and lifestyles of the parents and children (LeMasters & DeFrain, 1983). Whatever arrangement is chosen, the best interests of children as well as the rights and responsibilities of both parents should be the major consideration (Levine, 1976). While some men would not make competent single fathers, just as some women would not make competent single mothers, it is becoming increasingly important that fathers and mothers be judged on their merits and not on notions of sex-role bias (Orthner & Lewis, 1979).

## EFFECTS OF DIVORCE ON CHILDREN

Of course, children, like their parents, are severely affected by parental separation and transition to a single-parent family. Some research suggests that over time, the hurt appears to wane, and children seem to adjust to a normal family life with one parent at home (Schlesinger, 1982). Although outwardly most children appear to recover swiftly, new evidence suggests that they may never fully recover from the experience and in fact can carry their painful memories into adulthood.

Wallerstein (1982, 1984) followed a group of 131 children ranging in age from 12 to 18 for 10 years. At the time of the marital separation, the children experienced distress, worry, and depression. They wanted to undo the divorce and bring the family back together. Some research suggests that 3 months after marital separation in which fathers left the home, children appear to function as well as they had before his departure. A year later, children seemed happier than they were when the father was at home (LeMasters & DeFrain, 1983). Wallerstein (1982, 1984), however, discovered that 18 months postdivorce, many children who appeared to have survived the breakup began to show psychological decline. Problems were most frequent among boys less than 9 years of age who were vulnerable and had behavior problems at home and school and who typically were in their mother's custody. Five years after the divorce, Wallerstein found that the overall quality of life within the postdivorce family indicated good psychological adjustment. The continuity of the relationship with the visiting father contributed to the well-being of the child. At the 10-year mark, adolescents and young adults feared following in their parent's footsteps, of failing in their marital relationships. Their fears led to more cautiousness and postponement of marital and childbearing commitments in adulthood.

Children of divorce carry the experience into their adult lives as an integral part of their identity and vividly recall the painful memories of the past as a lesson to be avoided at all costs in their own adult relationships. A 22-year-old married student said to us, "I pray that our generation will try to keep the family together more than our parents did. I *never* want to go through what I did as a child during a divorce, nor what my parents went through as adults."

The aftermath of divorce takes its toll on every family member. Children, perhaps, have the greatest difficulty in adjusting, depending on their ages and developmental maturity (Hetherington, Cox, & Cox, 1976; Wallerstein & Kelly, 1980). For some it takes 1–2 years to recover from the divorce. For others, emotional scars remain a lifetime.

## EFFECTS OF DIVORCE ON SINGLE FATHERS

The problems that surface for single fathers are basically the same as those for single mothers (LeMasters & DeFrain, 1983). In the work of LeMasters and DeFrain, both fathers and mothers viewed the divorce process as stressful and described the reactions of friends and family in a similar way. Child-rearing philosophies were identical, and both fathers and mothers said their children were physically and emotionally well off at home and school. Men and women were interested in new social relationships and the potential for remarriage at some later time. Custody arrangements among all couples participating in the study were similar, with the ex-spouse usually having custody for holidays, weekends, and summers. More single fathers encouraged their children to take sides in disagreements with the ex-spouse. The authors speculated that this happened because fathers continued to harbor the stereotype that mother's were unlikely to disagree with the children if it meant risking losing them. Overall, the data of LeMasters and DeFrain consistently show that fathers are just as competent as mothers in rearing children alone.

Coordinating parental and adult roles, lack of patience, making decisions alone, and not having enough time to be with their children are problems that single fathers and mothers both share (Orthner *et al.*, 1976). Other problem areas identified by single fathers in one study were dating (57%), business trips (55%), and pursuance of job possibilities (45%). However, single fathers typically say that children do not interfere with their careers, and most report that they are able to continue their careers while caring for their children (Smith & Smith, 1981). They accomplish this by engaging in more flexible jobs, changing to more compatible work, or reallocating their time and priorities to domestic responsibilities (Hanson, 1981).

For many men who previously gave their careers top billing, single fathering is a welcome challenge. Like the father in the critically acclaimed film *Kramer vs. Kramer*, men who were mainly concerned with their careers during their marriages suddenly see their priorities differently. As solo parents, they begin to spend more time concentrating on relationships with their children, which acquire a new richer meaning. Many suddenly realize what an important experience they were missing (Smith & Smith, 1981). As these fathers become emotionally involved with their offspring, their interactions not only become more affectionate, but their parenting style may become less rigid and more democratic and easygoing (Gasser & Taylor, 1976; Lynn, 1974; Mendes, 1976a; Orthner *et al.*, 1976). Many single custodial fathers say the relationships with their children are better than before the divorce. "I would have never known the girls as well as I know them now had I stayed in the marriage. . . . Having the sole responsibility opens up all kinds of opportunities for having a closer family" are typical comments (Bartz & Witcher, 1978, p. 5). Even fathers who say relationships with their children have not changed say they always had close relationships with their children (Smith & Smith, 1981). Not only do single fathers see themselves as nurturing parents, but their children say their fathers are loving and concerned parents (Hanson, 1981).

Some evidence suggests that single fathers fare better than mothers in their relationships with children. Custodial single mothers in one study, for example, reported more problems with their children than did custodial fathers (Ambert, 1982). In contrast, children of custodial fathers expressed their appreciation for the father, whereas children of custodial mothers only rarely expressed appreciation of the mother. Custodial fathers had more positive interactions with their children than did mothers (for example, less disobedience, fewer arguments, etc.). Custodial single fathers also described a greater satisfaction with the parenting role than did custodial mothers.

## Swinging Single Stereotype

The image of the swinging single father, "foot-loose and fancy free" has been popularized by the media. This stereotype is so engrained that many people react to single fathers with distrust and suspicion.

One single father said that his neighbors would no longer let their adolescent daughter babysit his two small sons, and another said his neighbors quit associating with him after his divorce (Smith & Smith, 1981).

Research indicates that single fathers have basically the same emotional reactions and feelings as single mothers (LeMasters & DeFrain, 1983; Orthner et al., 1976). Contrary to the image of the swinging playboy after divorce, many practitioners report that single fathers—custodial and noncustodial—suffer serious emotional and physical side effects from the marital split (Greif, 1979; Roman, 1977; Silver & Silver, 1981). Typically, single fathers undergo a great deal of stress and describe an array of feelings such as anger, sadness, resentment, and depression (Greif, 1985; Keshet & Rosenthal, 1978; Mendes, 1976a; Miller, 1982; Schlesinger, 1978). One single father said, "I felt extremely depressed and unhappy about separating. I felt like it was right for all of us, but I still felt like a failure for breaking up the family" (Keshet & Rosenthal, 1978, p. 12). The emotional impact was also evident with the men we talked to, as the opening case illustrates: The aftermath of his separation left that father shocked, exhausted, and drained of his usual energies. Depression, stress, feelings of inadequacy and uncertainty about future relationships with children are also common. "During the first 5 years, my most memorable feeling was a perplexing gnawing question," one custodial single father told us, "Can I do it? Could I indeed feel I was doing a good job as a single parent raising children?"

Far from the image of "the bar-hopping swinger," single fathers and mothers tend to enjoy only occasional socializing (LeMasters & De-Frain, 1983). As the sole head of a household, most single fathers are too busy scheduling time with their offspring and managing their careers to find enough time for dating and socializing (Chang & Deinard, 1982). This holds true for custodial single fathers as well as noncustodial fathers. "I have to laugh every time someone asks me what I'm doing with all my new-found free time," a noncustodial father told us. "Any noncustodial parent committed to being as involved as before with the kids has little, if any, new-found free time."

Despite their busy schedules, loneliness from loss of companionship and social isolation are major problems reported by most men following divorce (Smith & Smith, 1981; White & Bloom, 1981). Loneliness and a sense of loss of a spouse and the children are especially hard for noncustodial fathers. A "weekend father" we know shared his biggest fears with us:

"Daddy, will your feelings be hurt if we decide to live with Mommy?" my 10-year-old daughter asked on the day of decision.

"No, Kristi," I lied. "My feelings won't be hurt. You choose what's best for you."

And so I left, with all my belongings, and enough fears to fill two suitcases. I remember saying, half-jokingly, to my 12-year-old son, Matt, "Promise me you won't become a screwed-up, miserable child of divorce."

"Don't be silly, Dad," he reassured me. Yet the knot of fear remained in my gut. I described my worst scenario to a friend.

"I'll see them only on weekends. They'll come dragging in, bent over from backpacks stuffed with a weekend's worth of clothes. They won't want to be there. It'll all be out of some misbegotten sense of filial obligation. They'll resent it. I'll be flitting around trying to make it fun, as if you can force fun. Meanwhile, during the week, their mother will be poisoning their minds against me. Eventually, they will drift out of my life, with bitter memories of their father, the deserter."

"Dale," my friend said, "that's wonderfully melodramatic, but you know it's bullshit. You have great relationships with your kids. Nothing will come between that." Regardless, during the first months, the knot of worry remained tightly tied.

I still remember the day, about 9 months after the separation, when the phone rang, and it was Kristi calling. I waited to find out where she wanted to be taken or what she wanted me to do for her. There was no request. She was calling just to chat. The memory of that phone call still brings tears to my eyes.

## Reactions to Stress

Emotional devastation quickly leads to other problems for many single fathers. Difficulties in eating, sleeping, and working are commonly reported by single men with and without custody. Physical complaints, brought on by stress, are also typical reactions. More than half the men interviewed by one practitioner developed physical symptoms after their marital separation, ranging from weight loss, eye and dental problems, high blood pressure, rheumatoid arthritis, backaches and footaches. There were also reports of problems of sexual performance—impotence or unusually frequent sexual activity or both—as well as alcohol abuse (Greif, 1979). Even though both men and women in one study described the divorce process and single-parenting experience as stressful, they said they would do it over again if they had to for the children's benefit as well as their own (LeMasters & DeFrain, 1983).

Many single fathers are able to cope with their initial feelings of loss, depression, and anxiety and usually do not feel the need for counseling (Chang & Deinard, 1982), whereas others do. Generally, single fathers quickly overcome the emotional and social obstacles—the most difficult time being the 1st year following the divorce (Mendes, 1976a). The man in the opening case said that nearly 18 months following his marital split, "We began to stabilize as a family and I learned to trust the feeling that I was succeeding—reaching for and achieving new heights as a human being, as a man."

Another single father told us his family was a "textbook" case:

> I've read that it takes a year to adjust to separation. This rule of thumb has seemed amazingly accurate in the case of myself and my children. It seemed as if I woke up one morning about a year after the separation, and everything was just fine. The children were dropping in and out of my place often and willingly; I was chauffeuring them hither and yon; we had numerous shared activities; our times together were filled with pleasant chatter, laughter, and tension-free affection. My wife and I are now discussing living together again, and the children are the biggest obstacle. Neither one is crazy about the idea. They remember, I'm sure, the times of preseparation conflict and don't want to risk a return to that awful state. They may be right. I told my mother on the phone the other night that we were thinking of getting back together. "You really should, you know," she said, and couldn't help adding that tired old phrase, "if only for the children." If she only knew!

### Caregiver Role

After the separation, single fathers have basically the same problems as single mothers (LeMasters & DeFrain, 1983). However, the chief problem men have that is not shared by women is the myth that they are incompetent single parents. For nearly a century, child custody decisions in the United States have been guided by the stereotype that mothers are better equipped to care for children (Santrock *et al.*, 1982). Men frequently feel compelled to prove that they can care for their children alone and can succeed in rearing their children without a partner (Smith & Smith, 1981). The comments from one single father we talked with indicate that overcoming this stereotype was one of the most difficult challenges of being a solo parent:

> I faced comments like, "What's a nice man like you doing with these children and no mama? Why don't you get married? Who cooks for these poor children?" I realized right away that society doesn't make it easy or even acceptable for men who are in my already difficult position. After a decade, being a single father became less an oddity (at least for myself) and there seemed to be less overt curiosity and a greater climate of acceptance. Part of this, of course, was probably my own self-acceptance in this new role. Nevertheless, relief and liberation from what others think or judge, from painful curiosity and from inappropriate prying, was truly a gift that I as a single father began to enjoy.

Admittedly, single fathers face the challenge of learning many domestic and child-rearing practices that previously had been the mother's responsibility (Smith & Smith, 1981). Having been socialized against participating in any form of child care and nurturing can hamper the single father's ability in this domain. Once they learn these skills, single fathers have few problems running their households and confidently carry out all the necessary homemaking activities for which the mother once had responsibility (Gasser & Taylor, 1976; Mendes, 1976a; Orthner *et al.*, 1976). Some men rely on the use of community support services such as day care centers, and others employ housekeepers or depend on relatives or friends for child care (Gersick, 1975; Mendes, 1976a; Orthner *et al.*, 1976; DeFrain & Eirick, 1981). Although single fathers report that the transition from professional concerns to domestic ones is not easy, they usually accomplish it on their own, as one single custodial father told us:

> The best I could do would be to fill my place in my children's lives as an available father, a male caregiver, care provider, a present parent, a loving approachable father, a man who though loving to fish, or carry a child on his back, or walk on a seashore, nevertheless, often had to dry a diaper, cook meals, and wash dishes—a job I have *always* hated above all others. "So what?" I asked myself, "Don't some mothers hate to wash dishes?"

## SUCCESSFUL SINGLE FATHERS

Research shows that a combination of certain financial, social, and emotional ingredients lead to successful single fathering. The average single father is in his 30s, well-educated, in managerial or professional positions, and earns an income equal to or above the national average (DeFrain & Eirick, 1981; Hanson, 1981; Orthner *et al.*, 1976). The fact that he has a slight edge over single mothers in income and education gives him definite advantages from the start (LeMasters & DeFrain, 1983). Financial hardships can further complicate a very difficult situation. Custodial mothers from lower income levels, for instance, have more parenting problems and their children have more behavior difficulties than children of custodial fathers or mothers from higher income levels (Ambert, 1982). Low-income mothers reported mostly problems from their children and few joys: truancy, disrespect toward teachers, premature sexual involvement, shoplifting, vandalism, juvenile delinquency, and "talking back" or even abuse from their children.

Aside from financial advantages, the typical single father who has chosen his role as such has personality traits that contribute to adjustment. He is independent, self-assured, open-minded, flexible, and supportive of the women's movement (Levine, 1976). Fathers who seek custody of their children tend to feel confident in their ability to rear children and view themselves as the better parent (Chang & Deinard, 1982; Gasser & Taylor, 1976; Orthner *et al.*, 1976). In fact, single fathers who actively seek custody of their children (sometimes called "seekers") tend to be better adjusted to their lifestyles, feel more positively about their experiences, and have fewer problems with their children than those single fathers whose position was thrust upon them by circumstance (sometimes called "assenters") (Greif, 1985; Mendes, 1976a, 1976b).

Prior experience is also an important ingredient. Men who, before their divorce, are actively involved in the rearing, discipline, and nurturance of their young ones; have some understanding of child development; and participate in managing a household usually adjust best (Greif, 1985; Hanson, 1981; Smith & Smith, 1981). By contrast, fathers who were preoccupied during their marriage with their careers rather than family interaction have more difficulty as single parents, compared to men who previously devoted a great deal of time and interest to their families (Mendes, 1976a). Still, because single custodial fathers are a select and self-motivated group of men, some experts believe they have an easier time meeting the demands of single parenthood than single mothers (Lamb & Bronson, 1980).

## CONCLUSION

The single father's biggest obstacle is not his "inability" to be a successful single parent, but the cultural views in this country. Many of his problems result from misunderstanding and discrimination arising from stereotypes held by members of the legal and helping professions. It is true that, as a rule, men have not been socialized for parenting responsibilities that include both breadwinner and domestic roles; neither have most women. Social conventions often place additional pressures on men and make them feel deviant and odd in a dual role. Single fathers are placed in the uncomfortable position of constantly having to prove themselves.

Research has shown that most single fathers overcome these obstacles with amazing success. Although emotional and physical side effects usually accompany their marital breakup, overall, single fathers experience positive and successful adjustment following separation and divorce. Increasingly fathers are receiving joint or even sole custody. These custodial fathers have shown that, as a select group, they are extremely competent parents. Coordinating their professional and domestic responsibilities, they confidently manage their households and homemaking activities with little outside support, except perhaps for day care services. Relationships between single fathers and their children become closer, more meaningful, and in some cases stronger than the relationships single custodial mothers establish with their children. Because of the single father's widespread success, we now know that men are equally capable of nurturing children. Today, more professionals are urging that custody decisions be considered from the standpoint of the best interests of children as well as the rights and responsibilities of both parents.

## SUGGESTIONS TO PROFESSIONALS

Despite discrimination against single fathers in custody decrees, a survey (Woody, 1978) of lawyers, psychiatrists, psychologists, and social workers revealed that practitioners do not adhere to stereotypes when evaluating the suitability of a mother or father for custody: "The implications are that mothers and fathers will be evaluated without obvious sex bias and, consequently, that fathers may be receiving custody in a greater number of cases than in the past" (p. 61). Although this is an encouraging sign, practitioners have few guidelines to use when working with single fathers. A survey (Nieto, 1982) of 90 helping professionals in Texas, for example, indicated that although practitioners are aware of the problem of single fathers and appreciate its magnitude, most of them wanted further information about this special group. The following suggestions will ensure high-level professional conduct, incorporate important legal concerns, and provide the best benefits to every family member:

*1.* Avoid treating single fathers as deviant. Because of the custodial single father's relative inexperience in child-rearing and domestic chores, single-father families are often viewed as more deviant than single-mother families. Some practitioners approach the single-father family as a social problem and apply a corrective model when working with them. This approach is "biasing, misleading, and overly simplistic" (Monaghan-Lackband, 1979).

*2.* Include the divorced father in therapy. Although divorce can end the relationship between husband and wife, it does not (or at least should not) end the father's relationship with his children or even his ex-wife. Many divorced couples continue to communicate in ways that are healthy, satisfying, and necessary for carrying out child-rearing arrangements (Ahrons, 1981). Despite this, many practitioners focus only on the problematic former couple relationships, and it is common practice for family practitioners to conduct sessions without the father, who is usually the parent living outside the home of origin (Wylder, 1982). Noncustodial fathers in particular are excluded from family therapy, yet their involvement is beneficial to the transition to single-family living because it ensures the father's contact with his children, helps resolve such practical problems as visitation rights and alimony, and aids in postdivorce adjustment for all family members.

3. Help single fathers deal with emotions following the marital breakup. Practitioners should be prepared to assist men in dealing with a wide array of feelings, ranging from loneliness and depression to self-doubt about coping as a single parent, and can also provide ways for men to keep communication channels open so that they can establish optimal relationships with their children and former wives.

4. Provide support networks for single fathers. A survey of one large urban city indicated that the community does not offer much in the way of support for single fathers (Nieto, 1982). Practitioners can offer single fathers needed support by putting them in contact with other local single fathers, establishing group sessions with several single fathers, or referring men to local chapters of Parents Without Partners or other support groups. Parent education classes for single fathers including child development classes, single parenting skills, meeting children's emotional needs, household management, and other workshops and growth groups all can help men develop role clarity and provide them an understanding of the attitudes and behaviors needed for successful single parenting.

Newsletters and other periodicals published by national or local organizations and books on single fathering and parent–child interactions can also be a source of support for men rearing children alone. A list of support systems and reading material are provided.

5. Keep an open mind about custody options and become prepared to make information about these options available. "The best interests of the child" can now include many types of custodial arrangements— including joint, sole, or split custody—in which single fathers have varying degrees of responsibilities. Where appropriate, practitioners should inform men of their rights and support them in pursuing their rights in the best interests of their children and the family as a whole.[1] In-service workshops on custody and domestic law will equip workers with current knowledge regarding legal decisions and the professional's role in these matters.

[1]See Barton Bernstein. Lawyer and counselor as an interdisciplinary team: Preparing the father for custody. *Journal of Marriage and Family Counseling*, 1977, 3, 29–40, for a checklist that prepares a single father for trial and objective testimony in custody disputes.

6. Work closely with school personnel to help children adjust to single-parent family structures. Workshops providing tips for classroom teachers on how to work with children from one-parent families can generate better understanding of the problems these children face, and thereby enable teachers to help children better adjust during their transition to single-family living. Encouragement of junior and senior high school males to become involved in family-life classes can prepare them for various possible consequences as fathers and especially for assuming the primary responsibility for their children in case of death or desertion of spouse or joint or split custody arrangements.

## PROFESSIONAL RESOURCES FOR WORKING WITH SINGLE FATHERS

### Books for Adults

Atkin, E., & Rubin, E. *Part-time father: A guide for the divorced father.* New York: Vanguard, 1976.

Cassidy, R. *What every man should know about divorce.* Washington, D.C.: New Republic Books, 1977.

Folberg, J. *Joint custody and shared parenting.* Rockville, Md.: BNA Books, 1984.

Galper, M. *Joint custody and co-parenting.* Philadelphia: Running, 1981.

Gardner, R. *The parents' book about divorce.* Garden City, N.Y.: Doubleday, 1977.

Gatley, R. *Single father's handbook: A guide for separated and divorced fathers.* Garden City, N.Y.: Doubleday, 1979.

Greif, G. L. *Single fathers.* Lexington, Mass.: D. C. Heath, 1985.

Grollman, E. *Explaining divorce to children.* Boston: Beacon, 1969.

Hunt, M., & Hunt, B. *The divorce experience.* New York: McGraw-Hill, 1977.

Jewett, C. *Helping children cope with separation and loss.* Boston: The Harvard Common, 1983.

Katz, S., & Inker, M. *Fathers, husbands and lovers: Legal rights and responsibilities.* Chicago: American Bar Association, 1982.

Kessler, S. *The American way of divorce: Prescriptions for change.* Chicago: Nelson-Hall, 1975.

Klein, C. *The single parent experience.* New York: Walker, 1973.

Krantzler, M. *Creative divorce.* New York: M. Evans, 1974.

McFadden, M. *Bachelor fatherhood: How to raise and enjoy your children as a single parent.* New York: Charter Communications, 1974.

Murdock, C. V. *Single parents are people, too!* New York: Butterick, 1980.

Napolitane, C., & Pellegrino, V. *Living and loving after divorce.* New York: Signet, 1977.

Oakland, T. *Divorced fathers: Reconstructing a viable life.* New York: Human Sciences, 1982.

Ricci, I. *Mom's house, dad's house: Making shared custody work.* New York: Macmillan, 1980.

Rosenthal, K., & Keshet, H. *Fathers without partners: A study of fathers and the family after marital separation.* Totowa, N.J.: Rowman & Littlefield, 1981.

Salk, L. *What every child would like parents to know about divorce.* New York: Harper & Row, 1978.

Shepard, M., & Goldman, G. *Divorced dads: A practical plan with seven basic guidelines.* Radnor, Pa.: Chilton, 1979.

Spanier, G. B., & Thompson, L. *Parting: The aftermath of separation and divorce.* Beverly Hills, Calif.: Sage, 1984.

Stein, P. S. *Single life: Unmarried adults in social context.* New York: St. Martin's, 1981.

Tessman, L. H. *Children of parting parents.* New York: Jason Aronson, 1978.

Turow, R. *Daddy doesn't live here anymore.* Garden City, N.Y.: Anchor Books, 1978.

Victor, I., & Winkler, W. A. *Fathers and custody.* New York: Hawthorn, 1977.

Wallerstein, J. S., & Kelly, J. B. *Surviving the break-up: How children actually cope with divorce.* New York: Basic Books, 1980.

Weiss, R. *Marital separation.* New York: Basic Books, 1975.

Weiss, R. S. *Going it alone: The family life and social situation of the single parent.* New York: Basic Books, 1979.

Woody, R. H. *Getting custody: Winning the last battle of the marital war.* New York: Macmillan, 1978.

Wooley, P. *The custody handbook.* New York: Simon & Schuster, 1980.

## Books for Children

Bach, A. *A father every few years.* New York: Harper & Row, 1977.

Blume, J. *It's not the end of the world.* New York: Bradbury, 1972.

Caines, J. *Daddy.* New York: Harper & Row, 1977.

Fox, P. *Blowfish live in the sea.* Scarsdale, N.Y.: Bradbury, 1970.

Gardner, R. A. *The boys and girls book about divorce: With an introduction for parents.* New York: Bantam, 1971.

Goff, B. *Where is Daddy?* Boston: Beacon Press, 1969.

Hazen, B. *Two homes to live in: A child's view of divorce.* New York: Human Sciences, 1978.

Kindred, W. *Lucky Wilma.* New York: Dial, 1973.

Klein, N. *Taking sides.* New York: Pantheon, 1974.

LeShan, E. *What's going to happen to me?* Four Winds, 1978.

Magid, K., & Schreibman, W. *Divorce is . . . a kid's coloring book.* Gretna, La.: Pelican, 1980.

Nahn, P. *My dad lives in a downtown motel.* Garden City, N.Y.: Doubleday, 1973.

Newfield, N. *A book for Jodan.* New York: Atheneum, 1975.

Perry, P., & Lynch, M. *Mommy and Daddy are divorced.* New York: Dial, 1978.

Richards, A., & Willis, I. *How to get it together when your parents are coming apart.* New York: David McKay, 1976.

Robson, B. *My parents are divorced, too.* Toronto: Dorset, 1979.

Rofes, E. *The kid's book of divorce.* Lexington, Ky.: Lewis, 1981.

Simon, N. *All kinds of families.* Chicago: Whitman, 1976.

Singberg, J. *Divorce is a grown-up problem.* New York: Avon, 1978.

Stein, S. B. *On divorce.* New York: Walker, 1979.

Troyer, W. *Divorced kids.* New York: Harcourt Brace Jovanovich, 1979.

## Periodicals

*Journal of Divorce.* 174 Fifth Avenue, New York, NY 10010. Editor: Craig Everett, Haworth Press.

*Family Relations: Journal of Applied Family and Child Studies.* Special issue on the single-parent family, January 1986. S. M. H. Hanson & M. I. Sporakowski (Eds.).

*Single Dad's Lifestyle.* P.O. Box 4842, Scottsdale, AZ 85258. "For Dads, whether single or remarried, who live with their children, want to gain custody, or simply want to enjoy more meaningful visitation experiences." An excellent source of legal information and moral support for men in these situations. Maintains a 24-hour national hotline to help single fathers locate resources in their area (602-998-0980).

*The Single Parent: The Journal of Parents Without Partners.* 7910 Woodmont Avenue, Bethesda, MD 20014. Editor: Barbara Chase.

## Handbook

*Joint Custody: A Handbook for Judges, Lawyers, and Counselors.* Association of Family Conciliation Courts, 10015 S.W. Terwilliger Boulevard, Portland, OR 97219.

## Audiovisuals

*Are you listening/single parents.* Single parents discuss the experiences, challenges, and rewards of single parenthood. They talk about the difference between being a male and a female single parent, the relationship between their children and others in the house, sex-role stereotyping, and other problems and concerns of being a single parent. Martha Stuart Communications, Inc., P.O. Box 127, Hillsdale, NY 12529. 16 mm, 29 minutes.

*Children of divorce—Transitional issues for elementary school age children of divorce* and *Transistional issues for junior high and high school ages.* These two films provide a foundation for discussions of divorce with each age group. They are good discussion starters for practitioners leading groups of children of divorce. American Personnel and Guidance Association, 1607 New Hampshire Avenue, NW, Washington, DC 20009. 16 mm, 12 minutes each, color.

*Daddy doesn't live here anymore: The single-parent family.* This four-part filmstrip includes the changing family, when parents divorce, living one day at a time, and the stepparent family. Human Relations Media, 175 Tompkins Avenue, Pleasantville, NY 10570. Sound filmstrip, 52 minutes, color.

*Divorce.* Parents and children are shown passing through the trauma of divorce. The film covers such topics as child support, property settlement, and visiting rights. Centron Films, 1621 West Ninth St., P.O. Box 687, Lawrence, KS 66044. 16 mm, 16 minutes.

*Divorce I* and *Divorce II.* These two films are designed to stimulate discussions regarding personal and interactional problems in divorce. The first focuses on individual issues of postdivorce identity, social explanations, and the formation of new relationships. The second deals with the management of former spouse problems, including anger, alimony and visitation, and child-rearing concerns. American Personnel and Guidance Association, 1607 New Hampshire Avenue, NW, Washington, DC 20009. 16 mm, 20 minutes each, color.

*The divorced family.* Children from broken homes reflect on the family breakup and deal with adjustment issues such as identity, peer relations, and parental attachments. This filmstrip is a good resource for practitioners to use to stimulate discussion among groups of children from elementary to high school. Barr Films, P.O. Box 5667, Pasadena, CA 91107. Filmstrip, 28 minutes, color.

*Home, sweet homes: Kids talk about joint custody.* In this thoughtful and totally candid exchange, five engaging children, aged 8 to 12, tell why they like alternately living with each of their divorced parents. Filmakers Library, Inc., 133 East 58th Street, New York, NY 10022. 16 mm, 20 minutes.

*Joint custody: A new kind of family.* This film discusses the joys and difficulties of shared custody. It profiles 3 different arrangements where divorced or separated couples take equal responsibility for raising their children and where the children divide their time between the homes. New Day Films, 22 Riverview Drive, Wayne, NJ 07470. 16 mm, 85 minutes in three parts, color.

*Not together now: End of a marriage.* In this film a recently divorced couple with three young children reviews aspects of their courtship and decision to marry and pinpoint differences that led to marital conflict and divorce. They present the divorce as a growth experience as they reflect on their postdivorce adjustment. Polymorph Films, 331 Newbury Street, Boston, MA 02115. 16 mm, 25 minutes, color.

*Raising a family alone.* A Puerto Rican father moves with five children to a Northeastern U.S. city. This film depicts tasks of maintaining a household alone. Much of the dialogue is in Spanish, as are the titles. National Center for Child Advocacy, Children's Bureau, Office of Child Development (DHEW), P.O. Box 1182, Washington, DC 20013. 16 mm, 9 minutes, color.

*Separation/divorce: "It has nothing to do with you."* In this film the son of a separating couple becomes entangled in an emotional confrontation between his parents. The final message is that the divorce has "nothing to do" with the son. CRM/McGraw Hill Films, 110 Fifteenth Street, Del Mar, CA 92014. 16 mm, 14 minutes, color.

*Single parent* (Parts I and II). This film, based on issues that are common to all single-parent homes, points out the complexity of problems that can arise within different families facing these situations. In Part I some of the issues covered are conflicts faced by the single parent in responding both to needs of children and the demands of a job; problems for a single parent in establishing new intimate relationships; rights of custodial parent to assistance from noncustodial parent; and special loneliness in facing serious problems involving children. Some other issues explored in Part II are the remarriage of an ex-spouse; the organization of social situations around a two-parent family; needs of a single parent for help from family and friends; and pressure from children to get a new spouse. Intertwined throughout these issues are problems encountered by the children. This film is valuable for providing a supportive environment for single-parent or parent–child discussion groups that will facilitate the rethinking of problems. Together with questions in its study guide, this film dramatizes issues to a level where new, objective resolutions to the problems will become clear to the discussion group participants. American Personnel and Guidance Association, Order Services Dept., Two Skyline Place, Suite 400, 5203 Leesburg Pike, Falls Church, VA 22041. 16 mm, each part approximately 22 minutes, color.

*Single-parent families.* This filmstrip examines several cases of single-parent families through the eyes of teenagers who are trying to cope with new responsibilities and changing roles in the family. Suggests that teenagers try to understand and accept their parents' needs and objectively assess and discuss their own needs with their parents. Discusses the assignment of household chores and care for younger siblings as well as the impact of a parent's dating and socializing. Sunburst Communications, Room JV, 39 Washington Avenue, Pleasantville, NY 10570. Filmstrip, color.

*What ever happened to dear old Dad?* This video profiles four families in which the fathers changed their lives to take more active roles in parenting, including a divorced father's co-parenting role. WHA-TV Distribution Department, 821 University Avenue, Madison, WI 53706. Videocassette, 30 minutes, color.

## Organizations

The Divorce Resource and Mediation Center, 2464 Massachusetts Ave., Cambridge, MA 02140. Helps fathers and mothers work out postdivorce parenting arrangements so that both can remain active in their children's lives.

Family Service Association of America, 44 East 23rd Street, New York, NY 10010. Has 260 affiliate agencies in the United States and Canada and provides counseling, advocacy, and self-help groups for single and noncustodial parents.

Fathers United for Equality, Kent Corner's Church, Riverside, RI 02915. Provides men legal and emotional support when seeking custody of their children and attempts to prevent sex bias against fathers in custody decisions. The names of this organization vary by state. In Boston it is called *Fathers United for Equal Justice*, and in California, *Equal Rights for Fathers*.

Offspring, P.O. Box 23074, Washington, DC 20024. Provides a referral service and support network for noncustodial mothers and fathers.

Parents Without Partners, International Headquarters, 7910 Woodmont Avenue, Bethesda, MD 20014. Has 1100 local chapters and functions as a support network for single parents and men and women without custody.

The Single Fathers Research Project, 2901 Jefferson Drive, Greenville, NC 27834. A clearinghouse for research on single-father families for social services personnel, lawyers, and researchers.

# REFERENCES

Abarbanel, A. Shared parenting after separation and divorce: A study of joint custody. *American Journal of Orthopsychiatry*, 1979, *49*, 320–329.

Ahrons, C. R. The continuing coparental relationship between divorced spouses. *American Journal of Orthopsychiatry*, 1981, *51*, 415–428.

Ambert, A. M. Differences in children's behavior toward custodial mothers and custodial fathers. *Journal of Marriage and the Family*, 1982, *44*, 73–86.

Bartz, K. W., & Witcher, W. C. When father gets custody. *Children Today*, 1978, *7*, 2–6.

Bernstein, B. E. Lawyer and counselor as an interdisciplinary team: Preparing the father for custody. *Journal of Marriage and Family Counseling*, 1977, *3*, 29–40.

Chang, P., & Deinard, A. S. Single-father caretakers: Demographic characteristics and adjustment processes. *American Journal of Orthopsychiatry*, 1982, *52*, 236–243.

Chapman, M. Father absence, stepfathers, and the cognitive performance of college students. *Child Development*, 1977, *48*, 1155–1158.

DeFrain, J., & Eirick, R. Coping as divorced single parents: A comparative study of fathers and mothers. *Family Relations: Journal of Applied Family and Child Studies*, 1981, *30*, 265–274.

Flake-Hobson, C., Robinson, B., & Skeen, P. *Child development and relationships*. Reading, Mass.: Addison-Wesley, 1983.

Gasser, R. D., & Taylor, C. M. Role adjustment of single parent fathers with dependent children. *The Family Coordinator*, 1976, *25*, 397–401.

Gersick, K. E. *Fathers by choice: Characteristics of men who do and do not seek custody of their children following divorce*. Unpublished doctoral dissertation, Harvard University, 1975.

Goldstein, J., Freud, A., & Solnit, A. *Beyond the best interests of the child*. New York: Free Press, 1973.

Greif, G. L. Single fathers rearing children. *Journal of Marriage and the Family,* 1985, *47,* 185–191.

Greif, J. B. Fathers, children, and joint custody. *American Journal of Orthopsychiatry,* 1979, *49,* 311–319.

Hanson, S. M. H. *Single custodial fathers.* Paper presented at the meeting of the National Council on Family Relations, Milwaukee, Wisconsin, October 1981.

Hetherington, E. M. Divorce: A child's perspective. *American Psychologist,* 1979, *34,* 851–858.

Hetherington, E. M., Cox, M., & Cox, R. Divorced fathers. *The Family Coordinator,* 1976, *25,* 417–428.

Hoffereth, S. L. Day care in the next decade: 1980–1990. *Journal of Marriage and Family,* 1979, *41,* 649–657.

Keshet, H. F., & Rosenthal, K. M. Fathering after marital separation. *Social Work,* 1978, *23,* 11–18.

Lamb, M., & Bronson, S. K. Fathers in the context of family influences: Past, present and future. *School Psychology Review,* 1980, *9,* 336–353.

LeMasters, E. E., & DeFrain, J. *Parents in Contemporary America: A sympathetic view.* Homewood, Ill.: Dorsey, 1983.

Levine, J. A. *Who will raise the children?* Philadelphia: Lippincott, 1976.

Lewis, K. Single-father families: Who they are and how they fare. *Child Welfare,* 1978, *57,* 643–651.

Lynn, D. B. *The father: His role in child development.* Monterey, Calif.: Brooks/Cole, 1974.

Mendes, H. A. Single fatherhood. *Social Work,* 1976, *21,* 308–312. (a)

Mendes, H. A. Single fathers. *The Family Coordinator,* 1976, *25,* 439–444. (b)

Miller, J. B. Psychological recovery in low-income single parents. *American Journal of Orthopsychiatry,* 1982, *52,* 346–352.

Monaghan-Lackband, K. Role adaptation of single parents: A challenge of the pathological view of male and female single parents. *Dissertation Abstracts International,* 1979, *39,* 7544A.

Nieto, D. S. Aiding the single father. *Social Work,* 1982, *27,* 473–478.

Orthner, D., Brown, T., & Ferguson, D. Single-parent fatherhood: An emerging lifestyle. *The Family Coordinator,* 1976, *25,* 429–437.

Orthner, D., & Lewis, K. Evidence of single father competence in child rearing. *Family Law Quarterly,* 1979, *8,* 27–48.

Parish, T. S., & Dostal, J. W. Relationships between evaluations of self and parents by children from intact and divorced families. *Journal of Psychology,* 1980, *104,* 35–38.

Roman, M. The disposable parent. *Conciliation Courts Review,* 1977, *15,* 1.

Santrock, J. W. The relations of type and onset of father absence to cognitive development. *Child Development,* 1972, *43,* 455–469.

Santrock, J. W., & Warshak, R. A. Father custody and social development in boys and girls. *Journal of Social Issues,* 1979, *35,* 112–125.

Santrock, J. W., Warshak, R. A., & Elliott, G. L. Social development and parent–child interaction in father-custody and stepmother families. In M. E. Lamb (Ed.), *Nontraditional families: Parenting and child development.* Hillsdale, N.J.: Erlbaum, 1982.

Schlesinger, B. Single parent. *Children Today,* 1978, *7,* 12–19.

Schlesinger, B. Children's viewpoints of living in a one-parent family. *Journal of Divorce,* 1982, *5,* 1–23.

Shepard, M., & Goldman, G. *Divorced dads: A practical plan with seven basic guidelines.* Radnor, Pa.: Chilton, 1979.

Silver, G. A., & Silver, M. *Weekend fathers.* Los Angeles: Stratford, 1981.

Smith, R. M., & Smith, C. W. Child rearing and single-parent fathers. *Family Relations: Journal of Applied Family and Child Studies,* 1981, *30,* 411–417.

Spivey, D., & Richards, M. Male single parent with custody. In S. Burden, P. Houston, E. Kripe, R. Simpson, R. Simpson, & W. Stultz (Eds.), *The single parent family.* Iowa City, Iowa: University of Iowa, 1976.

Spock, B. Joint custody and the father's role. *Redbook Magazine,* October, 1979, 77–79.

Steinman, S. The experience of children in a joint-custody arrangement: A report of a study. *American Journal of Orthopsychiatry,* 1981, *51,* 403–414.

Thompson, R. A. The father's case in child custody disputes: The contributions of psychological research. In M. E. Lamb & A. Sagi (Eds.), *Fatherhood and family policy.* Hillsdale, N.J.: Erlbaum, 1983.

U.S. Bureau of the Census, Current Population Reports, Series P-20, No. 349. *Marital Status and Living Arrangements: March 1979.* Washington, D.C.: U.S. Government Printing Office, 1980.

Wallerstein, J. S. *Children of divorce: Preliminary report of a ten-year follow-up.* Paper presented at the Tenth International Congress of the International Association for Child and Adolescent Psychiatry and Allied Professions, Dublin, Ireland, July, 1982.

Wallerstein, J. S. Children of divorce: Preliminary report of a ten-year follow-up of young children. *American Journal of Orthopsychiatry,* 1984, *54,* 444–458.

Wallerstein, J. S., & Kelly, J. B. *Surviving the break-up: How children actually cope with divorce.* New York: Basic Books, 1980.

Watson, M. A. Custody alternatives: Defining the best interests of the children. *Family Relations: Journal of Applied Family and Child Studies,* 1981, *30,* 474–479.

*Watts v Watts,* 350 NYS, 2d 285, (New York 1973).

White, S. W., & Bloom, B. L. Factors related to the adjustment of divorcing men. *Family Relations: Journal of Applied Family and Child Studies,* 1981, *30,* 349–360.

Woody, R. H. Fathers with child custody. *Counseling Psychologist,* 1978, *7,* 60–63.

Wright, M. D. Divorcing fathers love kids too. *The Charlotte Observer,* April, 1983, 4B.

Wylder, J. Including the divorced father in family therapy. *Social Work,* 1982, *27,* 479–482.

# CHAPTER SIX

## *Stepfathers*

**THE CASE OF A STEPFATHER**

I have been married twice and both times entered a marriage as a stepfather. My first stepchild was a boy and my second, a girl. Each stepparenting experience was as different as night and day.

My first stepchild was 15 months old when I married his mother. Our relationship just grew without any real effort on my part. My stepson probably looked up to me because I was the first man in his life. He had never known his father. So I really was his father even though I had no legal rights with him. He was quite a discipline problem. He was fairly active—even hyperactive. I disciplined him through spanking or verbal criticism. His mother began experiencing difficulties when she tried to toilet train him. I took over the job and proceeded to give him a bath and wash his hair each time he soiled his pants. I did this four times in one day! Because he didn't like having his hair washed, he was soon toilet trained.

I stayed married to his mother for 4 years, and he and I had formed quite an attachment when the marriage went on the rocks. This split was really emotionally hard for me, since I loved him but had no rights to spend time with him. At first my stepson's mother used him as a weapon to get at me. Eventually, because it was helpful to her, his mother allowed me to spend some time with him. Now that he's 13, he spends several weeks each year with my second wife and me.

My second marriage began when my new stepdaughter was 9. This relationship was much more difficult to get off the ground. My step-daughter wasn't a real discipline problem, but she was very sensitive and seemed to resent any intervention on my part. I felt terribly rejected and left out. She loved her father and I was a stranger to her. She obviously wanted her father back. Maybe the easier time with my stepson resulted from the fact that he was younger, and we soon established a strong bond of love with each other.

As time has gone by, I have developed a stronger relationship with my stepdaughter too. Even though she is now living with her father, she spends summers with her mother and me. With the maturation and realization that her father and mother won't get back together, she has come to accept me more. Also, I have gained more experience and confidence with my stepparenting role. It works better if I let my wife do the disciplining so as to avoid resentment and resistance. When my stepdaughter and stepson spend time with us in the summer, we get along quite well. The two children consider themselves brother and sister. Even though they get into some real battles, they also have fun together.

In looking back over my years as a stepfather, I now know that it is important to see children as individuals. What worked with my stepson didn't work with my stepdaughter, who didn't have a strong bond with me and resented my relationship with her mother. So when I tried to interact with her in the same way I did with my stepson, she was rebel-lious.

Being a stepfather hasn't been easy for me. Since I don't have any children of my own, I had to learn to be a parent from the ground up. Now that the children are teenagers, it's easier for me. I guess I just know how to interact with them better now that they are more like adults than babies.

**\*Anonymous**
*Columbia, South Carolina*

\*Reprinted with permission from Einstein, E. *The Stepfamily: Living, Loving, and Learning.* New York: Macmillan, 1982, p. 11.

As the case study illustrates, stepfathers may have the most difficult challenge of all the father roles we have discussed so far. They become part of an established family and must create relationships with children who may already have a father and/or who may see their stepfathers as intruders. In addition, in most cases the success of the marriage depends on the quality of fathering.

Demographers predict that by 1990 stepfamilies—sometimes called blended, reconstituted, or recoupled families—will become the pre-dominant family form in the United States, because divorce rates are skyrocketing and 75% of divorced people remarry (Herndon, 1982; Visher & Sager, 1982). During the 1960s and 1970s alone, the remarriage rate of widowed and divorced women rose by 40% (Glick & Norton, 1973). Approximately 83% of all divorced men remarry (Glick, 1980). More and more men will therefore become stepfathers.

The typical image of stepfamilies is of a mother, her child or children, and a new husband and father. Statistically, this kind of stepfamily is most common because courts routinely award custody of children to the mother (Macklin, 1980). Despite the prevalence of this stepfamily structure, recent reviews show that there is little factual information about stepfather families (Rallings, 1976; Robinson, 1984; Skeen, Covi, & Robinson, 1985; Skeen, Robinson, & Flake-Hobson, 1984).

## STEPFATHER FAMILIES COMPARED WITH NATURAL-FATHER FAMILIES

One week after his remarriage, a new stepfather we talked to went about his usual routine of dressing for work. As he opened his chest of drawers, he was horrified to see a photograph of his wife's first husband in a coffin. It was later discovered that the photograph had been placed there by one of his resentful stepchildren. This is a true, although extreme, case of how anger and jealousy can be expressed when two families blend together without adequate preparation. The stepfather and mother entered the remarriage with the same expectations they had in their first marriages. More realistic expectations and discussions about parenting might have saved this marriage, which ended after a year.

One of the most common mistakes made by members of stepfamilies is assuming that blended families are no different from biological families. Living in a stepfamily *is* different from simply moving from one primary family into another. Stepfather families may be as simple as a widow with one child who marries a bachelor, or as complex as four divorced individuals all with joint custody of their children trying to form new households. In the words of stepfamily expert John Visher, "Biological families have family trees, but stepfamilies have family forests" (Visher & Sager, 1982, p. 12). There are clear structural differences in how biological families and stepfather families interact (Perkins & Kahn, 1979; Visher & Visher, 1979). Rather than one interpersonal subsystem, the stepfamily has at least two. As Einstein (1982) notes, the stepfamily is not an imitation, carbon copy, or replacement for the biological family. Instead, part of the magic of melding the new stepfamily into a cohesive network is recognizing and acknowledging the differences:

> The major difference lies in the structure of its relationships. A host of extra people and pressures push and tug at the stepfamily, making the determination of its own destiny difficult. Some of the relationships that make it different are directly within the family unit and between the two joined nuclear families—former spouses, the other parents, step-parents, stepbrothers, and stepsisters. The stepfamily's success is determined largely by the quality of these old and new ties. (Einstein, 1982, p. 7)

Stepfathers enter into families where the mother and her children have had a lifetime to establish their relationship patterns. As the case study illustrates, stepfathers and stepchildren may find themselves having to create instant, intimate relationships with each other as they begin to live together. They may be virtual strangers and naturally resent each other from time to time. Or they may bury their anger under the guise of a friendship that is forced. Stepfamily members have different histories, memories, and habits. Solidarity must be reestablished, and status, duties, and privileges must be redefined within the context of the new family system (Duberman, 1973). The most common problem a stepfather experiences is uncertainty over his new stepfather identity (Fast & Cain, 1966; Messinger, Walker, & Freeman, 1978). Confronted with being both parent, nonparent, and stepparent and sharing role functions of parents in ways that are not clearly defined can lead to confusion.

Belief in the myth that stepfamilies should "instantly love" each other because they are now a family sets stepfathers and other family members up for failure (Visher & Visher, 1978). Some adults often mistakenly think that because they love each other, they are going to love each others' children (Visher & Sager, 1982). Other stepfamily members report they are unsure how they are supposed to feel and do not know how to interact with one another comfortably (Johnson, 1980). Is a stepfather, for example, supposed to automatically love a stepchild whom he hardly knows, and vice versa? If the stepfather and child do not love or even like one another (which is sometimes the case), do they feel guilty because the woman they both love as mother or spouse is so often caught between them? How will they compete for the love and attention of the mother? These are just some of the questions raised in the minds of stepfather family members as they try to integrate a new household.

Most stepfather families feel poorly prepared for the many problems they face in blending two households. Clinical reports suggest that there is a whole set of common problems unique to becoming a stepfather (Messinger, 1976; Mowatt, 1972; Visher & Visher, 1978). Problems around discipline, sex, jealousy, money, and the amount of time and attention given to one's children are problems that biological fathers in intact families share with stepfathers. But biological fathers generally have the opportunity to deal with these problems gradually as they occur developmentally in the household. Biological fathers have the luxury of time to negotiate each successive problem (Prosen & Farmer, 1982). Stepfathers, in contrast, instantly encounter all these problems at once and must face them collectively and immediately.

## CONFLICTS AROUND DISCIPLINE

One of the most commonly reported problems is discipline. How to discipline stepchildren and how to enforce rules are major problems for stepfathers, who often report that the transition from a friendly relationship to a parenting relationship is awkward. They frequently feel uncertain about how far to go in taking over the role of father (Mowatt, 1972). Some children are stunned when, after remarriage, the stepfather assumes the role of disciplinarian. Others will test stepfathers to see how they will react to some rule violation, sometimes to find out if the stepfather really cares about them. Einstein (1982) describes such an incident with her stepfather:

> As a youngster I wondered if my stepfather let me get away with so much because he didn't care about me. I recall clearly when he finally carried out a threat. At seventeen I had failed to do some job, so he told me to cancel a date with a boy named Ed. I assumed that the threat could be ignored, and I never called the boy. That evening I dressed for the date as though nothing had happened, but this time my stepfather held his ground. He greeted Ed, telling him that I had been a bad girl and could not go out. He elaborated that I had known of the punishment in the morning and should have called him earlier.
>
> I was furious and started to bolt out the door, but something stopped me. Despite the anger and embarrassment, I felt loved and cared about. But I never told my stepfather that. Instead, I ranted and raved and pouted. Today I understand the precarious position my stepfather and others like him are forced into. I sought boundaries; he feared overstepping his.*

---

*Reprinted with permission from Einstein, E. *The Stepfamily: Living, Loving, and Learning.* New York: Macmillan, 1982, p. 11.

Sometimes mothers suddenly may become protective of their children and feel personally attacked or inadequate when stepfathers criticize or attempt to discipline their children. Conflicts may arise between stepfathers and their wives over what is or what is not important to enforce. We met with a stepfamily, the Childers (a pseudonym), that is a case in point. The stepfather, Bill, who has custody of his three children from a previous marriage and whose wife has custody of her two children, told us, "My wife and I have used different guidelines for conduct and behavior with our respective children. I have been more rigid and strict. It's been difficult to moderate my expectations of her children in this regard." His wife agreed, saying, "It's really the little things in day-to-day living that become big problems—What time to go to bed? What to eat for lunch? Should my son drink all of his milk or leave the table without it?"

Johnson (1980), a social worker, also found this to be true of the stepfamilies with whom she worked. She identified the following nine items that become sources of conflict in stepfamilies because of preexisting lifestyles:

- Discipline: Who should enforce it, how should it be enforced, and when?
- Eating habits: Does the family eat together or separately in front of the T.V.?
- Division of labor: Whose responsibility is it to cook, clean, do the laundry, get the car fixed, and attend parent–teacher conferences?
- Attitudes toward sex: Should family members see each other undressed? Should teenage children engage in sex?
- Use of alcohol and drugs: Is such use acceptable for parents? For children? To what extent?
- Attitudes toward obligations: How important is it to pay bills, get to appointments, turn in homework, or call to let other family members know where you are?
- Manners: What behavior should be considered impolite?
- Household rules: What rules govern using the phone or keeping curfews?
- Expression of hostility, aggression, or disagreement: How much is acceptable? (Johnson, 1980, p. 307)

Because there are few guidelines for being a stepparent and even fewer for being a stepfather, men in this role, along with other stepfamily members, must create their rules based on individual personalities, living arrangements, and the ages and sexes of the children. The Childers stepfamily devised creative solutions to cope with these many conflicts. They set consistent behavior standards and systems of rewards and punishments for all five of their children. The stepmother said she took responsibility for decisions and discipline affecting her own children and her husband assumed responsibility for his. She told us:

> I try not to tell him how to raise his children and he does the same for me, although two of the most successful things we have done are setting up a chore chart for each week and each child and setting a point-reward system for high achievement in school. The children initially complained about living in a prison with too many rules. But with seven of us, two working parents, plus five active preteens, it's the only way we can avoid chaos and try to approach each child fairly about his or her behavior in the group and as an individual. These systems work after the kids figure out we mean it!

Therapists concede that agreement and unity between the remarried couple is also a key to minimizing conflict to stepfather families (Visher & Visher, 1978). When husband and wife are divided or inconsistent in their rules, stepchildren sometimes take advantage of this conflict. A positive relationship in which spouses back each other and support each other's authority in the household generally reduces such conflict. Bill Childers told us:

> We are both very strong individuals and we agree on basic life-styles but are totally different in our approaches. So we have had lots of discussion to find a middle ground. Somehow we manage to respect and to work around the other's opinion. Sometimes that involves settling our differences in front of the children. Other times we present a united front and then "fight it out" when they're not around.

## CONFLICTS OVER SHOWING AFFECTION AND SEXUAL FEELINGS

Stepfathers sometimes say they do not know how much affection to give stepchildren and how to show it. They sometimes report feeling awkward kissing their stepchildren and do not always enjoy playing games with them. As one mother told us, "My husband seems to be afraid of my daughter. It's as if she were a China doll and he doesn't know how or even if he should handle her. This is getting easier for him and he does seem more relaxed but for a while it was touch and go."

On the other side of the coin, sexual attraction can cause stepfathers to feel ill at ease around their stepdaughters. Stepfathers may have

fleeting sexual feelings toward adolescent stepdaughters, and stepdaughters can become attracted to stepfathers as well. Although data
are inconclusive on the sexual relationships between stepfathers and
their stepdaughters, statistics indicate that a higher proportion of
stepfathers are involved in incest than are natural fathers. One clinic
that specializes in the treatment of problems related to incest, reports
that 50% of the cases are stepfathers and stepdaughters (Visher &
Visher, 1979).

The sexual awakenings of teenage females that normally occur
during adolescence can be stimulated by their stepfather and mother's
active sexual life. As mentioned, teenage girls who are just becoming
aware of their own sexual feelings may find themselves attracted to
their stepfathers. Remarried mothers may fear, consciously or unconsciously, that a sexual relationshp between her husband and daughter is imminent.

Sexual feelings among stepfather families can cause members to
withdraw from one another and to erect thicker communication barriers. Unrecognized sexual tensions can erupt in other kinds of camou-
flaged conflict such as bedtime hours, curfews on date nights, and so
forth. Stepfamily therapists Visher and Visher (1983b) suggest that
these issues should be brought out and discussed openly. Family
members need to be made aware that sexual attractions among stepfamilies are not unusual, because the incest taboo is not as strong in
stepfamilies as it is in intact, biological families. The difference between feelings and behavior can be clearly distinguished, and the
notion that everyone has many different feelings upon which they do
not act can be discussed. Newly remarried couples may need to re-
strain their affections for one another when children are around.
Brooks (1981) also suggests that "stepfathers can respond warmly to
requests for affection but must be careful not to provide gratification
for erotic feelings" (p. 327).

## JEALOUSY AND COMPETITION

Although jealousy and competition exist in biological families, the
intensity of these feelings is magnified in stepfather families (Visher &
Visher, 1978). Jealousy and competition can run both ways. Children,
for example, may feel the new marriage is depriving them of their
mother's time and attention. This is especially true if children are not
included in the marriage plans or if the newly married couple concen-
trates on establishing their relationship at the expense of the children.
Following her divorce one mother told us:

Depression and despair came as I realized I was alone except for my child, and I'd cry for no reason. While this was wearing off I turned to my daughter and she became my constant companion, friend, and everything I seemed to live for. Since my remarriage, it has been hard for her to give me up and to share me with someone else whom I love. I'd given my love to her and only her for so long that jealousy is sometimes an issue at our house.

Stepfathers are in double jeopardy because there is no honeymoon. They must not only establish relationships with their spouses, they must also establish relationships with their stepchildren. Often this involves dealing with children's problems that are inherited as a part of the marriage package. Stepfathers may also feel that stepchildren are intruding on their marriages with their "unreasonable" demands for attention from the mother. Remarried couples may have little or no time alone together, and one or both may feel jealous of attention given to children (Visher & Visher, 1978). The more children involved, the more opportunities for jealousy and competition for the parent's attention.

## LOYALTY AND MONEY CONFLICTS

Stepfathers often report that they have divided loyalties between their own children, their stepchildren, and their wives. Guilt over leaving children from his previous family sometimes prevents the stepfather from giving openly to his spouse and stepchildren. Occasionally, the stepfather displaces guilt with resentment toward his stepchildren. He earns money and provides a home for children who may consider him an outsider. He may feel anger or shame or other emotions. He may feel cheated and taken for granted by the stepfamily and resent the time he gives to another man's children that limits the attention he can give to his own. Bill Childers told us, "I have done little to fill the void of a father since I'm not home much and when I am, I feel that I owe most of my attention to my own children." A stepfather may feel unappreciated in his new family. He may become a "Disneyland Dad," who through limited time, provides material gifts, trips to amusement parks, and overly permissive parenting (Shepard & Goldman, 1979). This in turn, can lead to concern and even antagonism toward the man who is raising his children, as a father reported to us:

Once I was told by the stepfather of my children that when the children were with him and their mother, he would see to it that they did not forget me! That seemed thoughtful and "good sport" enough. But that wasn't my concern. I told him I felt more deeply about the kind of lifestyle he led before them, the quality of modeling as a man and stepfather in their presence than I did their forgetfulness. I know my sons love me and don't worry that they will forget me, but I can't always be sure that those from whom my children take their life cues are persons whose integrity they can trust, whose positive lifestyle of loving and selflessness they can admire.

Money is often used as a symbol for how the stepfather feels about his biological children, his stepchildren, former spouse, or current spouse. Some stepfathers may be making support payments to their previous family. As a result of this added economic pressure, bitterness over money issues can become quite severe. Bill Childers told us: "A lot of times I feel overburdened with a wife, two stepchildren, three of my own, one here, two with child support, and ever-escalating alimony to my ex-wife. All of that makes me angry! Lucky for me, though, my former wife loves her work or our lifestyle would be drastically altered!" Since traditionally men have been the breadwinners, the ways in which they spend their money may be closely monitored by both families. As a result, a stepfather can be sandwiched between the competing demands of two famlies. The balance with which he allocates money may be used as a measure of his love and devotion among stepsiblings and spouse.

Marital quality in stepfather families is best in those situations where stepfathers have no children from previous marriages and where frequency of contacts with former spouses is moderate (Clingempeel, 1981). Obviously, the fewer previous ties men have, the less guilt, divided loyalties, money conflicts, and overall stress they will have. Frequent contact and close ties with the first marriage sometimes increase the stepfather's role confusion and his dependency on the first marriage to make his second marriage work (Clingempeel, 1981; Messinger *et al.*, 1978).

## CONFLICT OVER SURNAMES

Different surnames of stepfathers and their stepchildren can become a focus of tension. Some stepfathers strongly object to their stepchildren taking their surnames, while other stepfathers desire to adopt their stepchildren and to share their names. Stepchildren worry about this too and may fear they will be adopted by stepfathers who will not permit them to visit their biological fathers.

When children have different surnames from their mothers, stepfathers, and perhaps his children, it can be a subtle reminder that they are not really part of the family unit. Stepchildren may want to adopt the same last name so that they fit in with other family members. Acquiring the same last name as the stepfather can also prevent children's embarrassment and discomfort when in public. Of course, adoption alone does not ensure stepfamily integration. However, it can heal psychological wounds of isolation (Visher & Visher, 1983).

## RELATIONSHIPS BETWEEN STEPFATHERS AND STEPCHILDREN

Conclusions about the positive or negative impact of the stepfamily structure on parents and children and the stressfulness of the stepfather relationship in comparison with natural-father families must be regarded as tentative in light of the methodological limitations of research to date (see "Shortcomings of Stepfather Research" box). The following synthesis of the available information presents the factors that may affect the success of the stepparent–stepchild relationship.

### SHORTCOMINGS OF STEPFATHER RESEARCH

Many of the conclusions drawn in this chapter are tentative, due to numerous drawbacks in stepfather research. Only recently has the stepfather family become the subject of research (Robinson, 1984). Findings from the handful of studies that exist are inconsistent. The outcome predicted for family members depends on the type of research procedure employed.

Pioneer clinical studies (Fast & Cain, 1966; Mowatt, 1972) suggest that stepfather families have an array of role ambiguity, communication and stress problems. These studies generally employed small, volunteer samples drawn from families undergoing counseling, which may not be representative of all stepfather families (Robinson, 1984). The degree to which these same problems occur in nonclinical stepfather families is unknown. Families who seek counseling are a select group who may undergo more stress than those not involved in therapy. This high stress level seen clinically has led many practitioners to view *all* stepfamilies as pathological and to apply a therapeutic model for treatment that focuses on problems and fails to consider strengths of remarriage and stepfamilies (Chilman, 1983). To date researchers have not asked whether nonclinical stepfather groups have specific factor(s) not present in clinical groups or

whether clinical stepfather families survive longer than nonclinical stepfather families because of counseling support.

In contrast, more scientifically controlled studies (Bohannan & Erickson,
1978; Oshman & Manosevitz, 1976; Parish & Copeland, 1979; Parish &
Dostal, 1980a, 1980b; Wilson, Zurcher, McAdams, & Curtis, 1975) employ-
ing large representative samples of stepfather families (usually through
the use of questionnaires or cognitive and personality tests) tend to report
positive outcomes in terms of stepfather family functioning. This is especially true when stepfather families are systematically compared with
other family structures such as single-parent or father-absent families
(Chapman, 1977; Santrock, 1972; Wilson et al., 1975). A major shortcoming of most questionnaire research is that conclusions are based on the
perceptions of only one family member, usually the parent or child, but
not both (Robinson, 1984). As a result, mixed findings appear, depending
on which family member's viewpoint is studied. Age at onset of the
biological parent's absence, reasons for the biological parent's absence
(such as death or divorce), and the length of time the child has lived in the
stepparent family are important factors that have not been controlled in
family comparison studies. Another limitation of written questionnaires is
that researchers cannot be certain that respondents actually behave as
reported. In addition, preliterate children obviously are automatically
excluded from this type of research.

Behavioral studies provide the added benefit of including younger
preliterate children. The drawback of behavioral observation, which has
reported positive effects of stepfathers on their stepchildren's personality
and cognitive development (Santrock, Warshak, Lindbergh, & Meadows,
1982), is that competent stepfathers may be more willing to visit the
researcher's laboratory and submit to scrutiny than less competent stepfathers.

Stepfather research must develop further before conclusions can be
drawn with more confidence. A multimethod approach of study is
needed in which questionnaires from all stepfamily members are used in
conjunction with behavioral observations, clinical assessments, and personality and cognitive tests before a comprehensive picture of stepfather
families can be obtained. Multimethod assessments of stepfather families
have recently been initiated by Clingempeel (1981) and Clingempeel,
Brand, and Ievoli (1984). Such an approach would require that psychologists, sociologists, therapists, and the medical professions combine their
skills and work cooperatively.

Despite the structural differences in stepfather families that can
lead to conflict, heightened anxiety, and complex interactions, 64% of
all spouses in one study described the relationship between their own
children and the stepparent as excellent (Duberman, 1973). Other
findings show that stepfathers are more likely than stepmothers to
have successful relationships with their stepchildren (Bowerman &

Irish, 1962; Duberman, 1973). Many experts believe that this occurs because stepmothers must overcome a negative image (such as the wicked stepmother portrayed in fairy tales), which men do not (Visher & Visher, 1978). Others believe that many stepmothers have more problems because they attempt to become a second mother rather than trying to become the stepchild's friend (Draughon, 1975). Mothers traditionally are more involved in their children's upbringing than fathers. Sudden onset of "motherhood" without the benefit of having given consistent early nurturance can be more problematic for stepmothers than stepfathers.

Researchers have reported mixed findings in regard to the effect of the mother's previous marital status on stepfather family adjustment. Some researchers found that steprelations are more successful when previous marriages end in death (Duberman, 1973). The assumption is that the dead parent is not present to influence the new relationships in stepfather families. Others report that children adjust better when previous marriages are broken by divorce (Bowerman & Irish, 1962). In these broken families the belief is that divorce-induced tension may cause children to reject their natural parent and more readily accept the new stepparent. Since there is no consensus among investigators, clinicians recommend that therapists recognize that pain is present in both types of homes (Visher & Visher. 1978).

In many instances clinical reports from therapy groups and behavioral observations by researchers describe stepfathers as more effective parents than biological fathers. One therapist of stepfamilies who were experiencing trouble with children's behavior observed that stepfathers seemed more willing to involve themselves in the children's improvement than many of the natural fathers who had been involved in treatment (Mowatt, 1972). The therapist speculated that perhaps stepfathers felt less threatened (but just as annoyed) by their stepchildren's misbehavior than they would be by their biological children. Other practitioners have found that this objectivity is a real plus for stepfamily relationships (Visher & Visher, 1983b). Very often stepchildren love their stepfathers but also have a friendship with them that they do not have with their biological parents. This friendship encourages stepchildren to seek out the stepfather, who is less enmeshed with the child than is the biological mother.

Researchers have also observed that during interactions between stepfathers and stepchildren, stepfathers are more attentive to the needs of their children and are more democratic parents than biological fathers are with their sons (Santrock, Warshak, Lindbergh, & Meadows, 1982). Stepfathers also tend to be more self-conscious and self-critical than biological fathers about their effectiveness as a stepparent. Stepfathers, wanting to do a good job, set their standards high—measuring themselves against what an ideal father should be like (Bohannan & Erickson, 1978). Stepfathers assume the challenges of fatherhood with an awareness of the difficulties involved:

> I was really turned on by her—then I met her kids. They scared the hell out of me. I began to look at them in a very different way after I got serious. I kept asking myself, "What are they trying to do to me? What am I going to do to them?" Everybody warned me not to marry a woman with children. They said there'd be problems: There were. But the youngest goes off to college next month and I think we've won. (Bohannan & Erickson, 1978, p. 53)

Stepchildren tend to view their relationships with stepfathers differently depending upon how old they are when their mothers remarry. As the opening case study illustrates, stepfathers are more likely to have positive relationships when stepchildren are younger than in situations where stepchildren are older and have been reared for many years by their mothers (Visher & Visher, 1983b). Children less than 9 years old are more likely to accept a good stepparent than children between 9 and 15 years of age (Hetherington, Cox, & Cox, 1981). Stepchildren between ages 10–12 tend to view both their stepfathers and their natural fathers more negatively and less positively than children from intact families (Halperin & Smith, 1983). Stepchildren in junior and senior high school are more apt to describe their steprelations as more stressful, ambivalent, and low on cohesion than children from nonstepfamily homes. Stepchildren report the level of affection toward stepfathers as lower than children with biological fathers (Bowerman & Irish, 1962). Teenage children with stepfathers also tend to view their family as dysfunctional, compared to teenagers in natural-father families, who report better adjustment and greater satisfaction with their families (Perkins & Kahan, 1979). Older children are aware of their own awakening sexuality and do not want to view their parents as sex objects. In contrast, young boys often form intense attachments and warm relationships with stepfathers, which are reflected in more mature, independent, and controlled behavior both at home and in school (Hetherington, Cox, & Cox, 1982).

Although stepfather integration is typically more difficult when the children are older, this does not mean that stepfather families with older children are doomed. Many children whose biological fathers maintain contact or whose biological fathers abandoned them or died often feel that they have gained a father rather than lost a mother (Einstein, 1982). Some stepchildren never fully appreciate their stepfathers until they are grown and look back upon the experience with maturity and objectivity (Einstein, 1982).

Perhaps more important than the built-in advantage of having younger stepchildren is the way in which men approach these relationships. If the biological father has an interest in sailing, the stepfather should stay in dry dock (Visher & Visher, 1983b); stepfathers have more successful relationships when they do not compete in the same areas as biological fathers and when they make friends with their stepchildren. Stern (1982), through her intensive interviews with 62 persons in stepfather families, discovered the key to successful stepfather integration to be what she called "affiliation," that is, befriending the stepchildren. Unsuccessful stepfathers usually take on the role of disciplinarian, and the mother ends up intervening as go-between—separating her children and the stepfather physically and affectionately. In contrast, successful stepfathers tend to be cautious (not pushing the friendship too fast), gentle, and flexible in their interactions with stepchildren. This approach allows stepfathers and children to overcome friendship barriers and ultimately to become friends. Stern identified the ten following affiliating strategies that have led to successful stepfather–stepchild relationships.

1. *Spending quality time* with stepchildren provides opportunities for forming close relationships.
2. *Using proper timing* by saying and doing the right thing at the right time works better than forcing a relationship with a child who might not be ready.
3. *Spending money* or stinting (that is, withholding money) are measures some stepchildren use to judge their stepfather's true loyalty and devotion.
4. *Setting a good example* for stepchildren is more likely to attract their attention and their respect than poor modeling, which can turn them off altogether.
5. *Informal teaching* by sharing knowledge and skills with stepchildren (rather than supervising them as their superior) leads to a reciprocal sharing by children who let their stepfathers in on family secrets, jokes, or history.
6. *Following through* on promises and commitments is viewed highly by spouses and other stepfamily members, whereas unreliability leads to mistrust.
7. *Speaking the truth* about feelings, thoughts, and desires is an essential ingredient in cementing close stepfather–stepchild relationships, while concealing feelings creates barriers.
8. *Trusting* the stepchild's word, ability to carry out a job, or even the stepchild's basic honesty works better than constant doubting.

9. *Accepting* stepchildren as they are, including the bad with the good, leads to better relationships than rapidly imposing change.
10. *Liking,* when it is mutual between stepfather and child, pulls them together in a stronger bond.

Some men flounder in their steprelations because of a lack of specific stepfamily education, and they believe their feelings and stresses indicate that something is "wrong" with them. The need for the helping professions to better understand and offer assistance to remarried men and women is evident in the staggering fact that 40% of second marriages end in divorce in their first 4 years, with the presence of a child from a previous marriage a major factor in the breakup (Visher & Visher, 1983a). Sociologist Frank Furstenberg believes second marriages have such high divorce rates because remarried couples monitor their relationships more closely than couples in first marriages (cited in Cory, 1983). They have already experienced the demise of one marriage, and as similar signs emerge, they are less likely to stick around for the predictable ending. As one stepparent put it, "I'm willing to go through another divorce but I'm not willing to go through another bad marriage" (Cory, 1983).

Stern's (1982) strategies have been used successfully by the Stepfamily Foundation of California to teach men entering stepfamilies how to become friends with their stepchildren. Other clinical reports suggest that successful stepfathering can be achieved through remarriage preparation courses or group counseling that enable men to reduce their anxiety levels and clarify ambiguous roles in their new families (Fast & Cain, 1966; Messinger, 1976; Messinger et al., 1978; Mowatt, 1972; Visher & Visher, 1978, 1979). Before remarriage the entire stepfamily can more successfully blend as a whole when all members participate in a "rehearsal for reality" by expressing their feelings honestly and by anticipating potential problems that might arise after remarriage (Jacobson, 1980). A stepfather with whom we talked shared the advantages of his remarriage counseling:

> My wife and I experienced a type of counseling before we were married. We're both of the Lutheran faith and wanted a Lutheran wedding. My preacher said he would perform the ceremony but wanted to counsel us first. We went to his office and we took a test that involved sex, money, children, friends, religion, and activities. This was a multiple choice test. After we had taken it, the preacher divided the questions into categories and different sessions, and we spent about six sessions discussing each category and why we answered one way or another. This was in no way to stop us from marrying but to let us talk openly about things we might encounter in our lives together. Lynn has a degree in psychology and at times overanalyzes things that occur.

Either that, or I let it bother me when it shouldn't. Before we ever decided to marry, we had cleared the air about a lot of things that were discussed in the pastor's study.

## ADJUSTMENT OF STEPCHILDREN IN STEPFATHER FAMILIES

The myth that children suffer from maladjustment in stepfather families has been disclaimed (Burchinal, 1964; Oshman & Manosevitz, 1976). Perhaps the strongest and most consistent finding from the literature is that stepfathers generally have a positive effect on their stepchildren, despite the fact that the transition is not always easy (Robinson, 1984). A series of studies (Chapman, 1977; Santrock, 1972; Parish & Dostal, 1980a; Santrock *et al.*, 1982) has used a variety of personality and cognitive tests to compare children from stepfather families with those from intact or father-absent families. Although many adjustments must be made, the latest research concludes that having a stepfather is typically beneficial for children. The entrance of a stepfather into a previously father-absent home can have a positive effect on children's personality development. Generally, children prefer to live in a two-parent family even if it means the mother marries a man other than the biological father (Santrock, Warshak, & Elliot, 1982). Stepchildren tend to thrive in stepfather families. This is especially true for younger boys who become rapidly attached and flourish when raised by a stepfather (Wallerstein & Kelly, 1980). Older children derive benefits too. Adolescents from stepfather families tend to be equally as stable in their personality traits and equally socially involved as adolescents from intact and single-mother families (Burchinal, 1964; Wilson *et al.*, 1975).

The negative impact on children of divorce, father loss, and single parenting can be modified, especially if the child is a boy, when the biological mother remarries. Boys with stepfathers are just as psychologically healthy as boys from intact biological families and both have higher scores on psychological health than boys from father-absent homes (Oshman & Manosevitz, 1976). Boys from stepfather families are also more mature than boys from divorced families, and they are less anxious and angry, show more warmth, and have better self-esteem than boys in intact families where divorce is being considered (Santrock *et al.*, 1982). When stepfathers are present in a previously father-absent home, the cognitive development of boys of all ages is more likely to show improvement (Chapman, 1977; Santrock, 1972).

Girls seem to be affected differently. School-age girls in stepfather families tend to be more anxious than girls in intact families, and they seem angrier toward their mothers (Santrock et al., 1982). The entrance of a stepfather into a previously father-absent girl's home does not have an immediate positive influence on her cognitive development either. In fact, achievement test scores of school-age girls from stepfather families resemble those of father-absent girls more closely than those from intact families (Santrock, 1972). More recent research suggests that girls have more difficulty relating to stepfathers than do boys (Clingempeel, Brand, & Ievoli, 1984). Girls frequently view stepfathers as a rival for their mother's attention, while the boys welcome a male with whom they can play sports and about whom they can brag to their friends (Santrock, 1972; Santrock et al., 1982). The stepfather in the opening case study reported that he was able to take an active role with his stepson, who was eager to have a man in the family, sooner than with his stepdaughter. He felt compelled to maintain some distance with his stepdaughter, who resented him from the start. While father absence and remarriage might disrupt the cognitive development of stepdaughters during elementary school, the presence of a stepfather does seem to have long-range benefits. College-age females with stepfathers for example, are generally superior in intelligence to girls from either father-absent or intact families (Chapman, 1977).

Stepfathers have a profound influence on the self-concepts of stepchildren who live with them. Children from stepfather families evaluate themselves more positively, their absent fathers more positively, and their mothers less favorably than do children from divorced, nonremarried families (Parish & Dostal, 1980a). As a result of continuous comparisons and contrasts between themselves and their mothers and fathers, children align away from the absent parent and toward the remaining parents who continue to provide constant care. Within 2 years after their mother's divorce and remarriage, school children and young adults usually identify with their stepfathers and mothers and away from their biological fathers in an attempt to quickly overcome feelings of uncertainty and to seek stability that may have been lost during the breakup (Parish & Copeland, 1979; Parish & Dostal, 1980b).

## CONCLUSION

Stepfathers, just as men in other fathering situations, have been the subject of stereotypes. Stepfathers share many obstacles, such as transiton and identity problems, which they must overcome in order to function well. Because of its structural differences, the stepfather family system does not operate as well as a natural-father family—a fact of which most family members are initially unaware.

Tentative research (Robinson, 1984) presents a positive profile of the contemporary stepfather. Stepfathers are viewed as more successful in stepfamily relationships than stepmothers. Ratings of stepfathers by stepchildren and their mothers are just as positive as ratings of biological fathers by their natural children and their mothers. Stepfathers, in fact, tend to view themselves more critically than do their spouses and stepchildren. The overall marital quality in stepfather families is rated highest in remarriages where stepfathers have no children from previous marriages and where frequency of contacts with former spouses are moderate and fewer ties exist.

As a rule, the social–psychological characteristics of children in stepfather families are no different from those of children in intact families. In fact, clinical and experimental observations indicate that stepfathers are more attentive to the needs of their children and are more democratic parents than intact-family fathers. The personality development, self-concept, and maturity level for children with stepfathers, especially boys, are more positive than for children from father-absent homes. Stepfathers who enter into a previously father-absent home also have immediate positive effects on boys' cognitive development and long-range effects on girls' cognitive development. It appears that the presence of a stepfather counteracts the potentially negative effects of father absence and has a positive influence on children's psychological and cognitive attainment.

Although much of stepfamily life can be positive, it would be wrong to conclude that it is the preferred form of family life. Actually, much of the research compares stepfamilies to single-parent families or to intact families where separation is imminent. The additional strengths provided by two parents are considerable. Perhaps the critical factor in the complex processes of family living and fathering is not single-, step-, or biological fathering but a quality of fathering that is solid and consistent, based on love and mutual respect, and bounded by rules that are few and clear. Stepfathers, like all other kinds of fathers, often become successful fathers and provide a security and relationship that stabilizes the family as a whole and as individuals.

The structural difficulties in stepfather families may be reduced and roles may be clarified through remarriage preparation courses or group counseling. Stepfather families can blend more successfully once society in general and the helping professions in particular better understand and support stepfamilies in their efforts.

## SUGGESTIONS TO PROFESSIONALS

Despite the rise in the numbers of stepfamilies in this country, many human service workers have neglected this problem and know less about stepfamilies than any other kind of family: "Teachers, physicians, clergy, and others who deal with the children of divorce and remarriage remain uncomfortable and uninformed in their personal and professional relations with stepfamilies" (Herndon, 1982, p. 36).

Listed in the following paragraphs are some of the major problems that workers should be prepared to face.

*1.* Avoid taking a pathological approach to stepfamily intervention. Stepfather families who seek counseling are a select group who may be undergoing a great deal more stress than those who are not involved in therapy (Chilman, 1983; Robinson, 1984). The temptation to make generalizations from clinical groups who come for counseling to all nonclinical stepfather families should be avoided. Could, in fact, nonclinical stepfather families have a specific factor(s) that clinical groups do not have? Or do clinical stepfather families survive longer than nonclinical stepfather families because of their extra counseling support? To date, no attempts have been made to study these differences. Johnson (1980) wisely warns practitioners about the pitfalls of accepting social stigmas and associations that have been traditionally attached to stepfather families:

> ... the philandering husband who abandons his famly for a home-wrecking temptress; and round out the myth with an image of the innocent victims—that is, the children—who must endure years of pain and suffering because of their parents' behavior. (p. 304)

Practitioners must examine their own prejudices and realize that many of the stresses and tensions that stepfamilies experience result from social conditions arising from economic change and culturally conditioned beliefs and expectations. The mistaken notion that the nuclear family is the major family form in the United States can lead practitioners to view other family forms as deviant or even inferior. As a result, the well-meaning professional may look for pathology and apply a therapeutic model for treatment. Such a negative approach could reinforce the stepfamily's feelings that they are failures or even deviant because of their stepfamily status.

*2.* Take a positive approach to successful stepfathering. Practitioners can approach stepfamilies as a viable, potentially predominant family form that is here to stay. Workers can explore ways in which the stepfamily can grow and blend together in positive ways. While dealing with specific conflicts, workers can also focus on the benefits that can be derived within stepfather families, such as helping stepfamily members identify positive points about their families or exploring positive solutions to sources of conflict.

Special attention can be given to build the self-esteem of a stepfather who may lack confidence, become self-critical, or feel like an outsider. This positive approach can be used to help stepfathers deal with their range of emotions from guilt and elation to anger. The affiliation model developed by Stern (1982), which we discussed earlier, is a positive approach that uses 10 strategies to teach men to become successful stepfathers. Children will not love their stepfathers instantly. Through friendship with children, stepfathers can gradually establish a relationship and eventually gain their respect.

3. Treat stepfather families as a unique family system. Even though stepfamilies appear to resemble the typical biological family, they face situations that are rare in intact families. An awareness of the structural differences for both practitioners and family members can be beneficial. Research shows that stepfather families typically have ineffective communication patterns. Practitioners can best aid stepfather families by helping them open their interpersonal subsystems so that all members have mutual access (Perkins & Kahan, 1979). Each individual family member can discover the communication best for them. Because stepfather families are so different and few models exist, practitioners can help stepfather families to build their own guidelines before or after the remarriage. This can be done by helping individual members candidly think through, clarify, and spell out for themselves and for others their feelings and expectations. Family members can be encouraged to freely experiment with those guidelines and ways of relating that work best for them.

Stepfathers especially need self-clarification because of role confusion and anxiety they feel from entering relationships that are already cemented biologically. Stepfathers and stepfamilies need help to get at the root of their real feelings about their blended family. Honesty in expressing how they feel—even if it is anger, pain, hurt—is crucial for stable family development. Even if this involves the stepfather's openly admitting to himself that he does not like his stepchildren or does not like some aspect of the child's behavior, such honesty allows men to express their feelings of anger, confusion, or guilt. Once feelings are aired in a safe environment, resolution of problems can occur.

4. Encourage couples to seek counseling *before* remarriage. Clinical

reports have suggested that preventive counseling provides a stage for a "rehearsal for reality" before stepfamilies begin their live-in relationship (Herndon, 1982; Jacobson, 1980). All stepfamily members—stepfathers, wives, and children—are encouraged to air their grievances and anxieties and to keep lines of communication open. This approach helps to clarify a highly complex system of interactions and potential disruption in family functioning and to foster healthy ways of coping with highly complicated issues.

Practitioners can help stepfamilies systematically identify sources of conflict of which family members may be unaware. Written questionnaires with regard to Johnson's (1980) nine items of possible conflict, as mentioned earlier, might ask stepfamily members to indicate views of their own and other's roles, turf, benefits and losses, and so forth for each item. Having these responses in writing may provide the necessary feedback that will help stepfamily members clarify their concerns and expectations (Johnson, 1980).

5. Disseminate information to stepfather families. For example, sharing results from stepfather research discussed in this chapter could be beneficial. This might include pointing out the positive effects that stepfathers can have on children's personality and cognitive development, discussing instances in which stepfathers get very high ratings as a parent from their stepchildren and spouses, or reporting statistics on success in remarriages.

Other media such as filmed vignettes, pamphlets, or books can be useful informational tools. Prosen and Farmer (1982) recommend the use of filmed vignettes to help children and parents in stepfamilies to express and deal with situations that often emerge. Vignettes can be effective because they trigger reactions to experiences of children that are similar to those in the films and promote discussion. The films for children can also be shown to parents to help them understand their children's experiences.

Children and parents can also benefit from reading about stepfamilies. Newsletters from stepfamily organizations are valuable resources and may prevent feelings of isolation. Practitioners can refer families to local chapters of the Stepfamily Association of America, whose chapters in many states offer mutual education and support among families with similar backgrounds. A small library with selected books for stepparents such as Einstein's (1982) personal account of her upbringing in a stepfather family and later remarriage into a stepfamily is an excellent resource for adults embarking upon remarriage. Books for stepchildren also help children understand the complexities involved and other's feelings, as well as their own as two families merge. The resource list at the end of this chapter provides names of filmed vignettes, of stepfamily organizations and their publications, and other literature for adults as well as for children.

6. Establish separate counseling or family enrichment groups for stepchildren and stepparents as well as intergenerational groups. Counselors can initiate small group counseling sessions to let children see that other children are "in the same boat" and realize that they are not "oddballs." Children can provide a system of support and help one another understand and cope with situational stresses by expressing their emotions in direct ways and in a safe and supportive setting. Other groups similar to Parents without Partners can be established and might be named Parents with New Partners, Kids with New Parents, or Second-Time-Around Families (Johnson, 1980).

7. Work closely with school personnel in a concerted effort to provide in-service training. Classroom teachers often become the stabilizing figures in a child's life as the family goes through divorce and remarriage (Skeen, Robinson, & Flake-Hobson, 1984). Many of them are unprepared to devote the necessary attention, understanding, patience, and empathy these children need during this difficult time.

Years ago when one of the authors taught seventh grade, one of his 12-year-old students confided to him that her stepfather had been sexually abusing her. She needed most of all to know that there was someone to whom she could talk. She also needed to cry a great deal. She would never have shared the information with her mother, because she was afraid she would either be blamed for what happened or that her mother would never believe her, or view her as competition. She was too embarrassed to discuss this with friends and did not know the counselor well enough. This is only one example in which teachers, because of the relationships that are built from daily contact with children, must also be good counselors.

Becoming sensitive to a child's behavior changes, such as sudden acting out or extreme withdrawn behavior, can alert teachers that something is wrong. Paying attention to how school notes or invitations to special events or conferences are addressed to parents is also important so that all sets of parents are included and no one is excluded.

School counselors can help teachers structure special lessons on stepfamilies when teaching about families or talking about how the American family is changing or discussing "where I live." This way, children learn firsthand that it is all right to talk about having two families or living in two houses and that others have confused or conflicting feelings just as they do (Prosen & Farmer, 1982).

# PROFESSIONAL RESOURCES FOR WORKING WITH STEPFATHERS

## Books for Adults

Berman, C. *Making it as a stepparent: New roles/new rules.* New York: Doubleday, 1980.

Capaldi, F., & McRae, B. *Stepfamilies: A cooperative responsibility.* New York: New Viewpoints/Vision Books, 1979.

Cherlin, A. J. *Marriage, divorce, and remarriage.* Cambridge, Mass.: Harvard University Press, 1983.

Duberman, L. *The reconstituted family: A study of remarried couples and their children.* Chicago: Nelson-Hall, 1975.

Einstein, E. *The stepfamily: Living, loving, and learning.* New York: Macmillan, 1982.

Felker, E. H. *Raising other people's kids: Successful child-rearing in the restructured family.* Grand Rapids, Mich.: Eerdmans, 1981.

Furstenberg, F. F., & Spanier, G. B. *Recycling the family: Remarriage after divorce.* Beverly Hills, Calif.: Sage, 1984.

Hansen, J. C., & Messinger, L. (Eds.). *Therapy with remarriage families.* Rockville, Md.: Aspen Systems, 1982.

Lamb, M. E. *Nontraditional families: Parenting and child development.* Hillsdale, N.J.: Erlbaum, 1982.

Lewis, H. C. *All about families: The second time around.* Atlanta: Peachtree, 1980.

Lorimer, A., & Feldman, P. M. *Remarriage: A guide for singles, couples, and families, including stepchildren, in-laws, ex-spouses, possessions, housing, finances and more.* Philadelphia: Running, 1980.

Maddox, B. *The half-parent family: Living with other people's children.* New York: M. Evans, 1975.

Mayleas, D. *Re-wedded bliss: Love, alimony, incest, ex-spouses and other domestic blessings.* New York: Basic Books, 1977.

Messinger, L. *Remarriage: A family affair.* New York: Plenum, 1984.

Noble, J., & Noble, W. *How to live with other people's children.* New York: Hawthorn Books, 1977.

Reed, B. *Stepfamilies: Living in Christian harmony.* St. Louis: Concordia, 1980.

Reingold, C. B. *How to be happy if you marry again: All about children, money, sex, lawyers, ex-husbands, ex-wives, and past memories.* New York: Harper & Row, 1976.

Rice, F. P. *Stepparenting.* New York: Condor, 1979.

Roosevelt, R., & Lofas, J. *Living in step.* New York: Stein & Day, 1976.

Rosenbaum, J., & Rosenbaum, V. *Stepparenting.* New York: Dutton, 1978.

Sager, C. *Treating the Remarried Family.* New York: Brunner/Mazel, 1983.

Simon, A. W. *Stepchild in the family: A view of children in remarriage.* Indianapolis: Odyssey, 1964.

Spann, O., & Spann, N. *Your child? I thought it was my child?* Pasadena, Calif.: Ward Ritchie, 1977.

Thayer, N. *Stepping.* New York: Playbook Paperbooks, 1980.

Visher, E. B., & Visher, J. S. *Stepfamilies: A guide to working with stepparents and stepchildren.* New York: Brunner/Mazel, 1979.

Visher, E. B., & Visher, J. S. *Stepfamilies: Myths and realities.* Secaucus, N.J.: Citadel, 1980.

Visher, E. B., & Visher, J. S. *How to win as a stepfamily.* New York: Dembner Books, 1982.

Wald, E. *The remarried family: Challenge and promise.* New York: Family Service Association of America, 1982.

Westoff, L. A. *The second time around: Remarriage in America.* New York: Viking, 1977.

## Books for Children

Berger, T. *A friend can help.* Chicago: Children's, 1974.

Berman, C. *What am I doing in a stepfamily?* New Jersey: Lyle Stuart, 1982.

Burt, M. S., & Burt, R. *What's special about our stepfamily.* Garden City, N.Y.: Doubleday, 1983.

Clifton, L. *Everett Anderson's nine months long.* New York: Holt, Rinehart, & Winston, 1978.

Craven, L. *Stepfamilies: New patterns of harmony.* New York: Julian Messner, 1982.

Gardner, R. A. *The boys and girls book about stepfamilies.* New York: Bantam, 1982.

Green, P. *A new mother for Martha.* New York: Human Sciences, 1978.

Lewis, H. *All about families the second time around.* Atlanta: Peachtree, 1980.

Phillips, C. E. *Our family got a stepparent.* Ventura, Calif.: Regal Books, 1981.

Sobol, H., & Agre, P. *My other mother, my other father.* New York: Macmillan, 1979.

Stenson, J. *Now I have a stepparent and it's kind of confusing.* New York: Avon Books, 1979.

## Periodicals

*Family Relations: Journal of Applied Family and Child Studies.* National Council on Family Relations, 1219 University Avenue, S.E., Minneapolis, MN 55414. Special issue on remarriage and stepparenting, July 1984. Guest editors Kay Pasley and Marilyn Ihinger-Tallman.

*Remarriage.* G & R Publications, Inc., 648 Beacon St., Boston, MA 02215. This newsletter is for men and women who have married more than once. Its aim is to improve the quality of married life through increased awareness, understanding, insight, and thoughtful action.

*Stepfamily Bulletin.* Human Sciences Press, 72 Fifth Avenue, New York, NY 10011. Begun in 1981, the Bulletin is published quarterly by the Stepfamily Association of America. This newsletter is for stepfamilies and interested professionals and provides a rich source of facts and data about step relationships and remarriages when there are children from a previous marriage. It offers current information on state and national stepfamily meetings, professional training workshops, the location of established chapters, and guidelines for organizing local activities. The Bulletin is of value to stepfamily members and all professionals who work with stepfamilies, including social workers, psychologists, counselors, attorneys, and family therapists.

*Stepparents' Forum.* Westmount, P.O. Box 4002, Montreal H3Z 2X3, Canada. Publishes information and guidelines for stepparents.

## Manual

*Stepfamily Workshop Manual.* Stepfamily Association Sales Program, 28 Allegheny Avenue, Suite 1307 Towson Towers, Towson, MD 21204. An excellent resource for practitioners presenting guidelines, therapeutic suggestions, and references for those working with stepparents. By Emily and John Visher, 1983.

## Audiovisuals

*Step family.* This film deals with remarriage and the adjustments all must make. Contains a wealth of ideas for discussion and analysis. Centron Films, 1621 West 9th Street, P.O. Box 687, Lawrence, KS 66044. 16 mm, 13 minutes.

*Stepparenting.* This film helps define problems that occur in remarriage when children are involved. Scenes revolve around such issues as blending two different patterns of discipline for two different sets of children; and the issues that may develop between "his," "hers," and "our" children. The scenes easily elicit discussion of the issues dramatized. The audience can also generate alternative responses or ways of handling the same situation. American Personnel and Guidance Association, Order Services Department, Two Skyline Place, Suite 400, 5203 Leesburg Pike, Falls Church, VA 22041. 16 mm, 20 minutes, color.

*Stepparents and blended families.* This film points out the complexities of bringing children of different families into one household and shows it is possible to work through the inevitable rivalries and conflicts. Dramatizes the struggle of teenagers learning to accept the authority of a stepparent. Helps teenagers place some perspective on the new roles they must play as stepsiblings and stepchildren. Sunburst Communications, Room JV, 39 Washington Avenue, Pleasantville, NY 10570. Filmstrip and cassette.

*Stepparenting: New families, old ties.* This film shows the reflections of three middle-class, stepfamilies on their problems of blending their children into a new household. Issues such as discipline, household management, and role adjustments are discussed through the formation of a new family unit. Award-winning film from the National Council of Family Relations. Polymorph Films, 118 South Street, Boston, MA 02111. 16 mm, 25 minutes, color.

## Organizations

Stepfamily Association of America, 3001 Porter Street, N.W., Washington, DC 20008. Or 900 Welch Road, Suite 400, Palo Alto, CA 94304. A stepfamily support group that publishes the *Stepfamily Bulletin.*

The Stepfamily Foundation, 333 West End Avenue, New York, NY 10023. Provides a clearinghouse for information and research on stepfamilies.

## REFERENCES

Bohannan, P., & Erickson, R. Stepping in. *Psychology Today,* 1978, *11,* 53–59.

Bowerman, C. E., & Irish, D. P. Some relationships of stepchildren to their parents. *Marriage and Family Living,* 1962, *24,* 113–121.

Brooks, J. B. *The process of parenting.* Palo Alto, Calif.: Mayfield, 1981.

Burchinal, L. G. Characteristics of adolescents from unbroken, broken, and reconstituted families. *Journal of Marriage and the Family,* 1964, *26,* 44–51.

Chapman, M. Father absence, stepfathers, and the cognitive performance of college students. *Child Development,* 1977, *48,* 1155–1158.

Chilman, C. S. Remarriage and stepfamilies: Research results and implications. In E. D. Macklin & R. H. Rubin (Eds.), *Contemporary families and alternative lifestyles.* Beverly Hills, Calif.: Sage, 1983.

Clingempeel, W. G. Quasi-kin relationships and marital quality in stepfather families. *Journal of Personality and Social Psychology,* 1981, *41,* 890–901.

Clingempeel, W. G., Brand, E., & Ievoli, R. Stepparent–stepchild relationships in stepmother and stepfather families: A multimethod study. *Family Relations,* 1984, *33,* 465–473.

Cory, C. Second marriages: Better while they last. *Psychology Today,* 1983, *17,* 72.

Draughon, M. Stepmother's model of identification in relation to mourning in the child. *Psychological Reports,* 1975, *36,* 183–189.

Duberman, L. Step–kin relationships. *Journal of Marriage and the Family,* 1973, *35,* 283–292.

Einstein, E. *The stepfamily: Living, loving and learning.* New York: Macmillan, 1982.

Fast, I., & Cain, A. C. The stepparent role: Potential for disturbances in family functioning. *American Journal of Orthopsychiatry,* 1966, *36,* 485–491.

Glick, P. C. Remarriage: Some recent changes and variations. *Journal of Family Issues,* 1980, *1,* 455–478.

Glick, C., & Norton, A. J. Perspectives on the recent upturn in divorce and remarriage. *Demography*, 1973, *10*, 301–314.

Halperin, S. M., & Smith, T. A. Differences in stepchildren's perceptions of their stepfathers and natural fathers: Implications for family therapy. *Journal of Divorce*, 1983, *7*, 19–30.

Herndon, A. Do we know enough about the predominant family form of the 21st century. *Wake Forest*, August 1982, 36–37.

Hetherington, M. E., Cox, M., & Cox, R. Divorce and remarriage. Paper presented at the Society for Research in Child Development, Boston, April 1981.

Hetherington, M. E., Cox, M., & Cox, R. Effects of divorce on parents and children. In M. E. Lamb (Ed.), *Nontraditional families: Parenting and child development*. Hillsdale, N.J.: Lawrence Erlbaum, 1982.

Jacobson, D. S. Stepfamilies. *Children Today*, 1980, *9*, 2–6.

Johnson, H. C. Working with stepfamilies: Principles of practice. *Social Work*, 1980, *25*, 304–308.

Macklin, E. D. Nontraditional family forms: A decade of research. *Journal of Marriage and the Family*, 1980, *42*, 905–922.

Messinger, L. Remarriage between divorced people with children from previous marriages: A proposal for preparation for remarriage. *Journal of Marriage and Family Counseling*, 1976, *2*, 193–200.

Messinger, L., Walker, K. N., & Freeman, J. J. Preparation for remarriage following divorce: The use of group techniques. *American Journal of Orthopsychiatry*, 1978, *48*, 263–272.

Mowatt, M. H. Group psychotherapy for stepfathers and their wives. *Psychotherapy: Theory, Research and Practice*, 1972, *9*, 328–331.

Oshman, H., & Manosevitz, M. Father-absence: Effects of stepfathers upon psychosocial development in males. *Developmental Psychology*, 1976, *12*, 479–480.

Parish, T., & Copeland, T. The relationship between self-concepts and evaluations of parents and stepfathers. *Journal of Psychology*, 1979, *101*, 135–138.

Parish, T. S., & Dostal, J. W. Evaluations of self and parent figures by children from intact, divorced, and reconstituted families. *Journal of Youth and Adolescence*, 1980, *9*, 347–351. (a)

Parish, T. S., & Dostal, J. W. Relationships between evaluations of self and parents by children from intact and divorced families. *Journal of Psychology*, 1980, *104*, 35–38. (b)

Perkins, T. F., & Kahan, J. P. An empirical comparison of natural-father and stepfather family systems. *Family Process*, 1979, *18*, 175–183.

Prosen, S. S., & Farmer, J. H. Understanding stepfamilies: Issues and implications for counselors. *The Personnel and Guidance Journal*, 1982, *60*, 393–397.

Rallings, E. M. The special role of stepfather. *The Family Coordinator*, 1976, *25*, 445–449.

Robinson, B. E. The contemporary American stepfather: A review of literature. *Family Relations*, 1984, *33*, 381–388.

Santrock, J. W. The relations of type and onset of father absence to cognitive development. *Child Development*, 1972, *43*, 455–469.

Santrock, J. W., Warshak, R. A., & Elliott, G. L. Social development and parent–child interaction in father-custody and stepmother families. In M. E. Lamb (Ed.), *Nontraditional families: Parenting and child development*. Hillsdale, N.J.: Lawrence Erlbaum, 1982.

Santrock, J. W., Warshak, R., Lindbergh, C., & Meadows, L. Children's and parents' observed social behavior in stepfather families. *Child Development*, 1982, *53*, 472–480.

Shepard, M., & Goldman, G. *Divorced dads: A practical plan with seven basic guidelines*. Radnor, Pa.: Chilton, 1979.

Skeen, P., Covi, R. B., & Robinson, B. E. Stepfamilies: A review of the literature with suggestions for practitioners. *Journal of Counseling and Development*, 1985, *64*, 226–229.

Skeen, P., Robinson, B. E., & Flake-Hobson, C. Blended families: Overcoming the Cinderella myth. *Young children*, 1984, *39*, 64–74.

Stern, P. N. Affiliating in stepfather families: Teachable strategies leading to stepfather–child friendship. *Western Journal of Nursing Research*, 1982, *4*, 76–89.

Visher, J. S., & Sager, C. J. The new American (step)family. *Sexual Medicine Today*, 1982, 6–12.

Visher, E. B., & Visher, J. S. Common problems of stepparents and their spouses. *American Journal of Orthopsychiatry*, 1978, *48*, 252–262.

Visher, E. B., & Visher, J. S. *Stepfamilies: A guide to working with stepparents and stepchildren*. New York: Brunner/Mazel, 1979.

Visher, E. B., & Visher, J. S. *Stepfamily Workshop Manual*. Towson, Md.: Stepfamily Association of America, 1983. (a)

Visher, E. B., & Visher, J. S. Stepparents in modern America. Paper presented at the Southeastern Council on Family Relations, Atlanta, February 1983. (b)

Wallerstein, J. S., & Kelly, J. B. *Surviving the break-up: How children actually cope with divorce*. New York: Basic Books, 1980.

Wilson, K. L., Zurcher, L., McAdams, D., & Curtis, R. L. Stepfathers and stepchildren: An exploratory analysis from two national surveys. *Journal of Marriage and the Family*, 1975, *37*, 526–536.

# CHAPTER SEVEN

# Gay Fathers

## THE CASE OF A GAY FATHER

Being a gay father who has chosen to share parenting on an equal basis with my former wife seems to many people a contradiction in lifestyles. It certainly has proved to be complicated. For me, claiming an ongoing role in the parenting process was a logical step. Accepting my sexual orientation and my desire to share life with another man (if indeed it was to be shared in a committed adult relationship) meant that marriage must end. Both my wife and I had made a conscious decision that each of us wanted to be a parent. From the day she and my son came home from the hospital both of us shared the joys and responsibilities of parenting. We consciously avoided what we felt to be the stereotypical parenting roles prevalent in 1973, the year our son was born.

When our marriage ended 4 years later, it was unthinkable to me that I would give up my parenting role. Fortunately, my wife wanted us to continue to share the raising of our son. So we had no legal problems in establishing joint custody on an alternate week basis.

Six months after my wife and I separated, I began to live together with Hunter [a pseudonym], my first male partner in a committed relationship. He was very fond of my son and enjoyed caring for him. He frequently read him bedtime stories and helped in caring for him in other ways. My son's mother and I still made the major parenting decisions. For Hunter and me, those were very happy months. We had alternate weeks to devote exclusively to each other, and we had a supportive group of friends, both straight and gay. We had been living together 6 months when it became evident that professionally there was little future for either of us in the city where we lived. Furthermore, we wanted to live in an urban environment more receptive to our lifestyle. I was offered an excellent job opportunity in Washington, D.C. We decided that I should accept the job and that we would both move there. In considering the move the question of how to maintain a shared role in parenting weighed heavily on my mind. I knew there was little chance of my former wife moving to Washington. The only solution that she and I could agree upon was for my son to fly to Washington every other weekend and spend most vacations there as well.

This arrangement left him feeling abandoned and me wanting to cram 2 weeks of parenting and love into alternate weekends. The move was disruptive for everyone. Hunter seemed unable to replace the supportive group of friends we left behind. We had more time together than ever before but there seemed to be little focus to our relationship. At the beginning of the next school year, my former wife and my son moved to Washington, and we resumed alternate weeks of parenting. With the renewal of this arrangement, both Hunter and my son became jealous of my attention. I felt torn between the two; each person seemed to demand more of my time than I was able to give. This was an irritant in my relationship with Hunter, a relationship that already lacked focus. Four months into the school year our relationship had almost completely broken down. We still occupied the same apartment, but our love for

It is estimated that between 10% and 25% of homosexual men father children (Bell & Weinberg, 1978; Harry, 1983; Skeen & Robinson, 1984, 1985) and it is estimated that there are as many as a million gay fathers in the United States and Canada (Bozett, 1984; Fadiman, 1983). In the samples that have been studied, most of the men lived separately from their spouses and saw their children periodically.[1] Some marry and remain married, playing an important role in the socialization of their children. In some cases their spouses do not know they are homosexual (Voeller & Walters, 1978). Others never marry the mother of their child. Still fewer rear their children alone as single parents, because custody rulings in favor of gay parents are rare, just as they are for single fathers (R. Schwartz, personal communication, October 1982).

Despite this practice, in 1979 a gay man did win the custody of his two children, one of the first such rulings in Kansas. Upon remarrying, the children's mother (who did not want custody of her children) had become a victim of spouse abuse. The gay father said he had to take his children for therapy because of the violence they witnessed in his ex-wife's home. Before the judge ruled in the gay father's favor, it was each other which we had openly shared with my son had turned to hostility. He perceived this and became protective of me and I felt defensive about his habits, which I knew bothered Hunter. I also felt jealous of their mutual enjoyment of boating.

After several months we separated. My son expressed no feelings over this change. In fact, he delighted in being able to have my full attention! During the summers, my son spends much of this time with his grandparents. It wasn't until then that I felt comfortable dating other men. After the separation I worried about what signs of affection for another man would do to my relationship with my son. I was also afraid that my fitness as a parent might be brought into question by my former wife if there were signs of a new relationship.

During that summer I met Nick [a pseudonym], my present partner. Our relationship had a chance to grow for several months prior to my son's return. We have been in a committed relationship now for a year and a half although we have not lived together. On alternate weeks, the three of us are together several evenings with Nick staying over those nights. My son is 11 now, and I find myself trying to reinforce the bond of friendship and love between us so that when he understands my sexual orientation, he will be able to draw on the strength of our relationship to weather what I anticipate may well be a difficult time. My greatest fear is that he will reject me and choose to live apart from me. This is the one fear that I think is unique to being a single gay father. I look forward to the day when this fear is history!

**Michael Finch**
*Washington, D.C.*

necessary for two psychologists to testify that the father's homosexuality would not cause problems of gender identity for the children. According to Bruce Voeller, former coexecutive director of the National Gay Task Force and a gay father of three children, "screening out homosexuals is commonplace in foster care and adoption cases and, indeed, even in divorce proceedings where custody and visitation rights are being sought by a parent" (Voeller & Walters, 1978, p. 153).

In Washington, D.C., Massachusetts, and California, public policy forbids discrimination based on affectional or sexual orientations in foster care and custody decisions. In these states as well as a handful of others, the practice of placing homosexual teenagers with gay foster fathers has been met with some acceptance. When placed with gay foster couples, many of these gay adolescents—who have run away from home or were abandoned by their parents after learning of their

[1]Bozett (1980) reported that 17 of the 18 men he studied lived apart from their wives (94%); Miller (1979) found that 23 of the 40 men he interviewed lived apart from their wives (58%); and Skeen and Robinson (1984) reported that 22 of 30 men in their study were separated or divorced from their wives (73%).

child's homosexuality—experience their first positive relationships with an adult male (Harry, 1983). However, the children gay couples adopt are not always homosexual. In 1979, for example, a homosexual minister from Catskill, New York was awarded permanent custody of a heterosexual 13-year-old boy he had cared for. The boy is being reared by his adoptive father and his father's 40-year-old male partner. The judge in the case said, "The reverend is providing a good home, the boy loves his adoptive father and wants to be with him. Who knows in this world of ours? You do the best you can and hope it works out" (Maddox, 1982, p. 69).

But most state courts, like many service agencies, continue to make decisions based on myth and stereotype. Even with the recommendations of social workers, juvenile parole officers, psychiatrists, psychologists, and sociologists, judges may refuse such adoptions on the basis that they threaten the survival of the traditional American family as a way of life. It is interesting to note that this same argument has been used to prevent unmarried single heterosexual fathers from adopting children, as discussed in Chapter 5. In custody decisions where gay fathers are biological parents, it is practically impossible for men to gain custody. In fact, gay fathers are lucky if they can get visitation rights in contested custody cases (Hitchens, 1980). In many instances gay fathers are denied all visitation rights on the grounds that their character is immoral and unacceptable. When gay fathers are granted visitation privileges, as in the New York case of *Gottlieb v Gottlieb*, they are warned not to expose their children to other gay friends or to take them anywhere that homosexuals might be present (Fadiman, 1983).

Little is known about gay fathers because few research studies have been conducted. This neglect is characteristic of the general oversight of the role of fathers in the lives of their children (Pleck & Sawyer, 1974). In addition, the target group is difficult to reach, and obtaining a sample is therefore relatively costly and time consuming.

During the 1970s as researchers began to realize the important roles fathers play in the child's development and with the advent of changing sex roles and a greater acceptance of homosexuality among professional organizations, "the age of gay parenthood" emerged from the closet. We must point out that because of the inaccessibility of the target group, much of the available research takes the form of personal impressions or suffers from problems in sampling and research design (Fishel, 1983). The generalizations drawn in this chapter therefore are tentative. Nonetheless, the information that has emerged from these studies dispels many of the myths about gay parents that professionals have held in the past.

## CHILDREN OF HOMOSEXUALS

The most immediate concern about gay fatherhood is the effect on the sexual identities of children brought up in an openly gay household. One child who mistakenly revealed to her friends that her parent was gay said, "They didn't hang around me after that. . . . like they were scared they might catch germs from me or something" (Epstein, 1979, p. 45).

What has commonly been called the "germ theory" (Fishel, 1983) is a widely accepted belief that talking with or general exposure to a gay person will cause one to become homosexual. The term "homophobia" is used to refer to this emotional reaction of deep-seated revulsion and fear toward homosexuals and their lifestyles (Weinberg, 1972). A study by De Grescenzo and McGill (cited in Dulaney & Kelly, 1982) revealed that among mental health practitioners, homophobia was most prevalent among social workers, moderately so among psychiatrists, and least apparent among psychologists.

The homophobic fear that children will be "contaminated" by their gay fathers is the most pervasive, yet the most unfounded of all beliefs about homosexuals. Every study to date shows that the incidence of homosexuality among children of gays is not above that in the general population. One father we spoke with said, "My parents are heterosexual but I turned out to be gay. So why would anyone believe my homosexuality would 'rub off' on my son?" Evidence indicates, in fact, that most homosexuals were brought up in exclusively heterosexual households (Miller, 1979a; Robinson, Skeen, Flake-Hobson, & Herrman, 1982). Moreover, a study by the Kinsey Institute of Sex Research concluded from a sample of 1000 homosexuals and 500 heterosexuals that sexual preference results from many factors but begins with an early, probably biological, tendency toward homosexuality or heterosexuality (Bell, Weinberg, & Hammersmith, 1981). Other preliminary evidence indicates that parents' homosexuality has no bearing on their children's sexual orientation (Weeks, Derdeyn, & Langman, 1975).

Miller (1979a) assessed the sexual orientation of the 27 daughters and 21 sons of 40 gay fathers from cities across the United States and Canada. All the fathers were white, mostly middle class, and college-educated, and they ranged in age from 24 to 64. According to the fathers' reports, only 8% of the children were gay (one of the sons and three of the daughters). Although Miller's study was not randomized, second-generation homosexuals were rare in his sample.

Kirkpatrick, Roy, and Smith (1976) compared 20 lesbian mothers and their children with a similar group of divorced heterosexual mothers and children. A psychologist and a child psychiatrist who studied the children independently could not determine which children belonged to which group of mothers.

Psychiatrist Richard Green (1978) studied 37 children, ranging in age from 3 to 20, who were being raised by female homosexuals or by male and female parents who had sex-change surgery. After 2 years of study, 36 out of the 37 children showed clear heterosexual preferences or were developing them. Thirteen adolescent children were attracted to the opposite sex. Green (1978) concluded, "The children I interviewed were able to comprehend and verbalize the atypical nature of their parent's lifestyles and to view their atypicality in the broader perspective of the cultural norm" (p. 696).

Obviously, in the upbringing of children by gay parents problems do exist that further complicate the already difficult task of child rearing. For example, Lewis (1980) noted certain unfavorable outcomes experienced by children of lesbian mothers. She described these children as alienated from their peers, lacking enough maternal affection (most of which was described as directed toward the mother's partner), confused about their own sexual orientation, and uncomfortable with their mother's sexual behavior. Yet, they admired their mother's courage for sticking to her own set of values and felt a more satisfying relationship with their father could develop now that parental conflict was over. Moreover, Miller (1979a) presented evidence of adjustment problems among six daughters of the gay fathers in his sample. Two girls became pregnant and had abortions, one practiced prostitution, two faced problems in school, and one sought professional counseling for emotional difficulties.

Without exception, divorce is an emotionally painful and stressful event in the life of a child whether from a heterosexual or homosexual household. Carefully controlled research clearly shows that children from broken heterosexual homes react to divorce with sadness, fear, anger, and feelings of being deprived (Wallerstein & Kelly, 1980). Sometimes these children show marked changes in behavior such as acting out during school (Cantor, 1977). They show a shaken sense of identity and loneliness (Wallerstein & Kelly, 1976). Caution should, therefore, be exercised against interpreting the children's reactions in the Lewis (1980) and Miller (1979a) studies as a direct consequence of having a gay parent. Until the research on gay fatherhood is more exact, we can tentatively conclude, as Green (1978) did, that at this stage in the history of research in this area, children being raised by homosexual parents do not differ appreciably from children raised in more conventional family settings.

## SOCIETAL REACTIONS TO CHILDREN OF
## GAY FATHERS

A 10-year-old boy asked his homosexual father what to do about a playmate who said, "Your old man is a queer and you're going to be one too." The father discussed the issue with his son, and the next time the boy was teased about his father's sexuality, he replied, "So what?" (Miller, 1979b).

When gay fathers are open about their sexuality, their children usually face harassment from peers and even adults. Research shows that gay fathers are sensitive to the accompanying problems of being the child of a gay parent, and ordinarily prepare their children early to deal with ridicule, or take extra precautions to protect them from it (Bozett, 1980).

The most common and perhaps most effective preparation is for fathers to build within their children inner resources by teaching them tolerance of others. There is a tendency for gay fathers to instill in their children at an early age accepting and nonjudgmental attitudes toward all human beings, regardless of their race, religious beliefs, or sexual orientation. "If Eryn is gay, he should, unlike his father, have healthy gay role models to preserve him from self-hatred and isolation," says one gay father about his son, "If he is straight, he should have learned tolerance of sexual variation" (Fadiman, 1983, p. 80).

Another common practice of gay fathers in preparing children to deal with ridicule is to disclose their own homosexuality (Bozett, 1984). Bozett (1980) conducted depth interviews with 18 gay fathers who lived in or near San Francisco. The respondents, who were white, well-educated, professional men between the ages of 28 and 51, said that identity as a gay father is very important to them. A desire for close, intimate father–child relationships usually resulted in the father's divulging his homosexuality—either through indirect disclosure or direct disclosure. All but one respondent reported positive outcomes resulting from their openness. In the opening case study, indirect disclosure was chosen. The gay father intentionally presented himself as a positive gay parent model to his son. Openly affectionate with his lover, the father wanted to show his son that his behavior was not unusual. He also took his son to meetings of the Gay Fathers Coalition (see box), where there were other gay fathers with their children.

Other fathers are more direct about their sexuality. One gay father directly disclosed his sexuality to his 6-year-old son in this way:

You know your friend Christopher? Well, a lot of people won't like Christopher because his skin is black. Some people would like to see

## GAY FATHERS COALITION*

We are a group of fathers who are Gay. Our experiences have been varied, and we are united in our determination to integrate these two aspects of our lives. In the past our roles as fathers and gay men have been viewed as incompatible both by society at large and, all too often, by ourselves as well. We believe, on the contrary, that gay men can love and nourish children and provide a safe environment in which girls and boys can mature into loving and productive women and men.

We have formed this organization to help ourselves and others in similar situations to continue to grow and develop in ways which draw upon the rich experiences of both aspects of our lives. We intend to do this by forming mutually supportive groups for building a positive self-image and for creative problem solving, by locating other gay men who are fathers or are contemplating fatherhood and may be struggling alone, and by educating professionals and the general public both to our special strengths and our special concerns.

## STATEMENT OF POLICY

1. Membership and Community of Interest

Our affiliates include gay fathers groups, gay and lesbian parents groups and individuals acting as local contacts in areas where there are no such groups currently in existence.

At the present time we believe we can adequately represent only gay males in parenting situations. However, we have an active interest in the concerns of lesbian mothers and we want to assist and to cooperate fully with lesbian mothers who share our parenting concerns.

We support and welcome as members gay fathers, lovers of gay fathers and gay men who are committed to adopting children or providing foster care. Delegates to the Gay Fathers Coalition are presently limited to these categories. We recognize that local groups will continue to observe their own requirements for membership.

2. Support for Children

We support lesbian and gay parents in helping their children to deal with the effects of homophobic attitudes and myths.

We are committed to bringing about changes in the attitudes of society that cause confusion in our children about our worthiness as parents and our ability to love and nurture them or that cause them to be anxious about their own sexual development.

We affirm without qualification that we can and do serve as positive role models for our own children, as well as for all children, whatever their sexual orientation.

We are strongly committed to a non-sexist upbringing of our children.

We affirm that all children have the right to develop their natural sexuality free from stereotype, fear or coercion.

3. Support for Local Groups

In order to provide support for existing groups and to act as a catalyst to form new groups, we will:

- Prepare a support packet for gay fathers groups which will provide encouragement, assistance and information in existing, new and potential groups. This packet will later be expanded to meet the needs of other groups relative to gay parents, such as mental health workers, judges, attorneys and legislators, children, social action agencies, etc.
- Act as a clearing house for the collection and dissemination of information on gay parenting.
- Establish a national network of local representatives to assist individuals in forming new groups or to assist them on a one-to-one basis if group formation is not feasible.

4. Support for Individuals in Parenting Roles

In order to provide support for individual gay fathers or those who otherwise find themselves in a child-nurturing situation, we will:

- Provide information on parenting, such as the previously mentioned support packet.
- Put them in contact with other gay parents in their area.
- Act as a reference source for legal problems.
- Provide information, counseling and support to fathers estranged from their children because of court oders, geographic distance, homophobic attitudes in themselves or in others or any other reasons.

5. Educational Outreach

We plan to educate the general public as well as the gay community about the fact that there are substantial numbers of gay fathers and lesbian mothers and that we are fully effective parents.

To work toward educating professionals and the general public, we will:

- Encourage valid research on gay parenting and disseminate the results of this research.
- Provide and support speakers for gay and non-gay groups.
- Engage in outreach to the gay and non-gay media.

6. Legislation

We support the passage of legislation designed to eliminate the effects of discrimination on the basis of sexual orientation.

We are particularly committed to support laws and rulings that forbid the consideration of sex or sexual orientation in matter of divorce, separation, alimony, child support, child care, foster care, visitation and custody.

*Reprinted with permission from Gay Fathers Coalition International, Inc., P.O. Box 50360, Washington, D.C. 20009-0360.

Christopher dead. Others would just like to stay away from Christopher. Some people feel the same way about Michael and me because we are in love with each other, and usually a man will have those strong feelings for a woman. Both kinds of love are good. (Fadiman, 1983, p. 78)

Bozett (1984) found that disclosure—whether indirect or direct— tended to deepen the father–child relationship, whereas nondisclosure caused fathers considerable psychological stress.

Discretion in the father's overt expression of his own homosexuality and in teaching his children what is appropriate and what is not is also a frequent practice (Bozett, 1980). In her interviews with two gay fathers, Fadiman (1983) found that the children did not mention their unusual family at school. As one child put it, "When my friends are older, then I might try to explain it. I think they will like gay people O.K. because they'll like my daddy" (p. 96). In addition to his interviews with gay fathers, Miller (1979a) interviewed 14 of their children. The children who were between 14 and 33 years old already knew about their father's homosexuality. They reported learning early to exercise discretion with whom they discussed their father's homosexuality, minimizing the possibility of negative reaction. Several fathers said that their children's experience with homophobic harassment led them to become devoted champions of civil rights for minorities.

Other forms of protection exercised by gay fathers in Bozett's (1980) study may seem initially superficial, even awkward. For example, in some cases children were asked to refer to the father's partner as "uncle" or as a "housemate" to circumvent probing questions. In other rare instances where gay fathers had custody of their children, arrangements were made for children to attend a school outside their own neighborhood. That way the children would have two sets of friends—school friends and neighborhood friends. In the event the father's gay identity was discovered by one group of friends who might taunt the child, the child would still have a second set of friends. These strategies are perhaps trial and error methods by parents who have no answers, no models, and no support, trying to do what they feel is best for their children.

Among the homophobic attitudes children of gay fathers may encounter is the belief that sexual abuse of children is more likely to occur in a homosexual household. However, according to national police statistics, sexual abuse of children is a heterosexual crime in 90% of cases (Voeller & Walters, 1978). Miller's (1979a) interviews with gay fathers indicate that sexual exploitation of children was virtually nonexistent. This is also borne out by other social science research (Broth & Birnbaum, 1978), which concludes that "the adult heterosexual male constitutes a greater sexual risk to underage children than does the adult homosexual male" (p. 181).

Despite tactics such as those discussed above to protect children from homophobic attitudes and behavior, it is inevitable that children of openly gay parents—fathers or mothers—will experience pain. All the children of gays interviewed by Epstein (1979) had been hurt to some extent by prejudicial responses toward homosexuality. To avoid peer rejection and ridicule, they hid the truth about their mother's or father's sexual preference from friends, classmates, and strangers outside the house. There is not enough information on hand to assess what, if any, psychological damage this fear of rejection can cause. Tentative reports, however, indicate that the exposure to ridicule and the accompanying need for discretion has ironically given these children inner strength, sensitivity, and maturity well beyond their years (Epstein, 1979).

## MOTIVATION FOR GAY MEN TO BECOME FATHERS

Popular belief holds that homosexuals use their children as smoke screens to conceal their true sexual orientation. Yet, research indicates that the majority of gay fathers enter into marriage with an honest and true desire for successful family relationships. After marriage most gay fathers begin to experience conflict between their duality of homosexual feelings and heterosexual status of fatherhood and seek to reconcile this conflict.

Miller (1979a) found that at the time his respondents became parents, they did not think of themselves as homosexual. Although they reported having had sex with men, they had viewed themselves as heterosexual or bisexual. They had entered marriage with a genuine love for their wives and a desire to have children. During the course of their marriages, most men reported a metamorphosis in their sexual identity that eventually led to an exclusively homosexual orientation.

In another preliminary study of 30 gay husbands, Miller (1978) wrote that these men experienced a reformulation of their sexual identity not unlike the sexual awakenings of adolescents. Some of the respondents reported that their homosexual resocialization occurred as late as 50 or 60 years of age when they were grandfathers. Miller (1978) concluded:

> Homosexually oriented husbands tend to move from covert, highly compartmentalized lifestyles, with all the surface appearances of suburban matrimonial accommodation, toward open, often militant, gay stances. Although ruptured marriages are left in the wake of this movement, these men consistently maintain commitment to and responsibility for their children, insofar as the courts allow. Such resocialization and consequent adjustments to life in a differing cultural milieu are seen as resulting not only from a complex process of negotiating, in which cognitive dissonance is resolved, but also from the initiation of a homosexual love relationship. The latter appears stronger than any other factor in enabling the husband to reassess the potentialities of gay lifestyles and identities. (p. 229)

Miller (1979b) also found that when the men in his sample left their wives and acquired a homosexual lifestyle, they experienced an enhanced self-esteem, and some reported the disappearance of psychosomatic ailments—such as headaches, ulcers, or fatigue—that plagued them during their marriages. They also said that their gay relationships were more harmonious than their marital relationships, and that fathering was more important and fulfilling to them than ever before.

None of the fathers in Bozett's (1980) sample entered marriage for the purpose of putting up a heterosexual front. Most of the men, but not all, had sexual experiences with other males before marriage. They, like the men in Miller's (1979a) survey, married with the intention of maintaining a heterosexual marriage and having children. Similar to Miller's study, Bozett reported that the men he interviewed described a slow metamorphosis during their marriage, from identifying themselves as bisexual or heterosexual to exclusively homosexual:

> One man stated that he identified himself as "bisexual for a long, long time and I guess that maybe it was only in the last two or three years of the marriage that my subconscious would allow me to identify as being gay." Because of the strength of the defense mechanisms of denial and repression, conscious awareness of, and then acceptance of oneself as homosexual may take considerable time. (Bozett, 1980, p. 174)

This identity process is further complicated by the fact that gay fathers have two identities that are opposite extremes (Bozett, 1981a, 1981b). On the one hand is the identity of homosexuality (which carries a negative stigma) and on the other is the identity of fatherhood (which carries positive import). The major task for the gay father is to merge his two conflicting identities and the disparity between his feelings (homosexual) and his behavior (heterosexual). This is accomplished through a five-stage career that most gay fathers go through: (1) the period before marriage when they are dating women, (2) marriage, (3) fatherhood, (4) alteration in the spousal relationship, usually separation and divorce, (5) and the free activation of a homosexual lifestyle. As the gay father progresses through these stages, internal changes occur from awareness and unacceptance of his homosexual identity to acceptance of that identity. One gay father quoted by Fadiman (1983) described his emergence from "the closet" in this way:

> It was dark and cramped and narrow. . . . Just like its name. Inside, I did nothing but hedge and lie. Once I started stepping out of it a little, I began to realize how much energy I'd been bottling up. I laughed more and my whole body became more relaxed. It was like having the right terminals connected for the first time (p. 86)

Bozett's (1981a, 1981b) research indicates that gay fathers who were homosexually active before marriage tended to have an easier time reconciling their gay and father identities than those who were not. Apparently, early and varied homosexual experiences fostered the internalization of homosexuality as positive. In contrast, gay fathers who became homosexually active after marriage had a more difficult time resolving their identity conflict and perceived their gay identity as hopelessly incompatible with being a father. Not only must gay fathers resolve their identity in the heterosexual world, they must also come to terms with the homosexual world. This can be a problem in a culture that is characterized by single people, transient relationships, and youth orientation (Bozett, 1981a). Single gay men are often reluctant to become involved with a gay man with children whose time must be shared equally with offspring and sometimes a wife. A major irritant in the opening case study was the jealousy between the gay father's male partner and his son—a factor that played a role in the demise of the relationship between the father and his partner.

Despite the fact that unlike gay men in general, gay fathers must undergo an identity reconciliation, recent findings indicate that the sex-role orientation of gay fathers and gay nonfathers are virtually the same. Robinson and Skeen (1982) studied gay fathers from five regions in the United States and found that men who fathered children were no more masculine, compared with gay men who had not fathered children. A diverse pattern of sex-role orientation was found in which gay men, regardless of fatherhood status, were equally masculine, feminine, and androgynous.

## MENTAL HEALTH STATUS OF MARRIED GAY MEN

Pioneer psychoanalytic studies of the 1960s characterized homosexuals, particularly married gays, as pathological (e.g., Bieber, 1969) with the source of the pathology described as unhappy childhood experiences (Bieber, 1962) and poor parental relationships (Apperson & McAdoo, 1968; Evans, 1969). These early studies, riddled with methodological problems and investigator bias, have been severely criticized (Greenblatt, 1966; Hooker, 1969). Bieber (1962), for example, studied male adult homosexuals and heterosexuals under psychiatric treatment for various problems. Not surprisingly, pathological trends were noted in his subjects, since they were already under treatment. Bieber's study was further questioned because when analysts were called on to furnish information regarding the data, they knew in which category the patient fell (e.g., either homosexual or heterosexual). Thus, it was possible that their opinions were biased due to this information.

More recent and less-biased studies show that disturbed parental relationships are neither necessary nor sufficient conditions for homosexuality. Published interviews with homosexuals and heterosexuals by the Kinsey Institute for Sex Research revealed no association between early family experience and adult sexual preference (Bell *et al.*, 1981). More recently, from their nationwide sample of 285 homosexual men, Skeen and Robinson (1984, 1985) analyzed the responses of 30 respondents (or 10% of the sample) who had fathered one or more children. The fathers represented five regions of the United States. The profile emerging from the study was positive. Most gay fathers (80%) grew up in intact homes where heterosexual relationships were modeled, of which there were pleasant childhood memories, and there was practically no marital discord. Although relationships with mothers were perceived to be slightly better than those with fathers, both maternal and paternal parent–child relationships were more frequently described as adequate and positive than inadequate or negative. Most gay fathers believed that both their mothers and fathers viewed them as worthy individuals, although mothers did so slightly more than fathers.

It is not possible to determine from Skeen and Robinson's study (1984, 1985) what effect (if any) these positive early family experiences had on gay fathers' decisions to become involved in a heterosexual marriage and to subsequently father children. One half of the fathers cited stabilizing the relationships with their partners and children as the major task they hoped to accomplish during their lifetime. Thus, gay fathers seemed to carry over the value of stable family relationships from childhood into their adult lives. They placed the most value on their children, their male partners (and in some cases their wives). Asked "What is most important in your life right now?" many fathers listed both their children and male loved ones as important. Typical responses were "My two children, a new male friend"; "son, job, relationship"; "building my relationship with my daughter, parents, and lover"; "my children, parents, and church"; "family, friends, my son, and career"; "wife, child, career." Gay fathers rejected "Maintaining a heterosexist nuclear family system often with separate bedrooms for husband and wife, where each has a separate lifestyle" (Mager, 1975, p. 130), the method by which sexual incompatibility was reconciled 20 years ago. Instead, practically all fathers (73%) had dissolved their heterosexual marriages, in many instances in favor of a homosexual relationship (66%).

## CONCLUSION

Most gay fathers enter a heterosexual marriage with a genuine desire to establish successful family relationships—not to camouflage their sexual orientations. Those who disclose their homosexuality to their children tend to maintain close and open relationships with them. Gay fathers were usually raised in intact heterosexual families, and they seek to carry over the stable family relationships from their upbringing into their adult lives. Most gay fathers highly value relationships with their children and take extra precautions to protect their offspring from public harassment and embarrassment. Statistics indicate that the incidence of sexual abuse among children of gay fathers is practically nonexistent. Contrary to popular belief, gay fathers do not try to persuade their children to be homosexual. In fact, children of gay parents usually turn out to be heterosexual.

Despite these positive aspects, children of gay parents face an array of pressures that children of heterosexual parents do not, in addition to having many of the problems that all children of divorce parents have. Pain and confusion surrounding separation and divorce can lead to multiple childhood problems including sexual acting out, difficulties in school, feelings of isolation, and conflict regarding their identity. Adjusting to new multiple relationships within the family is an added problem for children of divorce. Like children from heterosexual divorced households, children of gay parents are likely to grow up in multiple relationships with adults. For example, perhaps the father and his male loved one and the mother and her male companion or husband are present (Bozett, 1980; Mager, 1975). Unbroken families have had a lifetime to establish their relationship patterns; children from broken homes are thrown into instant, intimate relationships with virtual strangers for whom they may not be ready (Kompara, 1980).

These complex relationships of divorced households can lead to what Elkind (1981) calls "the hurried child syndrome"—a condition in which children must grow up too fast socially and psychologically:

> We dress our children in miniature adult costumes (often with designer labels), we expose them to gratuitous sex and violence, and we expect them to cope with an increasingly bewildering social environment—divorce, single parenthood, homosexuality. Through all of these pressures the child senses that it is important for him or her to cope without admitting the confusion and pain that accompany such changes. Like adults, they are made to feel they must be survivors, and surviving means adjusting—even if the survivor is only four or six or eight years old. This pressure to cope without cracking is a stress in itself, the effects of which must be tallied with all the other effects of hurrying our children. (p. xii)

Children of gay parents are even more at risk of becoming hurried children because their parents' sexuality is a more present issue that requires a greater adjustment. Some children are uncomfortable with their parents' sexual orientation, often because they themselves become targets of ridicule and humiliation. This predicament sometimes thrusts children into circumstances requiring discretion and judgment beyond their level of emotional maturity. They are forced at an early age to understand the atypical nature of their parents' lifestyle and place this atypicality within a broader cultural perspective—a sometimes difficult task for even the most sophisticated adult.

## SUGGESTIONS TO PROFESSIONALS

Recently, one of our students chose the topic of gay fatherhood as her area of outside reading in a course on human development. In addition to her many hours in the library, she visited a local gay church. There, she met several gay couples, all of whom were parents, and invited them to class. Two of the couples were male and one couple was female. All had been involved in previous heterosexual marriages, and a man in one couple brought his two teenage sons.

Although the class had been prepared for the visit, the room was tense. The student questioned the adults about generally held myths about gay parents, while others questioned the teenage sons. Asked if they viewed themselves as heterosexual or homosexual, both sons (who lived with their gay father and his male partner) said they were "hopelessly" heterosexual. They were quick to add that they saw nothing wrong with being homosexual.

The class period became an open forum in which both students and guests candidly expressed their prejudices and fears. As the discussion progressed, a wave of calm and relaxation engulfed the room. Straightforward questions and honest responses were intermingled with good-hearted laughter. Afterward, some students remained in class to talk individually with the guests. The majority of students later said their initially uncertain and negative attitudes about gays as parents had become more positive.

Understandably, many well-meaning professionals experience homophobia because homosexuality has historically been a neglected area in the training of human services personnel at colleges and universities (Dulaney & Kelly, 1982). We believe there are certain points that workers should keep in mind when working with gay fathers, their wives, their children, and their partners.

*1.* Acknowledge that gay fathers exist, either openly or secretly, among all client populations with which human services personnel deal. It is estimated that 10% of all clients of mental health agencies are gay or lesbian (Woodman & Lenna, 1980). Yet, reports indicate that professionals have paid little attention to the needs of homosexuals in general and to gay parents in particular (Berger, 1977). Once this realization is made, the guiding principles for working effectively with gay fathers (or gay and lesbian clients in general) are the same principles followed in working with heterosexual clients: "Accept the client as a total human being, accept his or her sexual orientation, and do not pretend to have all the answers . . . if a worker is unable to accept a client's goals, he or she should transfer the client to another therapist" (Dulaney & Kelly, 1982, p. 180).

*2.* Examine your own homophobia and prejudices toward homosexuality and gay marriages. Recognizing uncomfortable feelings can be a valuable lesson and can be dealt with by gaining more knowledge about homosexual behavior and gay parenting. Perhaps the best and easiest way to do this is simply by reading about homosexual lifestyles and approaches to working with homosexual clients.[2] Other suggestions include talks with married gays with whom you can make contact or discussions with colleagues who have had experience working with homosexual couples or married gays. Visits to a gay bar, church,

[2]See, for example, Beane (1981); Berger (1977); Dulaney and Kelly (1982); Woodman and Lenna (1980); Weinberg (1972); and Winkelpleck and Westfeld (1982). Additional resources are presented at the end of this chapter.

or a gay support organization can be especially valuable. Many homosexual organizations also provide speakers for classrooms and professional organizations. A resource listing of national and regional organizations, support groups, contact persons, counselors, and toll-free nationwide hotlines can also be obtained by writing the National Federation of Parents and Friends of Gays, 5715 16th Street, N.W., Washington, D.C. 20011. Additional professional organizations established to prohibit discrimination toward clients on the basis of sexual orientation are listed at the end of this chapter. Workers can use this information as a resource bank for gay clients who have accepted their sexuality and wish to meet others to share their interests.

3. Use contemporary terminology when working with clients who are gay parents. The term "gay" is generally preferred to that of "homosexual"; homosexual women often prefer to be referred to as "lesbian."

4. Employ what is known as the advocate model when working with gay fathers and their families (Berger, 1977). In the past, courts, counselors, and psychiatrists have made decisions or acted on the basis of many of the myths and stereotypes discussed in this chapter. Miller (1979a) reported that a few of the men he interviewed were concerned enough about their homosexual feelings to seek counseling before entering a marital relationship. In each instance the man was led to believe that a heterosexual marriage and parenthood would "cure all his ills." In fact, when one of the men fathered a child premaritally, the psychiatrist underscored this as proof that the man was "genuinely heterosexual." A second respondent told of his eagerness to accept his counselor's assessments:

> The shrink told me what I was dying to hear: "A person as nice as you couldn't be homosexual." What he should have done was get me to accept my homosexual self rather than some imaginary heterosexual self. But I believed him because I desperately wanted a home and someone to love to come home to. I thought homosexuality offered only sordid one-night stands. Back then I never thought it possible for me to actually *love* another man and for us to share a home life together; I thought only heterosexuals could do that. Besides, [Susan] was lovable and available, so we got married. But it didn't take me long to figure out that, whatever the disadvantages of being a gay single were, they couldn't be more painful than being gay and married, living a lie and being unable to share my deepest feelings with those I was closest to. (Miller, 1979a, p. 546)

The advocate model recognizes homosexuality as a legitimate variation of traditional lifestyles—not as a psychological disturbance—without endorsing homosexual behavior per se.[3] In cases of child custody and adoption, the parent's homosexuality is viewed as one of a number of factors to be considered. This approach avoids the pitfall of leading a gay father to believe that all his problems will be solved if he adopts a heterosexual lifestyle. Instead, workers begin by helping clients accept their homosexuality (if this is a problem), and counseling can progress from there. Field experience has shown that use of this model results in stronger impact when providing services to homosexual clients (Berger, 1977).

5. Be aware of the confusion and guilt that sometimes accompanies resolving a homosexual identity within a heterosexual family context. As we pointed out, the "coming out" process for gay fathers can be lengthy and painful. Fathers need positive support and encouragement as they reformulate their sexual identity. Usually, this reformulation surfaces through turmoil and anxiety. The conflict can become so massive that it erupts in suicide attempts (Bozett, 1981a). Resolving the conflict is partly a consequence of helping the gay father accept himself and resolve his internalized negative stereotype of homosexuality. Self-acceptance is frequently resolved through disclosure and acceptance by loved ones. Of course, as shown in the opening case study, the haunting fear of rejection is always a possibility for which the gay father must prepare himself. However, research (Fishel, 1983) consistently shows that when gay fathers disclose their homosexuality to loved ones, the results are usually, quite surprisingly, positive. Helping the gay father establish social networks composed of both homosexuals and heterosexuals who accept both of his identities can help him resolve his conflict.

Workers should also be prepared to help fathers deal with the guilt that can emerge when their children become targets of harassment because of their father's sexuality. Additional problems that can emerge with gay father clients include marital tension between homosexual men living with their wives, difficulty adjusting to the role of part-time or single parent for gay fathers who have visiting rights or joint custody, and isolation from both gay and heterosexual support groups that provide resources to help fathers reconstruct an alternate family life (Miller, 1979a).

6. Give special attention to children and wives of gay fathers when appropriate. It is important to be aware of the bewilderment with

[3]In 1973 the American Psychiatric Association voted to no longer classify homosexuality as a mental disturbance, disease, or psychiatric disorder, and in 1974 the American Psychological Association removed homosexuality from its Diagnostic and Statistical Manual as a form of mental illness.

which children and wives of gay fathers are confronted. Be prepared to counsel family members who may experience conflicting feelings, social pressure, alienation from others or confusion regarding their self-image. Professionals will find that the same principles used in working with children from heterosexual broken homes also apply to children of gay fathers. However, the father's "socially unacceptable" sexual behavior can be an additional problem with which these children must cope. Workers can alert gay fathers to potential problems of harassment toward their children and help them prepare their young to work through any conflict and confusion. Strategies for preparing children to deal with harassment and for shielding them from it, based on our earlier discussion, can also be proposed. Most importantly, gay fathers can be encouraged to be salient figures in their children's lives—to participate in child care when possible and to share their feelings and affections and leisure activities—even if they must live separately from their children. It is also important to help gay fathers establish some structure in their lives to include all the ones they love—children, the significant man in their lives, and when appropriate, spouse.

Dulaney and Kelly (1982) recommend that professionals provide support to the wives of gay men, especially in arrangements where both partners wish to retain the relationship while allowing the homosexual partner a private sex life as well. In other cases, where the man abandons his spouse, she may feel rejected and angry. Or her self-concept as a sexual partner may be at stake. She may blame her own sexual inadequacy as the reason for the demise of her marriage. Professionals should be prepared to deal with all of these issues. Finally, some wives may even struggle with the fear that their children will become homosexual because of exposure to a gay father. Familiarity with the previously discussed research findings should enable professionals to allay the mother's fears.

7. Arrange group discussions, even if only two gay fathers. Groups allow the men to share their pain, failures, joys, and successes and can be helpful, especially during the rough early days of "coming out," resolving identity conflict, and separation from the children's mother. According to Mager (1975), "Such meetings would break down the isolation, would bring the feeling of self-confidence, and would open up alternatives which a person might not think of" (p. 132). Referrals to local branches of Gay Fathers Coalition is another way to achieve this end. Family groups, composed of gay fathers and their wives and/or children, can also be useful in conflict resolution. Occasionally, professionals will be called on to work with the father and his male

partner (and sometimes the wife) to help them work through the family transformation.

## PROFESSIONAL RESOURCES FOR WORKING WITH GAY FATHERS

### Books

Bozett, F. Gay men as fathers. In S. Hanson & F. Bozett (Eds.), *Dimensions of fatherhood.* Beverly Hills, Calif.: Sage, 1985.

Brown, H. *Familiar faces, hidden lives: The story of homosexual men in America today.* New York: Harcourt Brace Jovanovich, 1976.

Clark, D. *Loving someone gay.* Milluae, Calif.: Celestial Arts, 1977.

Curry, H., & Clifford, D. *A legal guide for lesbian and gay couples.* Reading, Mass.: Addison-Wesley, 1980.

Jones, C. R. *Homosexuality and counseling.* Fortress, 1974.

Jones, C. R. *Understanding gay relatives and friends.* Seabury, 1978.

Maddox, B. *Married and gay.* New York: Harcourt, Brace Jovanovich, 1982.

Ross, M. *The married homosexual man.* London: Routledge & Kegan Paul, 1983.

Silverstein, C. *A family matter: A parents' guide to homosexuality.* New York: McGraw-Hill, 1977.

Weinberg, G. *Society and the healthy homosexual.* New York: Doubleday, 1972.

Woodman, N., & Lenna, H. *Counseling with gay men and women: A guide for facilitating positive life styles.* San Francisco: Jossey-Bass, 1980.

### Audiovisuals

We could locate no media that pertain directly to gay fathers, but the following audiovisuals deal with many of the same issues:

*Counseling the homosexual person.* A broad background about homosexuality with specific counseling concern is presented. NCR Cassettes, Box 281, Kansas City, MO 64141. Two audio cassettes, 2 hours.

*Vir amat.* Two young men, who have lived together for over a year, share their relationship and sexual pattern—very explicit. 16 mm, 15 minutes.

*Michael, a gay son.* This sensitive film reveals the feelings and needs of a young man, his parents, and siblings when he tells his family that he is gay. This sympathetic portrayal will help professional and general audiences gain insight into the dilemmas facing the homosexual. It should be used by counselors, psychologists, social workers, and gay groups and their families. Filmakers Library, Inc., 133 East 58 Street, New York, NY 10022. 16 mm, color, 27 minutes.

## Organizations

American Psychological Association Task Force on the Status of Lesbian and Gay Male Psychologists, c/o American Psychological Association, 1200 17th Street, N.W., Washington, D.C. 20036.

Association of Gay and Lesbian Social Workers, c/o M. Weltmann, 1527 Spruce Street #33, Philadelphia, PA 19102.

Association of Gay Psychologists, 8430 Santa Monica Boulevard, Suite 200, Los Angeles, CA 90069.

Bay Area Physicians for Human Rights, Box 14563, San Francisco, CA 94114.

Caucus of Social Work Educators Concerned with Gay and Lesbian Issues, c/o James Kelly, 5675 Spreading Oak Drive, Los Angeles, CA 90068.

Committee of Black Health Workers, c/o National Coalition of Black Gays, Box 57236, Washington, D.C. 20037.

Gay Caucus of Members of the American Psychiatric Association, #28-C, 44 W. 62nd Street, New York, NY 10023.

Gay Fathers Coalition, Box 50360, Washington, DC 20009-0360.

Gay Fathers Unlimited, 625 Post Street, Box 283, San Francisco, CA 94109.

Gay, Lesbian and Bisexual Caucus of American Association of Sex Educators, Counselors and Therapists, Box 834, Linden Hill, NY 11354.

Gay Nurses Alliance, Box 1015, Brownsville, TX 78520.

Gay People in Medicine, 14650 Lee Road, P.O. Box 131, Chantilly, VA 22021.

Gay Public Workers, 206 N. 35th Street, Philadelphia, PA 19104.

National Association of Gay Alcoholism Professions, Box 376, Oakland, NJ 07436.

National Association of Gay and Lesbian Gerontologists, 3312 Descanso Drive, Los Angeles, CA 90026.

National Association of Social Workers Task Force on Gay Issues, 6th Floor Southern Building, 1425 H Street, N.W., Washington, DC 20005.

National Caucus of Gay and Lesbian Counselors, Box 216, Jenkintown, PA 19046.

Senior Action in a Gay Environment, 487-A Hudson Street, New York, NY 10014.

## REFERENCES

Apperson, L. B., & McAdoo, W. G. Parental factors in the childhood of homosexuals. *Journal of Abnormal Psychology*, 1968, *73*, 201–206.

Beane, J. "I'd rather be dead than gay": Counseling gay men who are coming out. *Personnel and Guidance Journal*, 1981, *60*, 222–226.

Bell, A. P., & Weinberg, M. S. *Homosexualities: A study of diversity among men and women*. New York: Simon & Schuster, 1978.

Bell, A. P., Weinberg, M. S., & Hammersmith, S. K. *Sexual preference: Its development in men and women.* Bloomington: Indiana University Press, 1981.

Berger, R. M. An advocate model for intervention with homosexuals. *Social Work,* 1977, *22,* 280–283.

Bieber, I. *Homosexuality: A psychoanalytic study.* New York: Basic Books, 1962.

Bieber, I. The married male homosexual. *Medical Aspects of Human Sexuality,* 1969, *3,* 76–84.

Bozett, F. W. Gay fathers: How and why they disclose their homosexuality to their children. *Family Relations: Journal of Applied Family and Child Studies,* 1980, *29,* 173–179.

Bozett, F. W. Gay fathers: Evolution of the gay-father identity. *American Journal of Orthopsychiatry,* 1981, *51,* 552–559. (a)

Bozett, F. W. Gay fathers: Identity conflict resolution through integrative sanctioning. *Alternate Lifestyles,* 1981, *4,* 90–107. (b)

Bozett, F. W. Parenting concerns of gay fathers. *Topics in Clinical Nursing,* 1984, *6,* 60–71.

Cantor, D. W. School-based groups for children of divorce. *Journal of Divorce,* 1977, *1,* 183–187.

Dulaney, D. D., & Kelly, J. Improving services to gay and lesbian clients. *Social Work,* 1982, *27,* 178–183.

Elkind, D. *The hurried child: Growing up too fast too soon.* Reading, Mass.: Addison-Wesley, 1981.

Epstein, R. Children of gays. *Christopher Street,* June, 1979, 43–50.

Evans, R. B. Childhood parental relationships of homosexual men. *Journal of Consulting and Clinical Psychology,* 1969, *33,* 129–135.

Fadiman, A. The double closet. *Life Magazine,* 1983, *6,* 76–100.

Fishel, A. H. Gay parents. *Issues in Health Care of Women,* 1983, *4,* 139–164.

Green, R. Sexual identity of 37 children raised by homosexual or transsexual parents. *American Journal of Psychiatry,* 1978, *135,* 692–697.

Greenblatt, D. Semantic differential analysis of the "triangular system" hypothesis in "adjusted" male homosexuals. Unpublished doctoral dissertation, University of California, Los Angeles, 1966.

Groth, N., & Birnbaum, J. Adult sexual orientation and attraction to underage persons. *Archives of Sexual Behavior,* 1978, *7,* 175–181.

Harry, J. Gay male and lesbian relationships. In E. D. Macklin & R. H. Rubin (Eds.), *Contemporary families and alternative lifestyles.* Beverly Hills, CA: Sage, 1983.

Hitchens, D. Social attitudes, legal standards, and personal trauma in child custody cases. *Journal of Homosexuality,* 1980, *5,* 89–95.

Hooker, E. Parental relations and male homosexuality in patient and nonpatient samples. *Journal of Consulting and Clinical Psychology,* 1969, *33,* 140–142.

Kirkpatrick, M., Roy, R., & Smith, K. A new look at lesbian mothers. *Human Behavior*, 1976, *5*, 60–61.

Kompara, D. R. Difficulties in the socialization process of stepparenting. *Family Relations: Journal of Applied Family and Child Studies*, 1980, *29*, 69–73.

Lewis, K. G. Children of lesbians: Their point of view. *Social Work*, 1980, *25*, 200.

Maddox, B. Homosexual parents. *Psychology Today*, 1982, *16*, 62–69.

Mager, D. Faggot father. In K. Jay & A. Young (Eds.), *After you're out*. New York: Gage, 1975.

Miller, B. Adult sexual resocialization. *Alternate Lifestyles*, 1978, *1*, 207–234.

Miller, B. Gay fathers and their children. *The Family Coordinator*, 1979, *28*, 544–552. (a)

Miller, B. Unpromised paternity: Lifestyles of gay fathers. In M. Levine (Ed.), *Gay men: The sociology of male homosexuality*. New York: Harper & Row, 1979. (b)

Pleck, J. H., & Sawyer, J. Men and children. In J. Pleck & J. Sawyer (Eds.), *Men and masculinity*. Englewood Cliffs, N.J.: Prentice-Hall, 1974.

Robinson, B. E., & Skeen, P. Sex-role orientation of gay fathers versus gay nonfathers. *Perceptual and Motor Skills*, 1982, *55*, 1055–1059.

Robinson, B. E., Skeen, P., Flake-Hobson, C., & Herrman, M. Gay men's and women's perceptions of early family life and their relationships with parents. *Family Relations: Journal of Applied Family and Child Studies*, 1982, *31*, 79–83.

Skeen, P., & Robinson, B. E. Family background of gay fathers: A descriptive study. *Psychological Reports*, 1984, *54*, 999–1005.

Skeen, P., & Robinson, B. E. Gay fathers and gay nonfathers' relationships with their parents. *Journal of Sex Research*, 1985, *21*, 86–91.

Voeller, B., & Walters, J. Gay fathers. *The Family Coordinator*, 1978, *27*, 149–157.

Wallerstein, J. S., & Kelly, J. B. The effects of parental divorce: Experience of the child in later latency. *American Journal of Orthopsychiatry*, 1976, *46*, 256–269.

Wallerstein, J. S., & Kelly, J. B. *Surviving the break-up: How children actually cope with divorce*. New York: Basic Books, 1980.

Weeks, R., Derdeyn, A., & Langman, M. Two cases of children of homosexuals. *Child Psychiatry and Human Development*, 1975, *6*, 26–32.

Weinberg, G. *Society and the healthy homosexual*. New York: Doubleday, 1972.

Winkelpleck, J. M., & Westfeld, J. Counseling considerations with gay couples. *Personnel and Guidance Journal*, 1982, *60*, 294–296.

Woodman, N., & Lenna, H. *Counseling with gay men and women: A guide for facilitating positive lifestyles*. San Francisco: Jossey-Bass, 1980.

# CHAPTER EIGHT

# *Teenage Fathers*

ON COLD FEET[*]

*The winter of the epidemic*
*they came in late evenings*
*on cold feet*

*One by one to knock*
*at her kitchen door*
*to rap inside*

*To talk about their loves*
*who were with child*
*a little or a lot*

*Trusting a trusted teacher*
*young fathers-to-be waiting*
*alone in a long night*

*Wondering worrying about*
*the three of them now*
*and what to do or not*

Douglas Powers

[*]Reprinted with permission of the author.

According to the Planned Parenthood Foundation, adolescent pregnancy is happening with greater frequency in epidemic proportions; boys under 18 are becoming fathers, and many are still in junior and senior high school (Abbott, 1978). Teenage males are responsible for 1.1 million pregnancies each year (National Center for Health Statistics, 1979).

The case study is a true instance in which a young boy felt alone and scared by the sudden realization that he was about to be a father—unprepared psychologically and financially. He was a child entering the stark reality of an adult world with little support from society, friends, or even his family. In the final moment he was denied the opportunity to make any decisions regarding the welfare of his unborn child.

Although teenage fatherhood takes many forms, in the typical case teenage mothers have their babies, decide to keep them, and never marry the father. Sometimes the mother insists on putting the baby up for adoption. Teenage boys and girls sometimes marry out of obligation or perhaps even desire, but these marriages usually do not last

### THE CASE OF THE UNWED TEENAGE FATHER

When my girlfriend told me she was pregnant, I wasn't really surprised. We'd been dating for 2 years and had been having sex a lot for the past 8 months. Oh sure, we talked about protection and sometimes we used rubbers. But mostly we just liked sex without even thinking about a baby. We talked about getting married after our senior year so the idea of a baby didn't seem so awful. The night she told me she'd missed her period both of us were scared. After talking about it we decided to go to a doctor in the next town to find out if she was pregnant or not.

Once we found out Janie was really going to have a baby, we had to make a decision. There was nobody I could talk to, so I pretty much stayed by myself and worried. Even though things seemed to be closing in on me, I dreamed about how fine things were going to be—how we'd get married and about being a father. I knew it wouldn't be easy, but I could work at the mill and we could live on my family's farm. I just knew we'd make it!

After hours of talking we decided to go to our parents, tell them everything, and to ask for their help. Graduation was 2 months off, and we planned to get married then. Janie would only be 4 months along and probably wouldn't be showing. Both of us had jobs; college would have to be put off, but we felt we had made good—and realistic—plans. We went to my parents first. Talking with them was hard because I knew I was really letting them down. Mom cried and Dad mostly yelled at both of us. But

(Furstenberg, 1976). Decisions about whether to abort, keep the baby, or put the infant up for adoption are usually made without the boy's permission. In unusual situations like that of Mike J in Wyoming, the teenage father becomes a single parent. When Mike's daughter was born, the 15-year-old mother wanted to give her away, but 18-year-old Mike is now raising his daughter as a single parent.

Throughout the 1970s there was a general concern about the growing number of teenage pregnancies. Out-of-wedlock births increased 50% in the last decade, meaning that at least one out of every six American babies was born to unwed parents. In 1970 there were about 399,000 out-of-wedlock babies born in the United States, accounting for almost 10.7% of all births. This figure rose to 17% in 1979, when 597,800 babies were born to unwed mothers. The Urban Institute in Washington has analyzed these figures, showing that 29% of births to white teens and 83% of births to black teens occurred outside marriage. In fact, adolescent pregnancies account for 46% of all out-of-wedlock births and 31% of all abortions in the United States (Alan Guttmacher Institute, 1982).

after lots of talk, they pretty much calmed down and agreed to think about our plans.

Things at Janie's house were different. Her mom and dad both blew up—and mostly at me! They refused to listen to anything we had to say and kept asking us how we let this happen and telling Janie what a no-good creep I was. Finally, after what seemed like hours, they told me to get out, so I left.

The next day Janie wasn't at school. As soon as classes ended, I went to her house to see what was going on. Her mom met me at the door and told me Janie was sick and needed to rest. She told me that this was normal and that Janie would call in a couple of days. Even though I didn't believe her, I didn't see that I had much choice. I worried a lot the next 2 days—I guess I knew something was wrong—and I was right!

After 2 days I went to Janie's and told her mom I wasn't leaving until I'd talked to Janie. Her dad came out and told me to get off their property and to never come back. He said they had taken her to a hospital where she had an abortion, and then she had gone to finish high school in another state! I couldn't believe it! I protested and tried to find Janie through her friends for weeks, but I never saw her again.

I felt put down by her family's lack of trust. Both of us had tried to be realistic and responsible. But her parents took all of that away from us, and I was robbed of my right to have some say in so what would happen to my child. I don't think I'll ever get over it.

**Anonymous**

   While these statistics indicate the scope of the problem, the consequences of being a teenage father are further complicated by the
stereotype. He is pictured as an irresponsible, perhaps even reckless
youth, who got himself into a bad situation because of an inability to
control his sexual desires. The odds are stacked against his ever being
a successful father. If he and his girlfriend are not married, he is
branded as uncaring and routinely absent, although in many cases the
teenage girl's parents forbid him to see their daughter (Connolly,
1978). Even when he wants to assume financial responsibility for an
abortion, society still regards him as irresponsible, out to save his own
neck.
   Partly as a result of this stereotype, in the past social and medical
services have not been concerned with the problems of teenage fathers. For the most part, human services support programs (Earls &
Siegel, 1980) and literature for counselors and other professionals
(Foster & Miller, 1980) have centered exclusively around adolescent
females. Earls and Siegel (1980) argue that the overall decrease in
regular contact between unmarried adolescent parents can be attributed to the failure of medical and social services to actively engage the
father. In most instances, there is a punitive and judgmental attitude
toward the male. His rights to make decisions about his child have
been ignored—except for his financial responsibility, which is generally the major legal concern of society (L. B. Johnson & Staples, 1979).
A 1972 Supreme Court ruling, *Stanley v Illinois*, established equal
protection and involvement under the law to unmarried, natural fathers in custody decisions. Even though the courts have tried to help
teenage fathers, most of these young men still are reluctant to come to
agencies that want to help them. In some parts of the country, however, social agencies have begun to offer help to adolescent fathers as
well as mothers (see box this chapter). Professionals have found that
these young men are eager to talk and become involved because they
have few friends with whom to share their feelings and fears (S. Johnson, 1978).
   Little is known about teenage fathers, for a number of reasons.[1]
They are not easy to find, and most of the research (e.g., Platts, 1968)
on them has been based on secondhand information from teenage
mothers. It is easy to imagine that some of the mothers might not
answer questions accurately. They might be angry with the father and
want to show him at fault. Or they might want to protect him and

---

[1]For a detailed critique of adolescent father research, see B. Robinson and
R. Barret, "Issues and Problems Related to the Research on Teenage Fathers: A
Critical Analysis," *Journal of School Health*, 1982, *52*, 596–600.

show him as being more responsible and involved than he really is. A good example of how these interviews can conceal or distort the facts was described by Lorenz, Klerman and Jekel (1977), whose sample of adolescent mothers occasionally responded with hostility or lack of cooperation when questioned about the adolescent father. Platts (1968) also reported instances in which adolescent mothers informed caseworkers that their relationships with the young fathers had ended when, in actuality, the mothers were trying to protect the father from "harassment" by the agency.

Another shortcoming in the research concerns titles (e.g., "Adolescent Pregnancy" or "Adolescent Parenthood") that routinely mislead the reader to believe both adolescent parents are included in the research. In 30% of the studies we reviewed, however, these rubrics are used to refer exclusively to the mother (Babikian & Goldman, 1971; Foster & Miller, 1980; Furstenberg, 1980; Lyons, 1968; McHenry, Walters, & Johnson, 1979; McMurray, 1968; Plionis, 1975; Scott, Field, & Robertson, 1980; Stickle & Ma, 1975).

Perhaps the most common problem in teenage father research is that of locating a representative sample. In the past, lack of representativeness was excusable due to expense and accessibility problems. Historically, fewer young unmarried fathers, compared with mothers, have maintained contact with human service organizations, which provide data pools through their work in this area (Leashore, 1979). Although sampling errors pervade previous studies, in many cases these methods were the most reasonable approaches at the time. Conducting studies with this population continues to be difficult because the subjects themselves are generally reluctant to come forward and the agencies that routinely interact with them often identify ethical principles (e.g., confidentiality) as reasons for not supporting well-planned research activities. Despite these drawbacks, enough information exists to provide a general picture of the adolescent father.

## SEXUAL NAIVETÉ

It is true that teenage fathers are sexually active early and have more frequent and more varied sexual activities than adolescent mothers. This early sexual activity leads to the notion that these young men know more about sexuality and reproduction than most teenage boys, which is untrue; young fathers are not worldly and are uninformed about sex and sexuality. Their sexual naiveté contributes to their dilemma. Most young fathers are as uninformed about sex and sexuality as young mothers (Howard, 1975). According to a report from the Alan Guttmacher Institute (1982), 12 million adolescents—7 million males and 5 million females—are sexually active starting at an average age of 16. Nearly 67% of sexually active teenagers have never practiced contraception or have used a method inconsistently. Forty-one percent thought—out of ignorance—that they could not become pregnant. The need for more information about sexuality in general and especially about birth control is greatest among black and Hispanic youths. Because they become sexually active at a younger age and have less access to information, they are more likely to father a child during their earlier teenage years (Finkel & Finkel, 1975; L. B. Johnson & Staples, 1979). In one study (Hendricks, 1980) 35% of the black adolescent fathers also had brothers who were unwed fathers.

From our own sample of 30 teenage fathers in the Charlotte, North Carolina area, 42% said they were having intercourse regularly before their girlfriends got pregnant (Barret & Robinson, 1982). Most of them never even discussed the possibility of pregnancy, and most never used contraception. Asked to complete the sentence, "I did not think she would get pregnant because, . . ." typical responses were "We had a lot of sex and she didn't get pregnant," "She didn't look like the type," "We only had sex once a week." Similar replies and the general trend of failure to use effective birth control led the Alan Guttmacher Institute (1982) report to conclude that adolescents need more information about sex, reproduction, contraception, and the responsibilities of parenthood *before* they become sexually active.

## RELATIONSHIP WITH THE MOTHER OF THE CHILD

The myth that teenage fathers do not care about the mother and baby has grown out of the convention of marriage as a sign of caring. Research suggests that the relationships between adolescent fathers and mothers are not casual (Lorenzi *et al.,* 1977). Unwed, adolescent parents have usually known one another for at least a year, and their feelings for one another range from affection to love—or at least what was felt to be love when sexual relations began (Hendricks, 1983; Howard, 1975).

A study conducted by the Youth Study Center of Philadelphia concluded that 75% of the adolescent fathers in a detention center did not seek desertion, detachment, or abandonment of their girlfriends or children (Connolly, 1978). In our own study we found that the relationship between the young father and his girlfriend is close and caring—

not a whimsical, one-time affair. The unwed mothers in our study usually informed their boyfriends directly about the pregnancy rather than concealing the fact or sharing it only with friends or family members. We found that although not married, the majority of teenage fathers we studied expressed strong emotional ties with the young women they impregnated.

Asked about their responsibilities in regard to mother and baby, an overwhelming majority expressed strong care and concern, as the following comments indicate:

- "I would try the best I could to make their life best for them!"
- "[I would] take care of them, being with them and giving the baby money for milk, doctor bills, and other things."
- "[I want] to stand behind the mother of my child even after the baby is adopted."
- "[I plan] to take care of my baby and my girlfriend and try to give them anything in the world they want."
- "[I want to take care of them] because I love both of them, they are my heart and I really care."
- "[I want to take care of them] because they are special to me and I do love them very much. Not only that, I care because only I am going to be able to take care of them."
- "[I look forward to] supporting [my] child and [the] mother of the baby because I love and respect her a lot and will do all I can for her and [the] child."

Strikingly similar kinds of emotional concerns were reported by Hendricks (1980), who interviewed 20 unwed teenage fathers in Tulsa, Oklahoma. Hendricks concluded that unwed adolescent fatherhood can be a very stressful experience, based on the wide range of problems the young men shared:

- "Providing financial support to the mother of my two children."
- "Sometimes [having a] misunderstanding with Mother [i.e., unwed mother] about various things."
- "Disadvantage to be young and try to raise kid in proper way."
- "She wants to marry before I finish school and I want to wait until I get myself straight."
- "Problems with her [i.e., unwed mother] father."
- "Money problems."
- "Not being able to buy clothes for the baby."
- "Finding a good nursery to take care of child."
- "Not being able to support the baby myself."

- "Can't see the baby when I want to."
  (Hendricks, 1980, p. 865).

These feeling-oriented comments are a stark contrast to the uncaring, irresponsible stereotype. Case workers have also reported that teenage fathers are interested in the mother and baby and that they are eager to talk and become involved in the fathering experience (Howard, 1975; S. Johnson, 1978; Pannor & Evans, 1975). They found

## REACHING ADOLESCENT FATHERS

Traditional programs for school-age parents have been directed toward adolescent mothers and have involved remedial rather than preventive efforts. It has been suggested that efforts to include fathers in services to mothers are more likely to ensure the father's long-term active and responsible participation in the care of his offspring (Parke, Power, & Fisher, 1980). More social agencies have consequently begun to extend services to include young fathers. Because of their awareness of the negative stereotype associated with teenage fathers, young men are hesitant to take advantage of programs unless special efforts are made to reach them.

The Char.-Em. Alternative Program in Ann Arbor, Michigan, has extended its services to reach teenage fathers through parental child preparation classes and instruction on child-care techniques for expectant parents. A special day for fathers was established and follow-up telephone calls provided many males the encouragement they needed to become involved. The Michigan Association Concerned with School Aged Parents (MACSAP) in Pontiac, Michigan, has involved adolescent fathers by providing advice on family planning, personal counseling, and LaMaze childbirth classes, and the program reportedly has been valuable (Fisher, 1979).

Recently, several innovative programs designed exclusively for teenage fathers have been implemented. In Cleveland, Ohio, the Teen Father Program at Hough-Norwood Youth Services helps teenage fathers stay more involved with their children and become more supportive of the children's mother. San Francisco's Teenage Pregnancy and Parenting Program teaches adolescent males how to change, feed, and hold their babies so that they can participate more fully in infant care. In the San Francisco program the young men can simultaneously train in a trade and finish school, increasing the likelihood of employment and reducing repeat pregnancies. Coed classes in natural childbirth and bottle feeding are held in Philadelphia at the Medical College of Pennsylvania Hospital, and the Teen Indian Parents Program in Minneapolis provides teenage fathers with instruction on how to play with their infants as well as that the service agency must take the first steps to reach unwed fathers, however, because fathers are not likely to come forth on their own. The box entitled "Reaching Adolescent Fathers" describes recent changes that social agencies have made to respond to this criticism. Research interviews bear this out. Hendricks (1980) reported that none of the young unwed fathers in his sample said they would seek out a particular social service agency, yet 95% said they would be interested in receiving services should an agency offer them.

information on nutrition and child abuse. At the Perdue Learning Center in Indiana, which houses the Teen Mother Program, prospective fathers are instructed on the male and female reproductive systems and are informed about conception, pregnancy, and birth. Additional topics include first aid, sick baby care, and tips on home safety.

The Young Males Pilot Project in California is a preventive program aimed at black, Hispanic, Asian, and Native American youth (L. B. Johnson & Staples, 1979). This program provides information on family life education, family planning, and parental concern with the goal of developing sexual responsibility and reducing repeated and unwanted out-of-wedlock pregnancies through goal-directed support and assistance to young and unwed fathers between the ages of 14 and 24.

The Males's Place is a new program developed by the county health department in Charlotte, North Carolina. Males between 15 and 24 years of age can get free medical examinations, sex counseling, and if needed, contraceptives. The department also employs 10 teenage males who go to the communities with the highest rates of teenage pregnancies. The teenagers talk to their peers about male sexual responsibilities, urge them to visit the clinic, and, if there is an apparent need, distribute contraceptives.

The Bank Street College of Education in New York City launched an innovative preventive program called "Oh, Boy! Babies." It provides a hands-on 6-week course in infant care for preadolescent boys between the ages of 10 and 12.

While these programs are promising, more preventive programs on family planning and responsibilities of parenthood are needed to reduce the number of adolescent fathers. Future programs must continue to include the teenage father and have both a preventive and remedial emphasis. More innovative programs are needed whereby social agencies take more assertive measures to serve teenage fathers. Contacts in parking lots, pool halls, basketball courts, barbershops, recreational centers; flyers on windshields at rock concerts or midnight movies; and ads on public transportation and displays at flea markets have been suggested as stronger ways of reaching teenage fathers and promoting sexual responsibility among adolescent males (Hendricks, 1983; McCallister, 1979).

## INVOLVEMENT IN THE SUPPORT AND REARING OF CHILDREN

Practically all reports show that adolescent fathers are unmarried at the time of their children's conception. Among the unmarried teenage fathers in one study, 64% continued to contribute financially to the support of the mother and baby 15 months after their baby's birth (Lorenzi et al., 1977). Although by 26 months this figure dropped to 49%, the duration of financial support implies a meaningful and extended relationship (Lorenzi et al., 1977).

Most young fathers also continue to see or talk to the mothers, their children, or both on a regular basis (Barret & Robinson, 1982; Lorenzi et al., 1977). The fathers we talked to, for example, said they saw or talked to the mother of their child daily or weekly. Other researchers report that half of the unwed adolescent parents being studied continued to date each other during the baby's 1st year of life (Nettleton & Cline, 1975). In another study 73% of the adolescent mothers described the teenage father as someone who "loves babies and helps care for them" (Fisher, 1979). Furstenberg (1976) followed a group of unmarried adolescent mothers in the Baltimore area and found that children of never-married parents were as likely to see their fathers regularly as those whose parents had been previously married. Some of the fathers visited their children at least once a week. Most of the fathers were maintaining contact with their children 5 years after childbirth. Approximately 40% of unmarried teenage fathers marry, but adolescent marriages tend to be shortlived (Nye & Lamberts, 1980). The divorce rate for school-age parents under age 18 is about two and a half times higher than for parents having their first child after 22 years of age, and it is greater for couples with premarital pregnancies than for those who conceive after marriage (Nye & Lamberts, 1980). Among the marriages that did occur in Furstenberg's sample of adolescent mothers, most did not last through the 5 years of his study; yet among the few stable marriages, father–child contact was most intense and the relationship was satisfying.

In a study (Furstenberg & Talvitie, 1980) that followed Furstenberg's teenage mothers and their children, the investigators concluded that when children bear their father's name, they are more likely to have regular contact with their fathers and to receive economic assistance from them. The investigators explained, "The bestowal of the father's name may be nothing more than an expression of prior sentiment, and acknowledgment of the father's willingness at the time of birth to play an active part in the child's upbringing" (p. 49).

The young fathers we studied were also highly motivated to participate in some way in the fathering experience. They believed they had certain responsibilities toward the mother and baby and usually described these responsibilities in terms of financial obligations. Most believed they were viewed in a favorable light by their girlfriend's family. Many had discussed financial support for mother and baby or the possibility of marriage with their girlfriend's family. A majority said both they and the mother would name the baby.


## EDUCATION AND EMPLOYMENT

A nationwide study of Card and Wise (1978) surveyed 375,000 boys and girls from 1,225 senior and junior high schools. They found that boys who become fathers and marry in their teens usually end up in low-paying, blue-collar jobs as adults and find themselves in work that provides little or no job advancement. The immediate need to support a family causes them to interrupt and usually to terminate their education.

Generally, both adolescent fathers and mothers attained less education than their classmates, and the younger the parent at childbirth, the more severe the educational setback. At age 15, the boys and girls who would later become teenage parents reported backgrounds characterized by lower income levels and lower academic abilities, and had lower educational expectations than their classmates. The investigators concluded that teenage parenthood at age 15 (regardless of background) is a direct cause of "truncated" schooling, which leads teenage fathers into lower prestige, blue-collar jobs and causes them to enter the labor force earlier than their unmarried classmates.

Card and Wise (1978) also found that teenage fathers generally were more likely than teenage mothers to be single at the conception and birth of their child. The proportion of teenage fathers and mothers who were separated or divorced was higher than that of their classmates at each follow-up period. At 5 and 11 years after high school, teenage fathers and mothers had been married more times than their classmates. Because teenage childbearers have longer reproductive careers, teenage fathers and mothers had more children than their classmates at the 5- and 11-year follow-up periods. Another survey of 78 adolescent fathers reported that 58% had either dropped out of school or had still not completed high school, and 48% were employed (Fisher, 1979).

From our own study we found that the majority of unwed teenage fathers (average age 18 years) were unemployed or already gainfully employed in blue-collar jobs such as shipping clerk, plastic recycler, or forklift operator. All were making minimum wage. Most of them described their grades in school as average; many reported making Ds and Fs.


## MENTAL HEALTH


Within the past 20 years, some social workers speculated that boys who father children in their teens do so out of psychological need:

> Vista Del Mar social workers are convinced that out-of-wedlock pregnancies result from intrapersonal difficulties, which manifest themselves in ineffective or inappropriate interpersonal relationships; that both unmarried parents in general are faced with intrapersonal and interpersonal difficulties; and that the unmarried father enters into the relationship because of his psychic needs, and not by accident. (Pannor & Evans, 1965, p. 56)

Studies designed to confirm this speculation, conversely suggested that adolescent fathers are psychologically normal (Pauker, 1971). Obviously, the psychological symptoms that counselors and social workers had observed were simply symptoms of depression or emotional conflict, which are natural reactions in young men to their unfortunate circumstance (Pauker, 1971). The words of a 17-year-old waiting while his girlfriend had an abortion are typical of the emotional conflict of teenage fathers:

> I thought I was a much more liberated man. I'd be able to walk in here and sit down and say, "here's an abortion" and that would be it. But now that I'm here, I'm a wreck. I don't think anyone could depend upon me in this situation . . . I'm shaken . . . I also feel that I was more experienced than her and that I should have tried to help more . . . I'm usually calm and analytical . . . my girlfriend has been surprisingly calm about this . . . I really want to know what they will do for her . . . what I wanted to hear was this big elaborate story of how the doctor is there all the time. I was looking for reassurance. . . . How about me? Do they have something for me to lay on while I die? (Rothstein, 1978, p. 208).

Other questions regarding psychological differences between teenage fathers and teenage nonfathers revolve around the degree of control young fathers have over their lives. Do adolescent fathers have control over their lives? Or are they bent and swayed at the mercy of their everyday worlds? A common working hypothesis used in the past to explain why some adolescents get pregnant (or impregnate someone) and some do not has been that adolescent fathers, compared with their nonfathering peers, have less control over their personal lives. This lack of internal control, so the speculation goes, places these young men in the control of external factors such as chance and fate (Earls & Siegel, 1980). This view suggests that teenage males who impregnate their girlfriends at a young age have externalized their responsibilities, resigned themselves to their circumstances, and, therefore, do not control their sexual urges.

We wanted to test the validity of this hypothesis with our sample of 30 adolescent fathers in Charlotte, North Carolina (Robinson, Barret, & Skeen, 1983). We therefore chose those young men who had completed the locus of control forms and who were less than 20 years of age. Ten of the young men did not meet one of the criteria. The remaining 20 adolescents, average age 17.5, met our criteria. We gave the same test to another group of 20 adolescent nonfathers, matched by age with the fathers, from a public school sytem in Virginia. The Virginia adolescents, average age of 17.2, came from intact middle-income families, and their parents worked in blue-collar or professional jobs.

We found that teenage fathers felt as much in control of their lives as the identical-age group of nonfathers. Having found no differences, we decided to go a step further. We took a closer look at the 12 older unwed fathers in our original sample (average age 21.4 years) who had not met the age criterion for inclusion in the teenage father analysis. We randomly selected 12 teenage fathers to compare with the older fathers. Despite an age difference of almost 4 years, we found that the adolescent fathers were equally in control of their lives, compared with the older fathers.

Our findings on fate control compare favorably with other studies of unwed adolescent mothers and fathers. One investigation (Silk, 1981) in particular showed unwed adolescent mothers (age 16.1) to have as much control of their fate as adolecent females (age 16.1) who were not mothers. Our findings were also similar to those of Hendricks (1980), who studied 20 adolescent fathers in Tulsa, Oklahoma and discovered that 80% felt that what happens to them is of their own doing and that their destiny is not governed by chance, fate, or by other people.

The 20 unwed adolescent fathers studied by Hendricks (1980) said that they felt were in control of their lives. Asked "Who would you go to first with a problem?" 95% of the young fathers said their family—mothers more than fathers. So while parents, especially mothers, were valued as a source of social support, peers, the clergy, and school teachers were all rejected, possibly because they were not equipped to deal with problems associated with teenage parenthood.

Despite their typically stable personality, teenage fathers are not psychologically ready for fatherhood. Interviews with 35 teenage males who accompanied their partners to the Bronx Municipal Hospital's abortion clinic, showed that 86% were psychologically uncertain about their readiness to assume the role of caretaker and provider of a family (Rothstein, 1978).

Other research suggests that because teenage parents are poorly prepared for parenthood, their offspring can suffer from severe negative consequences. Studies of married high school couples, for example, showed they had unrealistic expectations of their children and a general lack of knowledge about children (de Lissovoy, 1973). This lack of knowledge led to impatience and intolerance, which frequently resulted in physical means of disciplining children. In fact, statistics show that teenage parents are more likely than more mature parents to resort to child abuse (Kinard & Klerman, 1980). The fact that teenage parents usually express unrealistic child-rearing attitudes and misunderstanding of children's developmental milestones places their newborns at greater risk (Field, Widmayer, Stringer, & Ignatoff, 1980). Infants born to adolescent parents are more likely to be premature or suffer from a variety of health problems due to inadequate prenatal care and nutrition. For instance, 6% of first children and 10% of second children born to parents under 15 die before their first birthday— three to five times the mortality rate for other American babies (Phipps-Yonas, 1980).

## CONCLUSION

The unwed teenage father is unlike the stereotype often presented. Biologically, teenage fathers are men, yet in every other respect they are boys. They are as uninformed about sex as most teenage boys. They generally have close ties to their partners and express concern about the mother and baby. Many say they want to participate in the fathering experience and do so for long periods of time. Those who marry drop out of school early and are forced to take low-paying jobs to support their families.

Because teenage fathers are hard to find and do not participate in many studies, much about them is unknown. Studies are needed to determine whether teenage fathers differ from the boys in those couples who decide to abort the pregnancy; to establish whether teenage fathers continue to have contact with their children as they grow older; and to identify the kinds of boys who are most likely to become fathers while they are teenagers. More information is needed on how schools and agencies like Planned Parenthood can help these young men to understand what is happening to them and can give them information so they can choose when they want to risk fathering a baby. With this information it may be possible to reduce the number of unwanted pregnancies and improve the lives of teenage parents and their children.

## SUGGESTIONS TO PROFESSIONALS

Professionals can improve services for both unwed parents and further our understanding of teenage fathers. Although young fathers are often reluctant to identify themselves, perhaps more may come forward as agencies in the helping professions begin to respond to their needs.

*1.* Be prepared to help young fathers deal with depression, isolation, and alienation resulting from out-of-wedlock births, decisions to abort, or putting the child up for adoption. In the opening case study, the young man had an array of feelings to cope with. One of the authors counseled him. Often, just talking provides sufficient therapy for teenage fathers, but sometimes other techniques may be necessary. Professionals can alleviate feelings of isolation and depression by establishing social networks for teenage fathers. This can take the form of arranging informal meetings between two fathers or setting up ongoing support groups composed of several fathers. Outreach programs for school-age parents are also valuable resources (see the box entitled "Reaching Adolescent Fathers"). Another approach would be to establish a small lending library where easily read materials on sex, reproduction, contraception, and the responsibilities of parenthood are available to clients.

*2.* Provide information on prenatal care, nutrition, and child rearing to adolescent parents. In exceptional cases where teenage fathers gain custody of their children or are somehow involved in daily care of their children, professionals can provide information on child development and care. Even when fathers do not have sole custody, research suggests that most young mothers would like to see the fathers of their infants receive training in child-care techniques (Fisher, 1979). Health problems or deaths of infants of teenage mothers can be decreased when the mother receives good prenatal care and nutrition (Flake-Hobson, Robinson, & Skeen, 1983).

*3.* Encourage adolescent parents to participate in home-based infant stimulation programs that serve to educate teens about parenthood, decrease isolation, and encourage the infant's development. Research shows dramatic positive benefits for babies enrolled in these programs (Field *et al.*, 1980). These programs are also beneficial to the mothers. In one study social workers paid weekly visits to the home of adolescent mothers and instructed and guided them in infant care techniques for 2 years (Scarr-Salapatek & Williams, 1973). Mothers were interested in the social worker's help and sought their advice on personal problems, feelings of depression, and infant care.

4. Help young clients build positive self-concepts and feelings of self-worth and provide them with education about contraception and the consequences of teenage parenthood to prevent unwanted pregnancies (Flake-Hobson *et al.*, 1983). Programs in human sexuality can begin to address the emotional response of both males and females to pregnancy and emphasize the young father's often intense involvement in the pregnancy. Research indicates that 95% of the teen fathers interviewed said they would be interested in receiving services from a teenage parenting agency. In addition to sex education, they listed such needs as job training, job placement, and parenting information (Hendricks, 1980).

Perhaps the best option is to advocate for sex education in the early grades before children become sexually active, so they can make more responsible decisions regarding their sexual behavior. Counselors and teachers in public schools can work together to develop programs for males and females in sociology, psychology, and home economics that provide information on human reproduction, contraception, parenting, and life planning. Caseworkers can collaborate with school counselors to create imaginative programs that serve all school-age youth. Schools and churches are a natural place for parent education programs for parents of all ages as well as for young people who one day will be parents.

5. Note whether the infant has been given the father's name or mother's name. Use of the father's name may indicate a degree of father involvement (Furstenberg & Talvitie, 1980).

6. Cooperate, within the limits of legal/ethical confidentiality constraints, with research inquiries into the incidence and cause of teenage fatherhood. Trends indicate that adolescent parenting will continue to be a social problem of expanding proportions. Funding agencies, social agencies, and researchers can combine their resources to increase information about the teenage father. Funding agencies can be more sensitive to the many obstacles that confront professionals attempting to gather meaningful information on teenage fathers. These young men are difficult to reach, and research on teenage

fathers is more expensive and time-consuming than similar research on teenage mothers.

Agencies (e.g., Children's Home Society, Florence Crittenton Home) that routinely deal with unwed pregnancy and adoption can cooperate with research efforts and can begin to request interviews with fathers as a routine part of their services. Social agencies can also be more cooperative with researchers by coordinating group meetings of teenage mothers and fathers where data could be gathered. Schools, which deal with many of the results of adolescent pregnancy, could invite researchers to make presentations to student groups that probably include these young fathers. While it is important for agencies to protect their clients from exploitation by researchers, well-developed research activities conducted by ethical professionals will ultimately improve the nature and quality of services rendered. perhaps one solution is to use agency professionals as consultants. The consultant collaborates with researchers while simultaneously protecting the client's privacy.

With increasing awareness and inclusion of teenage fathers in social programs, researchers can then lead the way by well-planned studies that include representative samples and that avoid confounding variables. Although young fathers are often reluctant to identify themselves, it is believed that more of them will step forward once individuals and agencies in the helping professions begin to respond to their needs.

7. Carefully monitor any prejudices to characterize teenage fathers as aloof, unconcerned, and eager to avoid responsibility for involvement in the pregnancy. Agencies should involve the teenage father in the delivery of services as specified by each state. (For a more detailed discussion on ways of reaching and involving teenage fathers in providing services, see Pannor & Evans, 1975.) Many young fathers do want to become involved and to share the responsibility of their children. Still, many professionals, such as social workers, continue to be ambivalent toward including unwed fathers in adoption proceedings and still view the mother as the main nurturer of children (Pierce, 1981). One social worker from the Children's Home Society in California described an eye-awakening experience in this regard:

> I discovered that I was counseling with the expectation that the fathers didn't want to contribute. I wasn't confronted with my own values until I saw some natural fathers who really wanted to get involved, wanted to see their babies and wanted contact with the adopting couples so that they could clarify why they were doing this and prevent distorted information from being passed on. (Connolly, 1978, p. 42)

Professionals who become involved with unwed mothers can likewise actively respond to unwed fathers. Simply by understanding that adolescent fathers are as needy as young mothers, workers can provide more equitable services to teenage parents as a whole.

## PROFESSIONAL RESOURCES FOR WORKING WITH TEENAGE FATHERS

### Books

Alan Guttmacher Institute. *Teenage pregnancy: The problem that hasn't gone away.* New York: Alan Guttmacher Institute, 1982.

Barret, R. L., & Robinson, B. E. The adolescent father. In F. Bozett & S. Hanson (Eds.), *Dimensions of fatherhood.* Beverly Hills, Calif.: Sage, 1985.

Furstenberg, F. F. *Unplanned parenthood: The social consequences of teenage childbearing.* New York: The Free Press, 1976.

Furstenberg, F. F., Lincoln, R., & Menken, J. (Eds.). Perspective on teenage sexuality, pregnancy, and childbearing. Philadelphia: University of Pennsylvania Press, 1980.

Nye, F. I., & Lamberts, M. B. *School-age parenthood: Consequences for babies, mothers, fathers, grandparents, and others.* Washington State University: Cooperative Extension Bulletin 0667, 1980.

Pannor, R., Massarik, F., & Evans, B. *The unmarried father: New helping approaches for unmarried young parents.* New York: Springer, 1981.

Scott, K., Field, T., & Robertson, E. (Eds.). *Teenage parents and their offspring.* New York: Grune & Stratton, 1980.

### Periodicals

*The Family Life Educator.* National Family Life Education Network, ETR Associates, 1700 Mission Street, Suite 203, Santa Cruz, CA 95060. A quarterly magazine for senior high students and their parents to promote teen ability to discuss attitudes related to the roles of various family members. It teaches about family life and sexuality and can be used in schools or in the home.

*The Voice.* Joan Fisher, Editor, 3057 Beacham Drive, Pontiac, MI 48055. A newsletter concerned with all school-age parents, both mothers and fathers and published by Michigan Association Concerned with School Age Parents (MACSAP).

*Teenage Parents/Western Regional Educational Committee Newsletter.* Jeanne Lindsay, Editor, 6595 San Haroldo Way, Buena Park, CA 90620.

*Young Fathers-New Stuff.* Leo E. Hendricks, Institute for Urban Affairs and

Research, Howard University, 2900 Van Ness Street, N.W., Washington, DC 20008. An analysis of three select populations of black unmarried adolescent fathers from Chicago, Columbus, and Tulsa.

## Audiovisuals

*His baby, too: Problems of teenage pregnancy.* This group of filmstrips, titled *Dave's story, The choices,* and *Making the decision,* examines the feelings of the teenage father and argues against the stereotype that depicts him as an aggressive lover who unfeelingly leaves his sex partner. Outlines the limited choices available to the expectant teenage parent and emphasizes the need for both parents to share in decisions about the child's future. Examines the often overlooked emotional needs of the teen father regarding decisions on abortion and the role of the natural father in the child's upbringing. Appropriate for high school and community programs with audiences aged 14 years through adult. Multimedia kit includes a guide. Sunburst Communications (SUN), 41 Washington Avenue, Pleasantville, NY 10570. Three sound filmstrips, 38:30 minutes total, 1980.

*Me, a teen father?* Using voice-over reflections, this film conveys the guilt and anguish over teenage fatherhood and recreates a 17-year-old boys's romance ending in pregnancy. The unsupportive attitudes of the teens' parents toward their predicament are shown. Provides insight into the fears and feelings of adolescent fathers and demonstrates the depth of emotions that teenagers can experience. Appropriate for high school classes, youth programs, and adult viewers in the community. Multimedia kit includes a guide. Centron Films (CEN), 1621 West 9th, Lawrence, KS 66044. Film or video, 13 minutes, 1980.

*Teenage father.* This film presents interviews with real-life teenagers who had become involved in unwanted pregnancies. Provides a balanced account of the problems and traumas arising from such an experience. Covers the various options, legal rights, and lack of rights of young people in this predicament. Children's Home Society of California, 5429 McConnell Avenue, Los Angeles, CA 90069. 16 minutes, color, 1978.

*The teenage pregnancy experience.* This film is designed to prepare expectant teenage parents for birth and parenthoods; to discuss options for pregnant adolescents; to promote discussion on pregnancy; and to depict realistic situations for use with teen groups as well as in professional training. Parenting Pictures, 121 NW Crystal Street, Crystal River, FL 32629. 28 minutes, color, 1982.

*Wayne's decision.* This film dramatizes in realistic dialogue the crisis of becoming a teenage father. The protagonist's decision can help students and parents to recognize the tragic fact that there is no single ideal solution to teenage pregnancy. Useful in community and religious group programs for adolescents and in junior and senior high school guidance and family life classes. Memphis Association for Planned Parenthood (MAP), 1407 Union Avenue, Memphis, TN 38104. 6 minutes, 1980.

## Organizations

The Alan Guttmacher Institute, 360 Park Avenue, New York, NY 10010. This is a tax-exempt nonprofit organization that conducts projects in the areas of research, policy analysis, and public education. It publishes *Family Planning Perspectives*, a research journal devoted to the dissemination of information on all aspects of childbirth and family planning.

Planned Parenthood Federation of America, 810 Seventh Avenue, New York, NY 10019. This is a national organization with chapters in many cities. Its major services include pregnancy-related counseling, education services, workshops on family planning, and contraceptive and abortion clinics.

## Government Legislation and Services

*Demonstration Grants.* Title VI of P.L. 95-626 calls for the Office of Adolescent Pregnancy Programs (OAPP) to award grants to demonstration projects throughout the country to provide family planning services; primary and preventive health services, including pre- and postnatal care; pregnancy testing, maternity counseling, and referral; nutrition information and counseling; educational services in sexuality and family life; adoption counseling and referral.

*Federal Program Coordination.* Title VII of P.L. 95-626 requires the Secretary of The Department of Health and Human Services (DHHS) to coordinate all federal policies and programs relative to teenage pregnancy.

*Federal/State Cooperation.* The Interagency Task Force on Comprehensive Programs (Department of Education) assists school-age parent programs at state and local levels with curriculum development and resource material on parenting and early childhood programs. For more information, contact W. Stanley Kruger, Director, Parent/Early Childhood and Special Program Staff, Office of School Improvement, Room 2083, FOB #6 Building, 400 Maryland Avenue, S.W., Washington, DC 20202.

*Grants to States.* Bureau of Community Health Services (Public Health Services) provides formula grants to states for services to mothers and infants at risk, particularly to teenagers and their children. For more information, contact Dr. V. L. Hutchins, Associate Bureau Director, Program Office for Maternal and Child Health, Room 7-39 Parklawn Building, 5600 Fishers Lane, Rockville, MD 20857.

*Hyde Amendment.* By a one-vote margin, the Supreme Court affirmed the constitutionality of the Hyde Amendment, which prohibits the use of federal funds for adoptions for Medicaid-eligible patients, including indigent teenagers. (June 30, 1980. Private sponsorship of the program would cost $60 million annually.)

*Parental Consent to Abortion.* The Supreme Court ruled (and reaffirmed) that parents cannot veto a minor's decision to have an abortion. However, the upheld Hyde Amendment disallows federally funded abortion services, effectively closing the door to legal abortions for most pregnant teenagers.

*Rights of Unmarried Fathers.* The "illegitimate father" must be given the opportunity to consent to relinquishment of parental rights in adoption.

(Caban v Mohammed, 441 U.S. 380, 1979, Stanley vs. Illinois, 405 U.S. 654, 1972.)

*Services to Sexually Active Teenagers.* Title X Family Planning Program, in the Health Services Administration of Public Health Services (DHHS), P.L. 91-572 (1978), has been amended to include services for teenagers who are to expect to be sexually active. There are no income or age barriers. A handbook on counseling services to adolescents become available in mid-1981. For further information, contact William White, Associate Bureau Director, Program Office for Family Planning, Bureau of Community Health Services, Room 7-15, Parklawn Building, 5600 Fishers Lane, Rockville, MD 20857.

## Programs for Pregnant Teenagers

*Alternative School for Teenage Parents.* Sponsored by the Wayne County (Michigan) Intermediate School District, the school provides services outside the regular school setting to pregnant teenagers and/or teenage parents from 14 feeder districts. Students may stay as long as they feel they need to before returning to regular school. Young fathers may enroll, and free infant day care is provided both while mothers are in the program and when they return to school or go to work.

*A Comprehensive and Integrated Model of Services for Pregnant Adolescents, School-Age Parents and Their Families.* This was developed by the State of Michigan in April 1979 under the auspices of the Michigan Department of Public Health to overcome the dropout problem among pregnant teenagers. An advisory council in each school district promotes community and student awareness of the problems of pregnant teenagers, services available to them, and referrals to the program. Contact Bobbie Neff, Office of Primary and Family Education, P.O. Box 30008, Michigan Department of Education, Lansing, MI 48909.

*Comprehensive Services for School-Age Parents.* Developed by the Philadelphia School District, this program helps young mothers catch up with schoolwork missed during the months before and after birth, develop skills in parenting and family life, learn proper health care, and acquire coping skills. Some classes are geared specifically to pregnant girls and are held outside normal school hours; others are integrated into the regular school day.

*The Parent–Child Sex Education Program.* Funded in part through Title X, this program offers mother/daughter and father/son sex education programs to community groups. Five-week courses cover basic anatomy, reproduction, values clarification, and decision making regarding sexuality. Teaching methods include lecturers, films, discussions, and simulations. A training manual has been developed for use by health teachers. For information, contact Lynn Peterson, Family Life Education/Family Guidance Center, 200 Corby Building, St. Joseph, MO 64501.

*The Teen Research Program.* Funded by Title X of PHS Act, this program was initiated in New York City schools in April 1978 and extended to June 1980. It was aimed at preventing unwanted pregnancy among high school students by providing information on reproduction, contraception, risks of adolescent pregnancy, and responsibilities of parenthood. Outside personnel presented the program to eliminate possible threat to school staff. A Teen Research office was established in each school; all offices were staffed by paraprofessional women. Contact Donna O'Hare, Project Director, Maternity, Infant Care, Family Planning Projects, 377 Broadway, New York, NY 10013.

*TIPS (Teen Information and Peer Services)*. This is an information/education center where teenagers can go for information and counseling. It is staffed by both male and female teenagers trained as peer educators under the direction of a health counselor. For information, contact Elysa Fischette, 255 Greenwich Avenue, Goshen, NY 10924.

## Resource Organizations

*National Association of State Boards of Education*, 526 Hall of State, 444 N. Capitol Street, N.W., Washington, DC 20001 (*State Policies Related to Adolescent Parenthood*, a nation-wide study of existing legislation, policies of state boards of education, and of social service agencies as a step toward development of standard methods of dealing with problems of adolescent pregnancy and parenthood).

*National Clearinghouse for Family Planning Information*, P.O. Box 2225, Rockville, MD 20852 (information services bulletin: *Adolescent Pregnancy, Early Childbearing and Parenthood*).

*Office of Adolescent Pregnancy Programs*, Room 725-H, Hubert H. Humphrey Building, 200 Independence Avenue, S.W., Washington, DC 20201 (*Adolescent pregnancy and parenting: Federally funded studies, research demonstration and evaluation report number 1*).

*Population Institute*, 110 Maryland Avenue, N.W., Washington, DC 20002 (*Sex Education Action/Resource Bulletin*, free).

*U.S. Department of Health and Human Services, Public Health Services, Health Services Administration, Bureau of Community Health Services*, Rockville, MD 20857 (brochures, general information).

## REFERENCES

Abbott, M. Teens having babies. *Pediatric Nursing*, 1978, *4*, 23–26.

Alan Guttmacher Institute. *Teenage pregnancy: The problem that hasn't gone away*. New York: Alan Guttmacher Institute, 1982.

Babikian, H. M., & Goldman, A. A study of teenage pregnancy. *American Journal of Psychiatry*, 1971, *128*, 755–760.

Barret, R. L., & Robinson, B. E. A descriptive study of teenage expectant fathers. *Family Relations: Journal of Applied Family and Child Studies*, 1982, *31*, 349–352.

Card, J. J., & Wise, L. L. Teenage mothers and teenage fathers: The impact of early childbearing on the parents' personal and professional lives. *Family Planning Perspectives*, 1978, *10*, 199–205.

Connolly, L. Boy fathers. *Human Behavior*, 1978, 40–43.

de Lissovoy, V. Child care by adolescent parents. *Children Today*, 1973, *2*, 22–25.

Earls, F., & Siegel, B. Precocious fathers. *American Journal of Orthopsychiatry*, 1980, *50*, 469–480.

Field, T., Widmayer, S. M., Stringer, S., & Ignatoff, E. Teenage, lower-class black mothers and their preterm infants: An intervention and developmental follow-up. *Child Development*, 1980, *51*, 426–436.

Finkel, M., & Finkel, D. Sexual and contraceptive knowledge, attitudes and behavior of male adolescents. *Family Planning Perspectives*, 1975, *7*, 256–260.

Fisher, J. B. Developing a profile of the father of babies born to school-age mothers in Michigan. *The Voice*, 1979, 2–4.

Flake-Hobson, C., Robinson, B., & Skeen, P. *Child Development and Relationships*. Reading, Mass.: Addison-Wesley, 1983.

Foster, C. D., & Miller, G. M. Adolescent pregnancy: A challenge for counselors. *Personnel and Guidance Journal*, 1980, *59*, 236–240.

Furstenberg, F. F. *Unplanned parenthood: The social consequences of teenage childbearing*. New York: The Free Press, 1976.

Furstenberg, F. F. Teenage parenthood and family support. *Dimensions*, 1980, *9*, 49–54.

Furstenberg, F. F., & Talvitie, K. G. Children's names and paternal claims: Bonds between unmarried fathers and their children. *Journal of Family Issues*, 1980, *1*, 31–57.

Hendricks, L. E. Unwed adolescent fathers: Problems they face and their sources of social support. *Adolescence*, 1980, *15*, 861–869.

Hendricks, L. E. Suggestions for reaching unmarried black adolescent fathers. *Child Welfare*, 1983, *62*, 141–146.

Howard, M. Improving services for young fathers. *Sharing*. Washington, D.C. Child Welfare League of America, 1975.

Johnson, L. B., & Staples, R. E. Family planning and the young minority male: A pilot project. *The Family Coordinator*, 1979, *28*, 535–543.

Johnson, S. Two pioneer programs help unwed teenage fathers cope. *The New York Times*, March 1978, pp. 54.

Kinard, E. M., & Klerman, L. V. Teenage parenting and child abuse: Are they related? *American Journal of Orthopsychiatry*, 1980, *50*, 481–488.

Leashore, B. R. Human services and the unmarried father: The "forgotten half." *The Family Coordinator*, 1979, *28*, 529–534.

Lorenzi, M. E., Klerman, L. V., & Jekel, J. F. School-age parents: How permanent a relationship? *Adolescence*, 1977, *12*, 13–22.

Lyons, D. J. Developing a program for pregnant teenagers through the cooperation of school, health department and federal agencies. *American Journal of Public Health*, 1968, *58*, 2225–2230.

McCallister, S. Promoting adolescent male sexual responsibility. Paper presented at the Snow/WACSAP Conference, Washington, October 1979.

McHenry, P. C., Walters, L. H., & Johnson, C. Adolescent pregnancy: A review of the literature. *The Family Coordinator*, 1979, *28*, 17–28.

McMurray, G. L. Project teen aid: A community action approach to services for pregnant unmarried teenagers. *American Journal of Public Health*, 1968, *58*, 1484–1853.

National Center for Health Statistics. *Vital statistics of the United States.* Washington, D.C.: U.S. Government Printing Office, 1979.

Nettleton, C. A., & Cline, D. W. Dating patterns, sexual relationships and use of contraceptives of 700 unwed mothers during a two-year period following delivery. *Adolescence*, 1975, *37*, 45–57.

Nye, F. I., & Lamberts, M. B. *School-age parenthood: Consequences for babies, mothers, fathers, grandparents, and others.* Pullman, Washington: Washington State University Cooperative Extension Bulletin 0667, 1980.

Pannor, R., & Evans, B. W. The unmarried father: An integral part of casework services to the unmarried mother. *Child Welfare*, 1965, 15–20.

Pannor, R., & Evans, B. W. The unmarried father revisited. *The Journal of School Health*, 1975, *45*, 286–291.

Parke, R. D., Power, T. G., & Fisher, T. The adolescent father's impact on the mother and child. *Journal of Social Issues*, 1980, *36*, 88–106.

Pauker, J. D. Fathers of children conceived out of wedlock: Pregnancy, high school, psychological test results. *Developmental Psychology*, 1971, *4*, 215–218.

Phipps-Yonas, S. Teenage pregnancy and motherhood: A review of the literature. *American Journal of Orthopsychiatry*, 1980, *50*, 403–431.

Pierce, A. D. Adoption policy and the "unwed father": An exploratory study of social worker response to changing conceptions of fatherhood. *Dissertation Abstracts International*, 1981, *42*, 387A.

Plionis, B. M. Adolescent pregnancy: Review of the literature. *Social Work*, 1975, *20*, 302–307.

Platts, K. A public adoption agency's approach to natural fathers. *Child Welfare*, 1968, *47*, 530–537.

Robinson, B. E., Barret, R. L., & Skeen, P. Locus of control of unwed adolescent fathers versus adolescent nonfathers. *Perceptual and Motor Skills*, 1983, *56*, 397–398.

Rothstein, A. A. Adolescent males, fatherhood, and abortion. *Journal of Youth and Adolescence*, 1978, *7*, 203–214.

Scarr-Salapatek, S., & Williams, M. L. The effects of early stimulation on low-birth weight infants. *Child Development*, 1973, *44*, 94–101.

Scott, K., Field, T., & Robertson, E. (Eds.). *Teenage parents and their offspring.* New York: Grune & Stratton, 1980.

Silk, S. D. Cognitive and social correlates of adolescent pregnancy. Paper presented at the American Psychological Association, Los Angeles, August 1981.

Stickle, G., & Ma, P. Pregnancy in adolescents: Scope of the problem. *Contemporary OB/GYN*, 1975, *5*, 85–91.

# CHAPTER NINE

# Fathers of Disabled Children

MARY JANE BROTHERSON, PHD
ANN P. TURNBULL, EDD
JEAN ANN SUMMERS, BGS
H. RUTHERFORD TURNBULL, LLB, LLM

## THE CASE OF ONE FATHER WITH A DISABLED CHILD

My son, Jay, is 16 and moderately mentally retarded. I think the most important question is *not,* "What *is* mental retardation?" It is "What does mental retardation *mean*? What does it do to us?" Here, I would like to set out some of the answers I have to that question; of course, I keep learning as Jay and I grow older.

Mental retardation means Jay and I will never be able to share some of the experiences that most fathers and sons share. For example, he will not attend the family university, as did all of my male ancestors from 1876. Unlike my father and me, Jay and I will never enjoy certain types of recreation together; for example, we will never stand where our relatives played lacrosse at Johns Hopkins University or where Babe Ruth played baseball in Yankee Stadium. The normal stages of father–son development will not be ours. It is quite one thing to brag about a son's scholastic or extracurricular activities at school or college; I remember clearly my own father's admonition to follow in his footsteps as editor-in-chief of the college newspaper and his pride when I was elected to that position. It is quite another to proclaim that one's son has learned to read a clock at the age of 16. At 16, I acquired a driver's license and the right [at that time] to drink beer in New York, where I lived; at the same age, Jay amuses himself

Mary Jane Brotherson is at the University of Minnesota-Duluth. Ann P. Turnbull, Jean Ann Summers, and H. Rutherford Turnbull are at the University of Kansas.

by being driven everywhere he needs to go and ordering soft drinks.

*Mental retardation means a loss of part of fatherhood*: Jay will always be my boy but never fully my son. Mental retardation means I must make different assumptions about Jay than about his nonhandicapped sisters. I must rethink such matters as where he will live, how, and with whom; whether he will work and where; and whether my estate will be sufficient for him (with or without government benefits). Moreover, the difference in fatherhood of Jay and of our daughters is manifest daily. With my wife, Ann, I am the mediator of his behavior, always on guard (and therefore always experiencing overt or covert stress) that he not become too lethargic and withdrawn or too hyperactive. My nonhandicapped daughters, ages 8 and 5, usually instinctively regulate their own behavior and usually can judge its appropriateness without my intervention. Further, the advice and guidance I give Jay differs significantly from what I counsel my daughters to do; it is far more concerned with rudimentary behavior than with the subtleties of personal behavior. *Mental retardation means a different type of fatherhood.*

Mental retardation means I learn different things from Jay than I learn from anyone else. He has enabled me in my legal career. I would have remained a public law generalist if it had not been for Jay; but because I am his father I have been driven by myself and others (particularly Jay) to a career in disability law. Moreover, Jay is my impetus to develop competence in the application of ethics to professional practices involving mentally retarded citizens. In this vein he makes me more fully aware of my mission in life, of the reason for my existence. It is said that parents of mentally retarded children often find that their children intensify the existential aspects of their lives. That is true of Jay and me. In addition, Jay teaches me about the meaning of personal and professional integrity and about the merger of the two. Because of the way he relates to others and because of Ann, whom I met because of Jay through work in the Association for Retarded Citizens, Jay has taught me about unconditional love, about nonmanipulative relationships, and about tolerance. In short, Jay has contributed to my professional, moral, and personal growth in ways I could never have anticipated. *Mental retardation means a fuller type of fatherhood.*

Jay's mental retardation is not just a static condition of one person's disability. It is a process of development that, for a father, is full of contradiction. Jay forces me to deal with paradoxes: about how the exceptional in life (mental retardation) becomes the unexceptional by reason of its familiarity, about how a person's disability (Jay's) contributes to another's ability (mine) by stimulating growth, and about how the mysteries of life ("why me?") are answered, bit by bit, but ever so certainly.

**Rud Turnbull**
*Lawrence, Kansas*

Disabled children include children with mental retardation, visual impairment, hearing impairment, physical disabilities, learning disabilities, chronic illness, and emotional disturbance. Much research in the last three decades has focused on families with disabled children, that is, how families affect disabled children as well as how disabled children affect their families. This interest has grown in part as a result of deinstitutionalization (integrating disabled persons into their own homes and/or community, rather than placing them apart in public or private institutions). As a result of deinstitutionalization, many disabled children live at home with their families, thereby influencing everyone in the family, including fathers.

Research studies and intervention programs that focus on the role of fathers of disabled children are rare. Most research has focused on the mother–child dyad, and the bulk of parent training and intervention programs for parents with disabled children have mainly been "mother" programs with the greatest emphasis on young children (Berger & Foster, 1983). Bristol and Gallagher (1983) reported that a review of 60 studies of parent involvement in early education programs for disabled preschoolers revealed no studies assessing the effects of the fathers' attitudes or interaction patterns on their disabled children (Wiegerink, Hocutt, Posante-Lore, & Bristol, 1980). The few research studies that have been done have not involved direct observation of fathers and their disabled children but have mostly relied on the impressions of professionals and at best have involved interviews with the fathers (Lamb, 1983). As depicted in the opening case study the impact of a disabled child on fathers is great.

What do social service professionals know about fathers of disabled children? Are they the same or different from other fathers? How should we work with fathers of disabled children in order to offer the greatest assistance to them? A greater understanding of the father's role is needed in order to mobilize family strengths and develop programs that offer maximum benefit.

## REACTIONS OF FATHERS TO THE DISABLED CHILD

It is obvious that fathers of disabled children experience some benefits and drawbacks very different from those of fathers of nondisabled children. Obviously, within the group of fathers with disabled children there is a great variety of responses of fathers to children; the responses depend on the type and degree of the child's disability and the fathers' individual values and coping strategies. In a study that examined the successes and failures of involving fathers in early childhood special education programs attended by their children, Markowitz (1983) found through telephone interviews with program directors that the values and attitudes of the fathers was a key factor in their level of participation. Almost 50% of the interviewees reported that fathers who have a traditional concept of parenting roles (see Chapter 3 for a discussion of traditional fathering) are less likely to be involved in their children's programs. Fathers who value education, motherhood as a "creative role," participation in their children's activities as a "religious duty," or attach special meaning to children (for example, namesake, first boy, first live birth, etc.) are much more likely to be involved in their children's programs. Markowitz also found that fathers of severely disabled children were much more likely to participate in programs than fathers of mildly disabled children.

Not surprisingly, fathers with disabled children do not all experience the same amount of stress, nor do they respond to stress in the same way. Interviews from a sample of 29 "successful" and 21 "average" mothers and fathers of moderately and severely handicapped preschool children revaled that 48% of the fathers did not report any measurable stress, despite the presence of a disabled child in their families (Gallagher, Cross, & Scharfman, 1981). Assuming the validity of these data, these fathers were successful at adapting and coping with the stress of raising a disabled child. They did report that a change in vacations, social activities, and recreation was one of the major consequences of having a disabled child. These fathers used the strategy of informal support networks to reduce stress. Both fathers and mothers in these successful and average families regarded strong support from spouse and friends as very important in helping them adapt to their disabled child. Fathers and mothers regarded support from neighbors as less important.

Another coping strategy used by some fathers of disabled children to reduce stress is "reframing" (McCubbin & Patterson, 1981). Reframing is based on adopting a positive perspective and involves the ability to identify conditions that can be successfully altered, to initiate problem solving, and to identify conditions beyond one's control and make attitude adjustments to live with them constructively. Reframing is exemplified in a quote from one father of a mentally retarded son:

> I always felt and still feel that I'm fortunate to have a handicapped person in my family. It is through him that I've learned tolerance for other people of lesser abilities and different abilities. I know that my teaching has been deeply affected by him. I no longer judge a student on the basis of what he can do in mathematics. I try to look at him as a

person. I don't think less of a person because he lacks some physical ability, like jumping seven feet. So, Robin's handicap has been a very constructive influence in my life. (Helsels, 1978, p. 104)

Reframing is also exemplified by the father in the opening case. He solved such problems as future planning and made attitude adjustments like accentuating the positive effect his son has on his life, both personally and professionally.

There is limited evidence that the father's ability to reframe and accept his disabled child may set the pattern of acceptance or rejection of the disabled child in the family. Researchers studied ten families with mentally retarded children to examine their patterns of acceptance and rejection (Peck & Stephens, 1960). The authors found a high correlation between the father's acceptance or rejection of the child and the amount of acceptance or rejection by other family members. The correlation between the mother's acceptance and the amount of acceptance in the family was not significant. Two explanations offered for this finding were (1) that fathers set the pattern in the home or (2) fathers are better able than mothers to express their subjective feelings about their mentally retarded child.

Many researchers agree that most fathers are adversely affected by the birth or presence of a disabled child, particularly a retarded child (Cummings, 1976; Murphy, 1982; Price-Bonham & Addison, 1978; Ryckman & Henderson, 1965; Tallman, 1965). Cummings (1976) studied equal numbers of fathers of mentally retarded children, of chronically ill children, and of healthy children. He found that fathers of mentally retarded and chronically ill children experience a greater negative impact from fatherhood than fathers of healthy children, and fathers of retarded children revealed significantly more negative effects than fathers of chronically ill children.

The fathers of mentally retarded and chronically ill children experienced lowered self-esteem, depressive feelings, and lower confidence in their ability to be fathers, and also seemed to undergo long-term negative personality changes. Cummings proposed several factors that might account for the greater negative effect on fathers of mentally retarded and chronically ill children. One, fathers are confronted with daily reminders of their child's deficiency. Two, fathers usually have fewer opportunities than mothers to do something directly helpful for their disabled child, and thus counterbalance their sense of loss and frustration. Finally, fathers have fewer opportunities than mothers for services to reduce stress. They are less adequately served than mothers in supportive mental health and social service programs designed for parents who have disabled children.

Some fathers of disabled children report no measurable stress (Gallagher et al., 1981), while others are negatively affected by their child (Cummings, 1976). Some fathers do not experience benefits, whereas others are very clear about benefits experienced, as in the father in the case study, whose son taught him about integrity, unconditional love, nonmanipulative relationships, and tolerance. Fathers of disabled children do, indeed, experience very different reactions to raising their child.

## MARITAL RELATIONS

Many studies of families with disabled children have focused on the parent's marriage, but data on the specific effects of disabled children on the marital relationship are inconsistent. Divorce, marital disharmony, and the desertion rate of fathers all have been reported to be disproportionately high for parents of disabled children (Gath, 1977; Love, 1973; Reed & Reed, 1965). One research team assessed marital harmony in 59 families with a child with spina bifida initially following the birth of the child (Tew, Payne, & Lawrence, 1974). After maintaining contact with these families for 8–10 years, they found that the parents had lower marital harmony and twice the divorce rate of a control group with no disabled children. Other studies (Farber, 1959, 1960, 1962; Farber & Jenne, 1963) examined the impact of mentally retarded children on marriages and found a negative impact on marital integration and communication. Parents of children with cystic fibrosis have also reported severely strained marital relationships and lack of communication (Murphy, 1982). In a 12-family research study we conducted (at the Research and Training Center on Independent Living, University of Kansas), one father of a daughter with cerebral palsy told us how his daughter had affected the communication in his marriage:

> We've never been able to argue in front of her [the disabled daughter]. There have been no raised voices from the time she was very young. We couldn't raise our voices in front of her or she would cry. She felt her security rested between both of us—if we would argue, she felt insecure. We've never been able to get into some good hard arguments because it would upset her—you need a good hard argument every once in awhile.

Fathers, compared with mothers, have more difficulty coping with their severely retarded children, and they are especially vulnerable to social stigma and extrafamilial influences (Tallman, 1965). Differences between fathers and mothers in coping styles can be problematic for their marriage (Price-Bonham & Addison, 1978; Wikler, 1981). For example, a mother's primary coping style of using community and social support could increase the father's stress over potential social stigma and invasion of privacy. A father experiencing intense grief could be less responsive to the needs of his wife concerning the burden of physical care (Wikler, 1981).

Although much research indicates the existence of marital problems in couples having disabled children, Schufeit and Wurster (1976) found that when parents of mentally retarded children are matched for social class with parents of nondisabled children, divorce rate does not differ significantly. In a study comparing 30 parents of Down Syndrome infants with 30 parents with nondisabled infants, limited differences were found in the mental or physical health of the parents, but marital breakdown or severe marital disharmony existed in nine of the families with Down Syndrome children and in none of the controls (Gath, 1977). Almost half of the parents of disabled children in the study felt drawn closer together and felt their marriages were strengthened rather than weakened by their shared experiences. This was consistent with the findings of previous studies that were conducted with parents of older Down Syndrome children (Gath, 1973, 1974). Similar results were reported from fathers of children with fibrocystic disease. Fifty-three percent of these fathers believed that their problems and distress in raising a disabled child had brought them closer to their wives (Burton, 1975).

One couple we interviewed described the impact of their multihandicapped, 18-year-old daughter on their marriage. "We had been married 14 years when Rachel was born. Her presence in our famliy didn't exactly strengthen our marriage, but it added a new dimension. Our life has never been boring."

The conclusion of these mixed research results indicates that the disabled child in a marriage can be "the straw that breaks the camel's back." For those parents whose marriages are fragile, problematic, and unstable before the birth of their disabled child, their child may be the factor that causes their marriage to dissolve. For those parents who have strong and cohesive marriages before the birth of their disabled child, their child may bring increased closeness, strength, and happiness in the shared experiences of raising a disabled child.

## PARENTAL ROLES

Research with fathers and mothers of disabled children suggests that the presence of a disabled child in the family tends to highlight parental role differences in fulfilling family functions (Gallagher *et al.*, 1981;

Gumz & Gubrium, 1972; Tallman, 1965). Different family members assume varying degrees of responsibility for different functions such as, physical, economic, rest and recuperation, self-definition, affection, guidance, and education (Turnbull, Brotherson, & Summers, 1984).

Historically, whether a mother or father primarily fulfilled a given function has been influenced by a traditional concept of family roles. This concept of family roles led to the Parsons-Bales role theory (Parsons & Bales, 1955), which for many years was considered a framework to conceptualize the family as a social system involving complementary roles. As noted in Chapter 1, Parsons and Bales (1955) characterize the male role as primarily "instrumental," focusing on the external world and responsible for establishing the social and economic position of the family in society. They characterize the female role as primarily "expressive" in nature, responsible for the emotional and affective climate of the home as well as domestic and chlid-care activities. The father's role was initially considered unimportant during infancy, only becoming important as the child began to interact with the larger social world (Lamb, 1981). Instrumental family functions include those related to "external affairs" of the family (e.g., having stable employment, adequate shelter, formal education, and sufficient income). Expressive family functions include those related to the "internal affairs" of the family (e.g., giving affection, maintaining routine, and managing tension). Some researchers have confirmed that although sex differences along each function do not appear to be as dramatic and widespread as Parsons and Bales reported, this framework is useful for differentiating between maternal and paternal roles within the family (Lamb, 1981).

Three studies conducted with fathers and mothers of disabled children examined instrumental and expressive role functions in the family (Tallman, 1965; Gumz & Gubrium, 1972; Gallagher et al., 1981). Tallman (1965) interviewed and analyzed the responses of 69 fathers and 80 mothers of mentally retarded children and found that the presence of a severely retarded child in the family tended to highlight the parental role differences. His results established the existence of clear patterns of differentiation between mothers and fathers along the lines predicted by the Parsons–Bales (1955) role theory (see Chapter 1). Tallman predicted "that fathers will react most strongly to the impact of factors involving the retarded child which affect their image in the outside world, while mothers will react more to those elements which influence their interpersonal relations within the family unit" (p. 38).

Gumz and Gubrium (1972) also compared the attitudes and percep-tions of parents of mentally retarded children, using the instrumental–

expressive role framework. Their sample consisted of 50 fathers and 50 mothers from families of mildly and moderately mentally retarded children. They found that more mothers than fathers were highly concerned with the emotional crisis involved in having a retarded child; the additional care-of-child time, emotional strain, and ability to maintain family harmony and integration. Fathers showed a higher degree of concern about their child in roles outside the family than within the family. They also found that a high percentage of mothers were concerned about the severe financial problems associated with raising a retarded child, a concern that Parsons and Bales (1955) attributed to the instrumental role of the father. This would suggest that mothers, many of whom were employed, were assuming a more instrumental role in the area of economic planning. Concern over future economic problems, however, does seem to be a prevalent instrumental role stress of many fathers with disabled children (Hersh, 1970). This is evident in this chapter's case study, as the father is concerned about whether or not his estate will be sufficient to secure his son's future. Economic concern is also exemplified by another father of a mentally retarded son, who states:

> I suppose this [worrying about the future] is the biggest worry that a parent of a severely handicapped child has—what happens when I die? And there is no answer to that. As far as I know, there is no way to provide properly for him in the eventuality—at least, I don't know of any. (Helsels, 1978, p. 106)

Gallagher and his associates (1981), in a study with 50 fathers and 50 mothers of moderately and severely disabled children, found strong agreement between mothers and fathers on who was taking major responsibility for a particular role. Fathers predominantly played the roles of provider, protector, and outside home and equipment maintainer. Mothers predominantly played the roles of bookkeeper, food shopper, food preparer, inside home maintainer, social hostess, nurse, child transporter, and clothing selector. These authors stated that when parents were asked to check stressful life changes related to raising a disabled child, mothers checked "change in sleeping habits" as a stressful consequence much more frequently than fathers. This would indicate that it is the mother who has the major responsibility for child care, as is the case when the disabled child disrupts sleeping patterns.

These roles identified by fathers and mothers parallel the traditional spousal role differentiation of father-instrumental and mother-expressive. It is notable, however, that when asked to state the "ideal" role allocation, both fathers and mothers in this study indicated fathers should take a more active role in teaching, nursing, child discipline, transportation, clothing selection, and recreation. Fathers clearly believed they should be more committed to an active expressive role in their interactions with their child. The reason this does not or is not happening needs further investigation.

Gallagher and his colleagues (1981) state "the traditional father roles of physical playmate and model for the male child are largely diminished or not present at all with moderately to severely handicapped children" (p. 13). As in this chapter's case study, the father cannot take the male role with his disabled child that his father took with him. What then are the alternative role functions for fathers? As professionals we need to help fathers of disabled children identify and implement different or alternative role functions with emphasis on expanding expressive roles.

## EFFECTS ON FATHERS OF RAISING A DISABLED CHILD

Fathers of disabled children are much more negatively affected by raising a disabled son, as compared to raising a disabled daughter. However, research examining a sex-linked impact has almost solely been conducted with fathers of mentally retarded children.

Fathers, regardless of social class, experience a markedly greater initial impact if the retarded child is a boy, and mothers experience a slightly higher impact if the retarded child is a girl (Farber, Jenne, & Toigo, 1960). Fathers and mothers of retarded boys have shown a lower degree of marital integration than fathers and mothers of retarded girls (Farber, 1962). This may support the conclusion that the father sets the pattern of acceptance in the home; if a father experiences more stress from a male child, the marital integration of both parents suffers (Peck & Stephens, 1960).

Not only are fathers generally more adversely affected by a retarded son than a daughter, they are also less skillful than mothers in coping with their retarded children of either sex (Tallman, 1965). One researcher found that fathers tend to react in extremes (great involvement or total withdrawal) if the child is a boy and in routine fashion if the child is a girl (Tallman, 1965). He asserted that the greater the impact on the father, the greater the tendency to react in extremes.

Many fathers of mentally retarded children are more concerned about the roles their children play outside the home than within the home (Gumz & Gubrium, 1972) and are concerned about the attributes of their child that tend to stigmatize their family's social or community image (Tallman, 1965). Retarded children and youth, regardless of sex, often develop familial skills traditionally associated with the feminine role such as nonassertiveness, housekeeping, and domestic abilities. They are less likely to develop nonfamilial skills traditionally associated with the male role such as prowess in athletics, school achievement, and leadership. A father of a mentally retarded boy described to us the contribution of his son to family life on the farm.

> I had hoped to get Tom started in a project around the farm. I wanted to get him a sheep. But he was never interested—it just wasn't his cup of tea. Tom wasn't able to do outside work. We didn't want him to get hurt. He helped in the house on making beds.

Fathers may perceive their retarded sons as having greater role deviance than their retarded daughters. For example, it likely would be easier for them to feel pride over a 17-year-old daughter learning how to set the table, as opposed to a 17-year-old son. Their role expectations could more seriously be violated when sons are retarded, as compared to daughters. The father in our case study stated an expected role deviation when he compared what he had done at age 16—acquiring a driver's license and the right to drink beer—with what his son is doing at that same age—learning to read a clock. Fathers also may feel denied the opportunity to function as socializing agents for their sons in roles outside the home with more social stigma associated with sons as compared with daughters (Tallman, 1965).

One father of a severely disabled, nonambulatory son expressed to us his disappointment in not being able to share what he considered to be sex-linked hobbies with his son: "I would have liked to have taken him fishing and hunting. I try not to think about it. It is one of the things you put up with."

## LIFE STAGE TRANSITIONS AND STRESS

A widely held view in the literature is that fathers and mothers of disabled children experience an initial period of shock, denial, and guilt upon the diagnosis of a disabling condition and then move into a sustained period of reorganization (e.g., Simeonson & Simeonson, 1981; Wolfensberger, 1970). On the contrary, burden of care, lack of socialization, financial burdens and many other parental stresses triggered by raising a disabled child are chronic, while others emerge and reemerge over time (Wikler, 1981). One can expect fathers of disabled children to reexperience emotional upset and the need to readjust and reorganize as new stresses emerge at different points in the life cycle.

One father of a 22-year-old physically disabled daughter described to us his feelings in dealing with the life-long implications of his daughter's disability:

> It's not that simple [raising a disabled child], there are many days when I go to church and curse out the Lord and say what the hell are you doing—that goes on for a long time—and every time I have another problem, I go back and ask Him the same thing. But what it does do, however, is build up my faith with God—I build up stronger ties. But there is also a tremendous hatred as to why this is happening—why has he put such a burden on such an innocent child. It is a very hard thing to come to grasp with—I don't know if I ever have. I just accept it, I don't understand it.

The family life cycle can be divided into seven stages of family development: coupling, childbearing, rearing school age children, rearing adolescents, launching, postparental, and aging (Duvall, 1957; Olson, McCubbin, Barnes, Larsen, Muxen, & Wilson, 1983). Family life cycle stages often overlap, and families may dissolve before some stages occur (Hubbell, 1981). Nevertheless, most families seem to move through these seven stages. Transitions from one stage to the next frequently have been identified as major points of family stress and dysfunction (Carter & McGoldrick, 1980, Terkelson, 1980). Family theorists suggest that even greater stress is created when transitions occur off-time in light of the expected family life rhythm (Harkins, 1978; Neugarten, 1976). For many fathers of disabled children and youth, there are additional stresses at the transition points, when transitions occur off-time, or when they fail to occur at all.

Much of the literature on stages and stage transitions in families with disabled children has focused on mothers, or both parents, with very little attention being given directly to fathers (MacKeith, 1973; Travis, 1976). Entering school is a transition point that can cause reemergence of stress for both fathers and mothers. It is the time when they often have to deal with the "labeling" of their child and realistically face the level of their child's disability in terms of academic achievement (MacKeith, 1973; Travis, 1976). The father of a severely disabled child characterized stress at the transition point into school as follows:

> Underneath my well-adjusted surface, shock, denial, and fear remained, though they were buried and sublimated. At times these feelings found their way into the world again. Once it happened when Parnel and I were shopping for presents for Diana's fifth birthday.

> After we left the toy store, Parnel burst into tears. "I don't want to buy those infant toys for her. I want her to go to first grade this year like everyone else."
> "So do I, Parn, So do I," I answered. (Searl, 1978, p. 28)

Adolescence is another transition period of reemergent stress for fathers and mothers (see Chapter 4). Not only is it a time that often has physiological and psychological difficulties for the teenager, but it also brings to the forefront concerns about the permanence of the disability and concerns about future dependency (MacKeith, 1973). Parental aging can also cause a period of family transition and crisis. It is a time when both parents begin to have limited physical ability to care for a dependent son or daughter and begin to experience heightened concern over future financial stability.

Wikler (1981) suggests that stress reemerges for parents over the life cycle when there is a discrepancy between what parents expect of their son's or daughter's development and their own parenting in contrast with what actually takes place. She identified 10 critical potentially stressful periods for parents, five related to life-cycle transitions and five related to experiences occurring only in families of mentally retarded persons. The life-cycle transitions are (1) child should have begun walking, (2) child should have begun talking, (3) beginning of public school, (4) onset of puberty, and (5) 21st birthday (symbolic of independence). Results from interviews showed that 67% of both parents and social workers believed that parents experience chronic sorrow across developmental stages (Wikler, Wasow, & Hatfield, 1981). Interestingly, social workers tended to overestimate how upsetting the parents' early experiences were and to underestimate the stress of later life-cycle transitions.

Other findings justify focusing greater attention on the needs of fathers and mothers at later developmental stages (Bristol & Schopler, 1983). Older autistic children are more stressful than younger ones, and both community acceptance and services are lessened as children grow older. The varying needs of fathers and mothers over the life cycle are reflected in differential use of both personal and professional support networks at various stages of the life cycle (Suelzle & Keenan, 1981). Suelzle and Keenan reported that parents of older mentally retarded children were less supported, more isolated, and more in need of expanded services than were fathers and mothers of young retarded children.

Father–infant, father–child, father–adolescent and father–adult relationships represent different stages with different stresses in the evolution of a developing relationship between two individuals. We must understand the varying impact and stresses of this evolution on fathers in order to provide timely and effective assistance.

## CONCLUSION

Fathers of disabled children experience varying degrees of stress and respond to that stress with a variety of coping strategies to deal with the acute as well as the reemerging stresses over the life cycle. They experience various degrees of personal and professional growth as a result of raising a disabled child. Many fathers feel lowered self-esteem and ineffectiveness as fathers (Cummings, 1976), while others find their children to be a significant source of fulfillment and self-esteem (Lamb, 1983). Many fathers of disabled children experience greater marital difficulties, while others experience a heightened closeness and intimacy with their wives as a result of sharing the joys and sorrows of raising a child with special needs. Fathers of disabled children are a complex group with varying needs based on their own values and resources and on the particular characteristics of their disabled child.

Fathers of disabled children fulfill a mainly instrumental role in the family. However, they, like fathers in general (Eversoll, 1979; Young &

### INCREASING FATHER INVOLVEMENT WITH HANDICAPPED CHILDREN

Fathers as well as mothers of handicapped children need information on the unique needs involved in child care, and they need an abundance of psychological support to allay feelings of helplessness and depression resulting from the demands handicapped children place on a family.

A unique approach that is supporting parents of handicapped children has been initiated by the Cantalician Center for Learning in Buffalo, New York. Supported by a grant from the Handicapped Children's Early Education Program, staff members developed a comprehensive outreach program called The Family–Infant Program for families with handicapped children. This program stresses that father involvement can make a significant difference in the successful family adaptation to the handicapped child. From the initial telephone contact clients are told that fathers need to be present at the intake interview. The intake itself is directed to responses of the entire family to the handicapped child. Rather than seeking information solely from mothers, fathers are specifically asked to give information about their children. Fathers, along with other family members, are asked to identify their expectations and needs from the center. A treatment plan then is developed in response to the needs of each family member. A major aspect of this plan is the identification of the center's resources for the father and a clear list of goals that will be met by father participation in monthly training sessions. The father is

Hamilton, 1979), are seeking a greater expressive role in their interactions with their child. With a commitment to an expanded parental role and with assistance from professionals, fathers can learn to fulfill new and alternative roles for both disabled sons and daughters across all life-cycle stages.

A father's family involvement is vital to helping the family meet the added challenges and demands of raising a disabled child. Their participation in educational programs for young disabled children was reported by program directors to have had a positive effect on successful family functioning in such ways as reduced stress, better communication, more consistent child discipline, more shared responsibilities, and greater acceptance of the child (Markowitz, 1983). Fathers are an integral part of the total family system. It is a heartening trend that the effect of the father on the family with a disabled child as well as the effect of the disabled child on the father have become increasing concerns of both researchers and service providers. One such support program for fathers is described in the box entitled "Increasing Father Involvement with Handicapped Children."

expected to be present at monthly meetings.

To encourage father involvement, a male staff member models appropriate male behavior with children and reassures the father that not only female staff members will guide him. Since many fathers cannot be present during normal working hours, flexible hours are required.

New father participants are paired with fathers who have been active for several months. These "veteran" fathers attempt to create a relationship with new fathers to encourage them to be more aware of the benefits of father participation. This is done by telephone contacts, providing transportation to the center, and by sharing experiences about child care. These enthusiastic "veterans" seem to be a key ingredient in increasing father involvement.

Fathers are expected to participate in four teaching sessions annually, which are just for fathers and their infants. Fathers learn from each other as they become involved in the activities planned on these special days.

The fathers have become eager participants in their children's care and education. The Family–Infant Program is built on the recognition that fathers do have a great influence on their children's lives, and the program attempts to maximize this influence positively. Perhaps the most important reward of this program has been the reduction of family stresses and the generation of a positive and enthusiastic paternal attitude.

*Susan Zippiroli*
*Karen Schwabish*

## SUGGESTIONS TO PROFESSIONALS

*1.* To work effectively with fathers of disabled children, it is important for service providers to have knowledge about and experience
with disabled children. These fathers will be able to detect whether or
not you feel comfortable discussing their child's needs or interacting
with their child. One of the best ways to demonstrate your acceptance
of these fathers is to accept and respect their children. If you have
limited knowledge about disabilities, the resource list at the end of the
chapter will be helpful in providing you with information sources. If
you have had limited contact with disabled children, consider spending time in one-to-one relationships with the children of fathers with
whom you work. Many disabled children have limited invitations for
social outings, so it is likely that their fathers would especially appreciate your taking an interest, and it would provide you with a rich
learning opportunity.

*2.* Fathers of disabled children may need help in identifying ways to
make positive contributions to their children. You may need to encourage fathers to identify alternative roles that they can fulfill when
the paternal roles with which they are most familiar are largely diminished or inappropriate in light of their disabled child's needs. Fathers of
disabled children have few "role models" to provide information and
give them support in expressive roles or alternative roles of fatherhood. One way to address this need is to set up a father support group.
Another strategy is to arrange "mentor" relationships in which fathers
who have creatively devised meaningful roles are paired with fathers
who need assistance and guidance.

*3.* Assist fathers in developing effective coping strategies to deal
with the stress of raising a disabled child. One effective coping strategy
is reframing. Encourage fathers to examine and identify the positive
benefits that have occurred to them and other families members as a
result of raising a disabled child. Encourage fathers to approach new
problems from a positive perspective of: "How can I view this situation
in the most constructive way possible?" Assist them in developing and
using effective problem-solving skills.

*4.* Fathers may benefit from your assistance with future planning
to prepare them to anticipate changes and stresses that occur over the
life cycle. Future planning can identify high stress periods so that
additional supports can be provided from a proactive rather than a
reactive stance in those critical periods. Cummings (1976) found that
fathers of mentally retarded children, as compared with fathers of
chronically ill or healthy children, showed a significantly higher need
for orderliness, organization, and routine. This finding suggests that

future planning of activities, particularly for these fathers, can reduce the stress of father–child interactions. You might consider assisting fathers in identifying the residential and vocational settings in which their sons or daughters are likely to function as adults. Observations of such settings as group home, sheltered workshop, and competitive employment can be extremely helpful in identifying critical skills for success and developing a program to teach these skills.

5. Aid fathers in locating information to provide them with necessary knowledge. Many fathers of disabled children have a great need for information relating to disability; information on aspects of their own child's disability such as information on spina bifida, cerebral palsy, mental retardation; information on legal issues and policies relating to rights and benefits for disabled people; and information on estate planning, guardianship, and consent issues. In addition to reading professional literature, fathers may also benefit from information on the personal experiences of other parents concerning how they reacted to and coped with raising a disabled child. *Bibliotherapy* (the use of reading material for personal assessment, adjustment, and growth, see Mullins, 1983) is an under-used intervention strategy for many fathers of disabled children. Professionals need to be aware of and judiciously select readings that can provide fathers with information to meet their needs. Judiciously selected reading might reduce worry of fathers about the future by assisting them in learning about possible independent lifestyles for their child as well as how to personally and financially plan for life-cycle changes. Further information on using bibliotherapy with families having disabled children is described by Mullins (1983). A list of reading material from which selections can be drawn and matched to the individual needs of particular fathers is included in the resource list.

6. Help fathers understand the effects of the disabled family member on the entire family system (see Chapter 1). Fathers generally feel a responsibility for the well-being of the total family. Professionals should assist fathers of disabled children in understanding not only the impact of the disabled child on themselves, but also on their wives, other children, and extended family members. It is often difficult for parents to recognize the need to balance the interests of various family members and to realize that their own personal needs are as legitimate as the needs of every other member. For example, the father in the case study stated that he and his wife must be "mediators" of their son's behavior at home, and the mediation role results in covert or overt stress in always feeling as if they must be "on guard." They need opportunities to turn mediation over to someone else so they can be relieved of this responsibility. They also need support from service

providers in underscoring the legitimacy of the needs of all family members. The balancing of interests can require parents to make difficult choices; however, service providers can assist fathers in this process by helping them view the family as an interacting system, with the mental health of the family resting on a balance of meeting everyone's needs.

7. Assist fathers in developing and using both informal and formal support networks. Although support services are often available to fathers of disabled children, it is sometimes very difficult for them to use those services. Barriers include time conflicts with father's work schedule, the father's perception of being in the minority with most service recipients being women, fear over a public display of emotions, time needed to locate and/or coordinate services, invasion of privacy, risk of social rejection, potential for unsupportive responses, and the need to take care of the problem oneself or not to burden someone else.

Professionals need to support fathers in the effective use of available services and resources. They also need to support fathers in the realization that, because of the many additional demands on family function, parents "can't do it all themselves." Fathers, in partnership with mothers, should be encouraged to view themselves as the case managers or "orchestrators" of family functions and use supportive services responsive to their needs and the needs of their disabled child. One model program designed to reduce stress and barriers facing a family with a disabled child is Extended Family Resources in Seattle, Washington. This program mobilizes the use of informal support services by providing monetary incentives by aunts, uncles, grandparents, friends, neighbors and volunteers who agree to provide care or training to the disabled child. An uncle, for example, may agree to take the disabled child to a community park for 2 hours a week to work on some specified motor skills, thereby providing training to the child and respite care services for the parents. This program demonstrated that trained extended family members, friends, neighbors, and volunteers can provide a range of support services to families and reduce family stress related to raising a disabled child. Additional resources for fathers of disabled children are included in the next section.

## PROFESSIONAL RESOURCES FOR WORKING WITH FATHERS OF DISABLED CHILDREN

### Books

Anderson, W., Chitwood, S., & Hayden, D. *Negotiating the special education maze.* Englewood Cliffs, N.J.: Prentice-Hall, 1982.

Atwell, A. A., & Clabby, D. A. *The retarded child: Answers to questions parents ask.* Los Angeles: Western Psychological Services, 1975.

Baker, B. L., Brightman, A. J., & Blacher, J. *Steps to independence: Playskills.* Champaign, Ill.: Research, 1983.

Baker, B. L., Brightman, A. J., & Hinshaw, S. P. *Steps to independence: Toward independent living.* Champaign, Ill.: Research, 1980.

Dougan, T., Isbell, L., & Vyas, P. *We have been there.* Nashville, Tenn.: Abingdon, 1983.

Featherstone, H. *A difference in the family: Living with a disabled child.* New York: Penguin, 1981.

Fisher, J. *A parent's guide to learning disabilities.* New York: Scribner's, 1978.

Jeffree, D. M., McConkey, R., & Hewson, S. *Teaching the handicapped child: A guide for parents and teachers.* Englewood Cliffs, N.J.: Prentice Hall, 1982.

Kauffman, J. M. *Characteristics of children's behavior disorders.* Columbus, Ohio: Merrill, 1977.

McArthur, S. H. *Raising your hearing-impaired child: A guide for parents.* Washington, D.C.: Alexander Graham Bell Association for the Deaf, 1982.

Murphy, A. T. *Special children, special parents: Personal issues with handicapped children.* Englewood Cliffs, N.J.: Prentice-Hall, 1981.

Orlansky, M. D., & Heward, W. L. *Voices: Interviews with handicapped people.* Columbus, Ohio: Merrill, 1981.

Patterson, G. R. *Living with children: New methods for parents and teachers.* Champaign, Ill.: Research, 1976.

Pearlman, L., & Scott, K. A. *Raising the handicapped child.* Englewood Cliffs, N.J.: Prentice-Hall, 1981.

Perske, R. *New life in the neighborhood: How persons with retardation and other disabilities can help make a good community better.* Nashville, Tenn.: Abingdon, 1980.

Perske, R., & Perske, M. *Hope for the families: New directions for parents of persons with retardation or other developmental disabilities.* Nashville, Tenn.: Abingdon, 1981.

Turnbull, A. P., & Turnbull, H. R. *Parents speak out. Views from the other side of the two-way mirror.* Columbus, Ohio: Merrill, 1978.

Winton, P. J., Turnbull, A. P., & Blacher, J. *Selecting a preschool: A guide for parents of handicapped children.* Baltimore: University Park Press, 1984.

## Periodicals

*Exceptional Parent Magazine.* 296 Boylston St. (Third Floor), Boston, MA 02116. A magazine that deals with the kinds of problems faced by all parents of handicapped children. It provides practical information and an exchange of parent's ideas and experiences.

*Exceptional Children.* Council for Exceptional Children, 1920 Association Drive, Reston, VA 22091. The Council for Exceptional Children is the major professional organization in the field of special education. This publication includes research articles and position papers on a wide variety of issues related to the education of handicapped and gifted students from birth to young adulthood.

## Organizations

Alexander Graham Bell Association for the Deaf, 3417 Volta Pl., N.W., Washington, DC 20007.

American Council of the Blind, 1211 Connecticut Ave., N.W., Suite 506, Washington, DC 20036.

Association for Children and Adults with Learning Disabilities, 4156 Library Rd., Pittsburgh, PA 15234.

Association for Retarded Citizens, 2501 Avenue J, Arlington, TX 76011.

The Association for the Severely Handicapped, 7010 Roosevelt Way, N.E., Seattle, WA 98115.

Epilepsy Foundation of America, 4351 Garden City Dr., Landover, MD 29781.

National Association of Sports for the Cerebral Palsied, 66 E. 34th St., New York, NY 10016.

National Easter Seal Society, 2023 W. Ogden Ave., Chicago, IL 60612.

National Handicapped Sports and Recreation Association, 4105 East Florida Ave., Denver, CO 80222.

National Mental Health Association, 1800 North Kent St., Rosslyn, VA 22209.

The National Society for Children and Adults with Autism, 1234 Massachusetts Ave., N.W., Suite 1017, Washington, DC 20005.

Spina Bifida Association of America, 343 S. Dearborn Ave., Suite 319, Chicago, IL 60604.

United Cerebral Palsy Associations, 66 E. 34th St., New York, NY 10016.

Closer Look, Box 1492, Washington, DC 20013. This is a national information center for disability-related information and is one of the best sources of information for parents and professionals.

## Reference Guides

Bisshopp, P., *Books about handicaps: For children and young adults.* Meeting Street School, 667 Waterman Avenue, E. Providence, RI 02914. An annotated bibliography of books (mostly fiction) with characters having various handicapping conditions. Each book is thoroughly described and evaluated.

Bookbinder, S. R. *Mainstreaming: What every child needs to know about disabilities.* Exceptional Parent Bookstore, 296 Boylston St. (Third Floor), Boston, MA 02116. This is a guide for elementary school teachers and parents to use in preparing disabled and nondisabled children for social and instructional interaction.

Moore, C. B., & Morton, K. G., *A reader's guide for parents of children with mental, physical or emotional disabilities* (DHEW Publication No. HSA 79-5920). Washington, D.C.: U.S. Government Printing Office, 1979.

*National catalog of films in special education.* Ohio State University Press, 2070 Neil Avenue, Columbus, OH 43210. An annotated bibliography of more than 700 films about children with disabilities.

## Programs

Atlanta Institute for Family Studies. The Atlanta Institute for Family Studies provides services for fathers through working with families and social network members of families with a disabled child. An ecological model is used combining strategic and structural family therapy and social network intervention. Training and consultation is also provided to service providers in the application of family therapy theory and techniques to working with families with disabled children. For information contact Michael Berger, Family Therapist, Atlanta Institute for Family Studies, 61 Eighth Street, N.E., Atlanta, GA 30309.

Extending Family Resources (EFR). This project is designed to reduce barriers to raising a disabled child by extending the family's support systems. Families are assisted to incorporate under-involved relatives, friends, and neighbors into the family's support network. For information write Judith Moore, Program Director, Children's Clinic and Preschool, Spastic Aid Council, Inc., 1850 Boyer Avenue East, Seattle, WA 98112.

Families with Infants in Networks of Interactional Support (FINIS). This family-focused early intervention program is designed to enhance the development of disabled infants. Services are designed to facilitate father–infant interactions and promote effective family functioning. For information contact Damon L. Lamb, Project Director, Project FINIS, 502 North 12th Avenue, Marshalltown, IA 50158.

The Family–Infant Program: Programming for Dads. This is an educational program for developmentally delayed infants and is described in detail in the box entitled Increasing Father Involvement. It is based on the belief that fathers are an untapped natural resource for early childhood programs and are an important part of the educational team. Fathers are involved in all aspects of the program. For information write Sister Raphael Marie, CSSF, Cantalician Center for Learning, 3233 Main Street, Buffalo, NY 14214.

Supporting Extended Family Members (SEFAM). The primary focus in SEFAM is on fathers of young disabled children. There are also programs for siblings and grandparents. The father program meets twice each month on Saturday mornings to provide fathers an opportunity to learn from other fathers, hear guest speakers about services and issues that will affect them and their families, and broaden their repertoire of activities appropriate for their child. SEFAM has developed a curriculum guide to aid interested service providers in developing a father's program. For information write Rebecca Fewell, Project Coordinator, Experimental Education Unit WJ-10, Child Development and Mental Retardation Center, University of Washington, Seattle, WA 98195.

## REFERENCES

Berger, M., & Foster, M. Applications of family therapy to research and interventions with families with mentally retarded children. Paper presented at NICHD Conference on "Research on Families with Retarded Persons," Rougemont, N.C., September 1983.

Bristol, M. M., & Gallagher, J. J. Psychological research on fathers of young handicapped children: Evolution, review, and some future directions. Paper presented at NICHD Conference on "Research on Families with Retarded Persons," Rougemont, N.C., September 1983.

Bristol, M. M., & Schopler, E. Stress and coping in families of autistic adolescents. In E. Schopler & G. B. Mesibov (Eds.), *Autism in adolescents and adults.* New York: Plenum, 1983.

Burton, L. *The family life of sick children.* London: Routledge & Kegan Paul, 1975.

Carter, E., & McGoldrick, M. The family life cycle and family therapy: An overview. In E. Carter & M. McGoldrick (Eds.), *The family life cycle: A framework for family therapy.* New York: Gardner, 1980.

Cummings, S. T. The impact of the child's deficiency on the father: A study of fathers of mentally retarded and of chronically ill children. *American Journal of Orthopsychiatry,* 1976, *46,* 246–255.

Duvall, E. *Family development.* Philadelphia: Lippincott, 1957.

Eversoll, D. A two generational view of fathering. *Family Coordinator,* 1979, *28,* 503–508.

Farber, B. Effects of a severely mentally retarded child on family integration. *Monographs of the Society for Research in Child Development,* 1959, *24*(2, Serial No. 71).

Farber, B. Family organization and crisis: Maintenance of integration in families with a severely retarded child. *Monographs of the Society for Research in Child Development,* 1960, *25*(*1,* Serial No. 75).

Farber, B. Effects of a severely mentally retarded child on the family. In E. P. Trapp & P. Himeleston (Eds.), *Readings on the exceptional child.* New York: Appleton Century-Crofts, 1962.

Farber, B., & Jenne, W. C. Family organization and parent–child communication: Parents and siblings of a retarded child. *Monographs of the Society for Research in Child Development,* 1963, *28*(7, Serial No. 91).

Farber, B., Jenne, W., & Toigo, R. Family crisis and the decision to institutionalize the retarded child. *NEA Research Monograph Series* No. A-1. Washington, D.C.: Council for Exceptional Children, 1960.

Gallagher, J. J., Cross, A., & Scharfman, W. Parental adaptation to a young handicapped child: The father's role. *Journal of the Division for Early Childhood,* 1981, *3,* 3–14.

Gath, A. School age siblings of mongol children. *British Journal of Psychiatry,* 1973, *123,* 161–167.

Gath, A. Sibling reactions to mental handicap: A comparison of the brothers and sisters of mongol children. *Journal of Child Psychology and Psychiatry and Allied Disciplines*, 1974, *15*, 838–843.

Gath, A. The impact of an abnormal child upon the parents. *British Journal of Psychiatry*, 1977, *130*, 405–410.

Gumz, E. J., & Gubrium, J. F. Comparative parental perceptions of a mentally retarded child. *American Journal of Mental Deficiency*, 1972, 77, 175–180.

Harkins, E. Effects of empty nest transition on self-report of psychological and physical well-being. *Journal of Marriage and the Family*, 1978, *40*, 549–556.

Helsels. The Helsels' story of Robin. In A. P. Turnbull & H. R. Turnbull (Eds.), *Parents speak out: Views from the other side of the two-way mirror.* Columbus, Ohio: Merrill, 1978.

Hersh, A. Changes in family functioning following placement of a retarded child. *Social Work*, 1970, *15*, 93–102.

Hubbell, R. The family impact seminar: A new approach to policy analysis. In H. C. Wallach (Ed.), *Approaches to child and family policy.* Boulder, CO: AAAS, Westview, 1981.

Lamb, M. E. Paternal influences on child development: An overview. In M. E. Lamb (Ed.), *The role of the father in child development* (2nd ed.). New York: Wiley, 1981.

Lamb, M. E. Fathers of exceptional children. In M. Seligman (Ed.), *The family with a handicapped child: Understanding and treatment.* New York: Grune & Stratton, 1983.

Love, H. *The mentally retarded child and his family.* Springfield, Ill.: Thomas, 1973.

MacKeith, R. The feelings and behavior of parents of handicapped children. *Developmental Medicine and Child Neurology*, 1973, *15*, 524–527.

Markowitz, J. Partipation of fathers in early childhood special education programs: An exploratory study of factors and issues. Unpublished manuscript 1983.

McCubbin, H. I., & Patterson, J. M. *Systematic assessment of family stress, resources and coping: Tools for research, education and clinical intervention.* University of Minnesota, St. Paul: Family Stress and Coping Project, Department of Family Social Science, 1981.

Mullins, J. B. The uses of bibliotherapy in counseling families confronted with handicaps. In M. Seligman (Ed.), *The family with a handicapped child: Understanding and treatment.* New York: Grune & Stratton, 1983.

Murphy, A. T. The family with a handicapped child: A review of the literature. *Developmental and Behavioral Pediatrics*, 1982, *3*, 73–82.

Neugarten, B. Adaptations and the life cycle. *The Counseling Psychologist*, 1976, *6*, 16–20.

Olson, D. H., McCubbin, H. I., Barnes, H., Larsen, A., Muxen, M., & Wilson, M. *Families: What makes them work.* Beverly Hills, CA: Sage, 1983.

Parsons, T., & Bales, R. F. *Family, socialization and interaction process.* Glencoe, Ill.: Free Press, 1955.

Peck, J. R., & Stephens, W. B. A study of the relationship between the attitudes and behavior of parents and that of their mentally defective child. *American Journal of Mental Deficiency,* 1960, *64,* 839–844.

Price-Bonham, S., & Addison, S. Families and mentally retarded children: Emphasis on the father. *The Family Coordinator,* 1978, *3,* 221–230.

Reed, E. W., & Reed, S. C. *Mental retardation: A family study.* Philadelphia: Saunders, 1965.

Ryckman, D. B., & Henderson, R. A. The meaning of a retarded child for his parents: A focus for counselors. *Mental Retardation,* 1965, *3,* 4–7.

Schufeit, L. J., & Wurster, S. R. Frequency of divorce among parents of handicapped children. *Resources in Education,* 1976, *11,* 71–78.

Simeonson, R. J., & Simeonson, N. E. Parenting handicapped children: Psychological aspects. In J. L. Paul (Ed.), *Understanding and working with parents of children with special needs.* New York: Holt, Rinehart & Winston, 1981.

Searl, S. J. Stages of parent reaction. *The Exceptional Parent,* 1978, *8*(2), F27–F29.

Suelzle, M., & Keenan, V. Changes in family support networks over the life cycle of mentally retarded persons. *American Journal of Mental Deficiency,* 1981, *86,* 267–274.

Tallman, I. Spousal role differentiation and the socialization of severely retarded children. *Journal of Marriage and the Family,* 1965, *27,* 37–42.

Terkelsen, K. G. Toward a theory of the family life cycle. In E. Carter & M. McGoldrick (Eds.), *The family life cycle: A framework of family therapy.* New York: Gardner, 1980.

Tew, B. J., Payne, E. H., & Lawrence, K. M. Must a family with a handicapped child be a handicapped family? *Developmental Medicine and Child Neurology,* 1974, *16*(Suppl. 32), 95–98.

Travis, G. *Chronic illness: Its impact on child and family.* Stanford, Calif.: Stanford University Press, 1976.

Turnbull, A. P., Brotherson, M. J., & Summers, J. A. The impact of deinstitutionalization on families: A family systems approach. In R. H. Bruininks & K. Lakin (Eds.), *Living and learning in the least restrictive environment.* Baltimore, Md.: Brookes, 1984.

Wiegerink, R., Hocutt, A., Posante-Lore, R., & Bristol, M. Parent involvement in early education programs for handicapped children. In J. J. Gallagher (Ed.), *New directions for special education* (Vol. 1). San Francisco: Jossey-Bass, 1980.

Wikler, L. Chronic stresses of families of mentally retarded children. *Family Relations,* 1981, *30,* 281–288.

Wikler, L., Wasow, M., & Hatfield, E. Chronic sorrow revisited: Attitude of parents and professionals about adjustment to mental retardation. *American Journal of Orthopsychiatry,* 1981, *51,* 63–70.

Wolfensberger, W. Counseling the parents of the retarded. In A. A. Baumeister (Ed.), *Mental retardation.* Chicago: Aldine, 1970.

Young, J. C., & Hamilton, M. E. Paternal behavior: Implications for child rearing practice. In J. Stevens & M. Matthews (Eds.), *Mother/child/father/ child relationships.* Washington, DC: National Association for the Education of Young Children, 1979.

# INDEX